HIPPO EATS DWARF

Also by Alex Boese
The Museum of Hoaxes

3/66

Alex Boese

HIPPO
EATS
DWARF

A Field Guide to Hoaxes
and Other B.S.

A Harvest Original | Harcourt, Inc.

Orlando Austin New York San Diego Toronto London

Requests for permission to make copies of any part of the work should be
mailed to the following address: Permissions Department, Harcourt, Inc.,
6277 Sea Harbor Drive, Orlando, Florida 32887-6777.

www.HarcourtBooks.com

Library of Congress Cataloging-in-Publication Data
Boese, Alex.
Hippo eats dwarf: a field guide to hoaxes and other b.s./Alex Boese.
p.   cm.
1. Impostors and imposture.   2. Fraud.   I. Title.
HV6751.B63   2006
001.9'5—dc22   2005026349
ISBN-13: 978-0-15-603083-0   ISBN-10: 0-15-603083-7

Text set in Bernhard Gothic
Designed by April Ward

Printed in the United States of America

First edition
A C E G I K J H F D B

To Beverley

Contents

We live in a hippo-eats-dwarf world.

I don't mean we live in a world in which little people suffer constant, vicious attacks by hungry hippos (at least not to my knowledge). What I mean is that we live in a world that's fake and growing faker every day, in increasingly bizarre ways.

For the past decade versions of the following news clipping have circulated around the world:

> A circus dwarf, nicknamed Od, died recently when he bounced sideways from a trampoline and was swallowed by a yawning hippopotamus waiting to appear in the next act. Vets said Hilda the Hippo's gag reflex caused her to swallow automatically. More than 1000 spectators continued to applaud wildly until they realised the tragic mistake.

This sensational news item has been reported in the *Manchester Evening News,* Thailand's *Pattaya Mail,* and the Sydney *Daily Telegraph.* It resurfaces periodically, kept alive by the Internet (that vast repository of weird information) until it reappears in print again. In one version the circus is located in Austria; in another, northern Thailand. But whenever it's reported, the tale is presented as fact. The catch is that it's almost definitely not.

The story's original reporting is often credited to the *Las Vegas Sun,* but when I contacted the *Sun* they could find no record of it in their archives. I suspect the Hippo Eats Dwarf tale was first invented, years ago, as a joke. At some point it was mistaken for news and thus began its career as bogus fact. Credit goes to the *Daily Telegraph* for dreaming up the headline HIPPO EATS DWARF in 1999, helping to fuel the tale's popularity. Nowadays a Google search for the term pulls up hundreds of hits. A band in New Zealand even adopted the phrase as its name.

The hippo-eats-dwarf story is (a) bizarre, (b) almost certainly fake, and (c) masquerading as real. This set of attributes describes quite a lot in the modern world. We live in an age in which you can rent an imaginary girlfriend for a month, find instructions on the Internet for growing a "bonsai kitten" in a jar (a hoax), and buy what is supposedly Britney Spears's used chewing gum on eBay.

To say that we live in a fake or hoaxy age, or that "we live in fictitious times" (as the director Michael Moore put it), doesn't do justice to the full-blown weirdness of the pervasive phoniness that surrounds us. Our world isn't just fake or phony. Any society that produces Michael Jackson's nose, breast-enlarging mobile-phone ring tones, and human-flavored tofu has gone well beyond that. Our world is hippo-eats-dwarf.

Zoomout Moment, n.: When you suddenly see the big picture and realize you had no clue how things really are.

Reality Index, n.: The ratio of the time you spend in an unreal environment versus a real one. For instance, how much time you spend watching TV versus talking with friends. Coined by Kalle Lasn in *Culture Jam: The Uncooling of America.*

Living in a hippo-eats-dwarf world requires hippo-eats-dwarf survival skills. It's easy to lose your way amid the bewildering array of Botox masks, Milli Vanilli–like musicians, Internet hoaxes, and unreality TV shows constantly trying to convince us they're real. Given the preponderance of fake stuff and the fact that reality itself has taken a turn for the weird, telling the difference between the genuine and the fake has become a constant challenge. That's where this book comes in. It will teach you the art of defense against dwarf-eating hippos—or, to put it another way, how to survive in an insane world in which the line between truth and fiction has completely blurred.

Assembled in the following pages are thousands of examples of the hoaxes, urban legends, spoofs, scams, advertising ploys, political doublespeak, and other forms of b.s. that lurk in the modern world. Later, when you're trying to figure out if a website selling dehydrated water is for real, or if that photo of a two-hundred-pound cat that just arrived in your in-box is genuine, these examples should provide some guidance on which to base your decision. I offer reality rules for navigating the treacherous landscape of reality. And I also define new terminology—because while Eskimos may not actually have invented one hundred words for snow, twenty-first-century popular culture has definitely generated thousands of terms for bullshit (or should I say hipposhit?). Finally, I've thrown in some reality checks. As you go along, use them to test your ability to differentiate the authentic from the bogus.

This field guide to modern (un)reality is comprehensive. It begins with birth, ends with death, and covers just about everything in between—including eBay. The last thing I would want is for a reader to be stuck in a reality jam without some kind of guidance to be found within these pages. But inevitably there were examples I didn't have space to include. Thanks to the Internet, this extra material has a place to call home. Check out my website, museumofhoaxes .com (or hippoeatsdwarf.com), where I keep track of all the hoaxy things in the world on an ongoing basis (with a lot of help from an always entertaining community of regulars and visitors).

Reality-Based Community, n.: Those who prefer to view the world as it is, rather than how they'd like it to be. A play on the term "faith-based community."

Patina of the Real, n.: The coarse, well-worn quality real things have, versus the overly smooth, processed look of fake stuff.

There are some topics this field guide doesn't cover. You won't find a survey of the most famous hoaxes of all time. The Piltdown Man, the Cardiff Giant, the War of the Worlds panic broadcast, and other classic hoaxes are covered in my first book, *The Museum of Hoaxes. Hippo Eats Dwarf* focuses entirely on present-day popular culture.

Similarly, while pseudoscience, Bigfoot, UFOs, or belief in ghosts may be lacking a firm connection to reality, I don't discuss them here. These topics belong more in the genre of error, superstition, and unexplained mysteries, rather than deliberately fake things. I also don't offer much advice on spotting scams, frauds, or counterfeits, except for a few cases in which these criminal activities have ventured into the realm of the bizarre, or hippo-eats-dwarf-ness. The majority of the fake things discussed in this book are not actually criminal. They're just weird.

From a sociological perspective, the question of why our world has become so hippo-eats-dwarf is an interesting one, but that's another topic I don't address at length. However, if you're asking, I'd say our culture has a love affair with fakery for the following reasons. First, going fake is often more entertaining and fun than always confronting the bitter truth (i.e., the illusory world inside the Matrix was preferable to the real world outside it). As Carl Jung said, "People cannot stand too much reality." Second, fake stuff is cheaper and more convenient than the real thing, an important consideration in this age of the mass market. We can't all afford to live like royalty, but a lot of us can afford the facade of doing so. Third, there's a core group of people (advertisers, politicians, TV producers, et al.) who will always want to b.s. the public for self-promoting reasons. And, finally, people have always faked stuff, but advances in technology have allowed more of them to do it in more aggressive and elaborate ways, propelling the phenomenon into the hippo-eats-dwarf zone. A number of works explore this subject in a more scholarly fashion—see Daniel Boorstin's *The Image: A Guide to Pseudo-Events in America* or *Travels in Hyperreality* by Umberto Eco.

Philosophers might also want me to address the ontological question of what is reality since I spend a lot of time discussing what is not reality. But I duck that loaded issue entirely. I stick with the fairly simple principle that those things are unreal that are not what they seem to be, or not what someone wants us to believe they are.

Finally, I describe many websites throughout the book. However, rapid change being in the nature of the Internet, I make no guarantee that the URLs I provide will still work, or will still lead to where they once did. (Operators of adult sites have a disconcerting habit of buying up discarded URLs.)

And with these caveats out of the way, you're ready to begin. Happy hippo hunting.

Hyperreality, n.: The kind of reality fake things acquire when they become valued for their own sake, not merely as substitutes for real things. In the words of Umberto Eco, when they become "authentic fakes." For instance, people often find holographic images more interesting than the objects they represent. Likewise, a plastic Christmas tree decorated entirely with Elvis ornaments (such as the one my sister puts up every year) could be regarded as more authentic, in its own hyperreal way, than a real tree.

BiRTH 1

Two thousand years ago, scholars recorded stories about women who had given birth to elephants and mothers who had borne over thirty children (none of whom were elephants, thankfully). We may think we're too sophisticated to believe such tales today, but that's not so. Instead of elephant-bearing women, modern legends have progressed to human clones, pregnant men, and online supermodel egg auctions.

REALITY RULE 1.1

Just because a woman looks pregnant, it doesn't mean she is.

Foam-Pad Pregnancy, n.: What you get when a woman stuffs some padding under her shirt and claims to be pregnant. More generically, any fake pregnancy.

The Fake Pregnancy Scam

You meet a pregnant woman—one who not only looks pregnant, but also says she is. How do you know she really is pregnant? The odds that she's faking it aren't very high. Unlike fake tattoos, fake tans, and fake hair, the fake pregnant look is a fashion that's never caught on. When fake pregnancies happen, the motivation is usually fraud, not fashion.

The scam goes like this: a woman claims to be pregnant, then persuades an adopting couple to support her while they wait to become the proud parents of her nonexistent child. By the time the couple figures out what's going on, the con artist is long gone, looking for the next pair of suckers.

For instance, in early 2004, authorities charged Maya-Anne Mays with deceiving at least three couples who hoped to adopt her child. Maya-Anne wasn't pregnant, but her heavyset build made her look like she was, and a recent miscarriage allowed her to test positive on a pregnancy exam. The couples who were paying her rent (and food, and travel money) only grew suspicious when, as the months rolled by, Maya-Anne stubbornly declined all medical care. In hindsight, her only mistake was sticking around for too long.

If you think a woman's growing belly owes more to foam padding than to a fetus, what can you do to verify your suspicions? Not much. That's the beauty of the scam. Start poking her stomach, and you open yourself up to charges of assault and battery. Ask that she subject herself to a medical examination, and she's well within her rights to refuse. The most reliable fake-pregnancy-debunking method is to wait nine months. If no baby appears, then you might consider your suspicions confirmed.

case file: Erin McGaw

Although most fake pregnancies are pulled off by con artists, occasionally you come across a "fake pregnancy as fashion choice" or "fake pregnancy as research project." Take the case of Erin McGaw.

Erin's classmates at Penn Manor High could scarcely believe this wholesome seventeen-year-old was pregnant. She was the kind of girl who hung out after school with her church group, not with boys. But the evidence of her growing belly was undeniable. And anyway, she said she was pregnant.

But Erin wasn't. Early in fall 2003 she had hatched a plan to fake a pregnancy as a way of completing a senior-year independent study project on child development. (Why didn't I think of that? It would have beat my senior-year study of nineteenth-century Romantic poetry hands down.) She imagined experiencing how pregnant teenagers are treated in our society and then reported her findings at the school's year-end Festival of Learning. Her teacher, Mindy Rottmund, approved the project and promised to keep it a secret.

Each week Erin carefully stuffed a little more padding into the swimsuit she wore beneath her clothes. Pretty soon boys were commenting that she looked fat and girls were whispering behind her back that she must have had a one-night stand. Erin found herself shunned by her peers, but she soldiered on, determined to complete her project. Even when her priest voiced concerns to her family, she didn't give up.

Erin could probably have gone for nine months without anyone realizing what was up, but after three months Ms. Rottmund squealed to the headmaster, who immediately called a halt to the whole thing and forced Erin to confess to her classmates.

That should have been the end of it, but one year later Erin's fake pregnancy bore fruit of a different kind. A camera crew from MTV rolled into town and asked the entire high school to reenact what had happened so MTV could film it for *High School Stories: Scandals, Pranks & Controversies*. Erin didn't reprise her role, though she did appear as an extra. Nevertheless, the school got to witness the surreal spectacle of a girl pretending to be pretending to be pregnant, while everyone around her pretended that they didn't know she was pretending.

Given all the pretending going on at Penn Manor High, it's not surprising that a cynical and ugly rumor soon spread claiming it was all a hoax within a hoax—that Erin had actually been pregnant all along and had only pretended to be pretending as a way to explain away her condition and its sudden conclusion. There is absolutely no evidence to support this rumor.

Empathy Belly, n.: A strap-on belly manufactured by Birthways, Inc. The device simulates pregnancy so that anyone (but particularly fathers-to-be) can experience all the wonder and joy of the symptoms expectant mothers feel, including weight gain, shortness of breath, bladder pressure, backaches, fatigue, and, as the manufacturer promises, "much, much more!"

REALITY RULE 1.2
Human women give birth to human babies.

Pull a Mary Toft, v.: To pretend to give birth to a nonhuman species. The phrase derives from the case of the eighteenth-century Englishwoman who claimed to have given birth to eighteen rabbits. It was only when a doctor announced his desire to operate on her to examine her astounding uterus that Mary Toft admitted she was lying.

case file: The Woman Who Gave Birth to a Frog

Imagine you're a news editor at the prestigious British Broadcasting Corporation and across your desk comes a story about a woman in Iran who has given birth to a frog. Details are sketchy, but an Iranian newspaper has theorized that the woman picked up a frog larva while swimming in a dirty pool, and that the larva then grew into an adult frog inside her body. What do you do with this story? Do you (a) leave it to the likes of *Ananova* or the *Weekly World News*, noting to yourself not only the possibility that the woman is "pulling a Mary Toft," but also the story's similarity to a well-documented urban legend, decades old, about a girl who gave birth to a live octopus after getting octopus eggs inside of her while swimming? Or do you (b) publish the story on the BBC website, accompanied by a picture of a surprised-looking frog? If this is real life, then the answer, of course, is (b). The BBC really did publish such a story on June 27, 2004. After becoming the butt of jokes on account of it, the BBC lapsed into a strange silence on the subject. No more details were forthcoming about the woman or the frog.

REALITY RULE 1.3

People will make jokes about anything. Even babies. Even dead babies.

Modest Proposal, n.: A satirical salvo that uses as its ammunition one of the few sacred cows in modern culture—babies. (In a pinch, kittens can serve as a substitute.) A few people always fail to get the joke, thereby making the modest proposal a guaranteed controversy generator. The term derives from Jonathan Swift's 1729 satire, *A Modest Proposal for Preventing the Children of Poor People in Ireland From Being a Burden to their Parents or the Country, and For Making Them Beneficial to the Public,* in which he made a case for the social and economic benefits to be gained by feeding the unwanted babies of the poor to the rich.

Modest Proposals on the Internet

While publishers might hesitate before printing nausea-inducing jokes about dead babies, the Internet knows no restrictions. The most disgusting baby-related satire is always just a few mouse-clicks away. What follows is a sampling of the tamer stuff.

EatBabies.com: an Internet-based guide for cooking with babies, because those who want to take Jonathan Swift up on his suggestion that the rich eat the children of the poor can't be expected to consume the delicacy raw. Recipes at this site include Spicy Baby Tortillas, Baby Flambé, and, of course, the ever-popular Baby Baby Back Ribs.

ChrissyCaviar.com: a site where performance artist Chrissy Conant offers "human caviar" for sale—eggs harvested from her own body. She's just joking, right? Unfortunately, no. The human caviar is quite real. Each jar really does contain one of Chrissy's eggs swimming in human tubal fluid. She claims this delightful delicacy is just for display. (The FDA might have a few things to say about it if she actually were to start selling this stuff as food—though as long as it's art, it's fine.) Chrissy also says she hopes Chrissy Caviar will one day "surpass Beluga caviar as the current ultimate in luxury, consumable items." Here's hoping that day never comes.

BabySmashers.com: a practical exploration of how the baby-changing stations that fold down from many public restroom walls can serve double duty as a means of smashing the baby violently against the wall. As the site enthuses, "Baby Smashers are an efficient, convenient, and fun way to dispose of unwanted babies." Visitors to the site can print out illustrations and decals that can then be pasted onto baby-changing stations to rebrand them as Baby Smashers. Thankfully the underlying purpose of the site is to expose, through satire, how unsafe the baby-changing stations can be.

Reality Check: **Foreskin Face Cream**
Is there a brand of face cream made from the
foreskins of circumcised infants?

The correct answer would be yes. Kind of. Although it sounds like an urban legend, TNS Recovery Complex (the TNS stands for Tissue Nutrient System) does contain ingredients derived from the foreskins of circumcised infants. But if you're imagining foreskins ground up in a blender, that's not the case. Instead, foreskin cells are grown in a medium, and nutrients are siphoned off from this brew. The product was originally developed to help burn victims, but eventually made its way into the beauty market. Reportedly it works quite well.

REALITY RULE 1.4

Women give birth to children. Men don't. This rule is subject to future revision.

Male Pregnancy

Crazy Uncle Ed calls to tell your family the good news: He's pregnant! Should you tell him he needs to start taking his medication again, or begin planning the baby shower? Is there a chance he's telling the truth?

Rumors of pregnant men have floated around for years, and on the Web you'll discover an entire subculture that fetishizes the idea of pregnant men. But, to date, there's never been a scientifically documented case of a man "in the family way."

Obviously a man could not get pregnant in the same way that a woman does. In theory a surgeon could transplant a fertilized egg into a man's abdominal cavity and then give the man female hormones to encourage blood vessels to grow around and feed the developing egg. In practice, getting this to work would be very, very difficult, and there aren't a whole lot of research dollars flowing into efforts to crack this problem.

During the 1960s Dr. Cecil Jacobson, a researcher at George Washington University Medical School, claimed he had successfully implanted a fertilized egg into a male baboon and allowed the egg to develop for four months before terminating the pregnancy. Of course, Dr. Jacobson didn't show the baboon to any other scientists and never published his results, so you have to take his word for it that this happened. Since Dr. Jacobson was later arrested for secretly impregnating seventy-five patients with his own sperm at his fertility clinic, you might want to think twice before taking his word for it.

More recently the website malepregnancy.com purported to document the first case of a man to bear a child. Although the site looked real and featured video clips and pictures of the father with child, it was in reality an art project dreamed up by conceptual artist Virgil Wong. But in 2002 a Beijing doctor, Chen Huanran, based at the Chinese Academy of Medical Sciences, really did recruit volunteers to participate in a "male mother" study. He said his goal was to help transsexuals realize their dreams of giving birth. As of his last public announcement, he had four volunteers. So don't be too surprised if you wake up one day soon to the headline WORLD'S FIRST PREGNANT DAD. As for crazy Uncle Ed, for now I'd tell him to get back on his medication.

Milkman, n.: 1. A man who earns his living by delivering milk. **2.** A man whose breasts produce milk, allowing him to breastfeed a child. Widely rumored, seldom seen.

Reality Check: **Male Lactation**
Can men really produce milk from their breasts
by stimulating their nipples?

If you surf the Internet you might stumble across sites waxing eloquent about the joys of being a milkman (see definition). Or you might come across the case of Mr. B. Wijeratne from Sri Lanka who discovered after his wife's death that he was able to breastfeed his daughter. Are such claims real? I won't vouch for Mr. Wijeratne since I've never met him, but male lactation is a real enough phenomenon. The fact is that men possess all the biological equipment necessary to produce breast milk. But how do men unlock this hidden talent? The evolutionary biologist Dr. Jared Diamond notes that "mere repeated mechanical stimulation of the nipples suffices in some cases, since mechanical stimulation is a natural way of releasing hormones." However, in most men mechanical stimulation alone is very, very unlikely to do the trick. (So you can go easy with the breast pumps, guys.) Starvation will more reliably trigger lactation because it interferes with the liver's ability to flush out excess hormones. Dr. Diamond writes that "thousands of cases [of spontaneous lactation] were recorded among prisoners of war released from concentration camps after World War II." But by far the easiest way to make a man produce milk is to inject him with female hormones—though that seems like cheating. If you happen to be a domesticated goat or a wild Dayak fruit bat, you don't need any of these tricks. Male members of these species produce milk relatively often and without any obvious external stimulus. Lucky them.

REALITY RULE 1.5

Extraordinary claims about advances in reproductive science require extraordinary proof. Demonstration of the ability to hold a press conference does not constitute extraordinary proof.

Babytron, n.: An artificial, out-of-body womb supposedly being developed by the Raelians, a quasi-religious group that believes humankind was genetically engineered by space aliens. Someday, the Raelians promise, we will all grow clones of ourselves in Babytrons, download our memories into these clones, and thereby live forever. The existence of a Babytron in any stage of development has yet to be proved.

Phony Clones

If everything you hear at press conferences is true, then sixteen human clones are alive in the world—one for each time the birth of a clone has been announced to the media. But, of course, it's doubtful that any of these press releases heralded the delivery of anything more than a load of hot air.

It's possible that by the time you read these words a true human clone will have made its way kicking and screaming into the world. So how is one to tell the difference between a phony clone and the real thing? Simple. All phony clones share a distinctive trait: No one is ever allowed to see them.

The honor of the first birth-of-a-human-clone announcement went to David Rorvik, a respected science journalist who startled his peers with news of a clone birth in 1978. Rorvik was vague about the top-secret project that produced the clone, but he was willing to say it took place on a faraway tropical island and was funded by an eccentric millionaire codenamed Max. The clone, Max's exact genetic match, couldn't be introduced to the public so that scientists could verify the claim because of concerns about the child's privacy, etc. Instead Rorvik asked that everyone simply take his word for it that the clone did exist.

It must have seemed like a good idea to Rorvik at the time: Invent a tale about the world's first human clone, throw in a few exotic details, write a book about it (*In His Image: The Cloning of a Man*), and then laugh all the way to the bank as the book became a bestseller. Unfortunately, one of the scientists whose research Rorvik cited in the book sued him for libel. The court ruled that Rorvik's book was a "fraud and a hoax," and most of his earnings vanished to pay legal fees.

But Rorvik's clone was just a warm-up for the phony clones that materialized after the 1997 announcement of the birth of Dolly, the world's first cloned sheep. The scientifically verified birth of a cloned mammal gave credence to the idea that a human clone was possible. What resulted was a mad rush to cash in on the publicity that would flow to the first group to produce a human clone.

First at bat was Dr. Severino Antinori, an Italian physician who announced in late November 2002 that a woman under his medical supervision would give birth to a human clone within the next two months. This put a fire under the feet of the Raelians, a previously obscure group of alien-worshipping clone enthusiasts, who convened a press conference a month later to announce that they already had a clone. Delivering the news was Dr. Brigitte Boisselier, a woman whose peculiarly bright red hair and manic grin became as celebrated in the media as the clone announcement itself. According to her, scientists at Clonaid, a Raelian-funded biotech company, had helped a client give birth to a healthy girl clone named Eve in late December.

Raelian clones followed thick and fast. By February 2004 the Raelians had announced the birth of six more clones, with seven more on the way. All these clones, of course, remained offstage, unexamined by the scientific community.

Rael, the titular leader of the Raelians, later halfway admitted that their clones were a hoax when he remarked, "Even if you want to think that we did all that only for publicity, it is wonderful. If that is the case, we are promotional geniuses...But if what we say we did is true, we are also scientific geniuses. In any case, we are geniuses! Wonderful! In any case, we win!" And he was right. The Raelians achieved worldwide notoriety (and a steep rise in their membership) on account of the clone mania they generated.

It's a safe bet any would-be clone that hasn't been examined by the scientific community to make sure its DNA matches the DNA of its parent-donor is a phony. But researcher Gabriel Weinberg has proposed a way to produce a fake clone that would pass any test the scientific community could throw at it: Fertilize an ova via in vitro fertilization, then divide the resulting embryo to produce identical twins (perfectly doable). Allow one embryo to develop, be born, and grow up, but freeze the other. Eighteen years later implant the frozen embryo into the womb of the grown-up twin and allow her to give birth to it. The resulting child would be an exact genetic match of her mother/sister: an apparent clone, though in reality just a twin.

If another two decades pass before anyone produces a clone they're willing to allow the scientific community to examine, one might suspect Weinberg's strategy is involved.

REALITY RULE 1.6

When seeking medical advice about birth, it's better to rely on a doctor than on a backroom miracle worker.

Hysterical Pregnancy, n.: A medical condition in which a woman falsely believes she is pregnant, sometimes to the point of developing pregnancy symptoms.

Miracle Births

During the summer of 2004, hundreds of Muslims flocked to a west German university clinic to see a woman who had given birth to Allah's chosen son. Their source for this information? A rumor posted on a Turkish Internet site. They had read it online, so it had to be true. (See Rule 6.1.)

The woman was said to have been burned across her entire body—except for her breasts—while giving birth, and to have died of these wounds. She had then been buried, but was dug up when someone realized that Allah had brought her back to life so that she could breastfeed the Messiah for forty days before dying again. The staff at the German clinic were at first confused, then amused, and then frightened by the steady stream of pilgrims. Some had traveled all the way from the Netherlands. Eventually the clinic hired extra security to turn away the pilgrims who refused to believe that there really, truly was no one there matching the description of Allah's chosen son and his mother.

This case illustrates that though this is (supposedly) an age of science and reason, it is also an age of faith, and many people are quite willing to believe that miraculous, supernatural forces can intervene directly in the process of birth.

The year 2004 also saw the bizarre case of Archbishop Gilbert Deya and his holy ghost babies. This self-styled archbishop (he gave himself the title) convinced numerous female followers in Britain that they had been impregnated by Jesus. He then whisked these women away to Kenya, where they gave birth in a backstreet clinic. There was just one problem. Most of the women were either postmenopausal or infertile. Furthermore, the holy ghost babies had developed within their wombs in record-breaking time. Deya helped one fifty-six-year-old woman give birth thirteen times in three years. That's about one baby every three months. But the really bizarre thing was that living, screaming, kicking babies did appear at the end of these rapid-fire pregnancies. Where were they coming from?

The Kenyan government had an explanation. They accused Deya of baby trafficking—gathering up infants in the slums of Kenya and depositing them into the hands of British women. Strangely, the women appeared unaware of any illegality or deception. Their desire to give birth was so strong that they allowed Deya to convince them they were pregnant. A video of one "miracle" birth shows a semiconscious woman, clearly unaware of what is happening, being handed a child while "doctors" cut an umbilical cord that looks suspiciously like a wire. Which goes to show that there truly is nothing people can't be made to believe if they want to believe it badly enough.

REALITY RULE 1.7

The Internet is not a reliable source of information about birth or babies.

Reality Check: Fetal Footprint

A photograph shows the outline of a fetus's foot pressing against the inner wall of its mother's stomach. Is the photo real or fake?

This photograph began circulating on the Internet in mid-2004. Its source remains a mystery, making it impossible to say with 100 percent certainty that

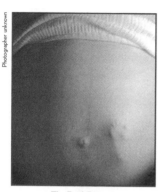

The Fetal Footprint
(aka "Bend It like Beckham")

the image is real or fake. However, although a woman will often see her belly bulge when a baby thrusts out a limb, the abdominal wall is simply too muscular and thick to allow a footprint to be seen with this clarity. The only way a fetal footprint could be seen in this way would be in the rare case of an ectopic pregnancy, which involves a fetus developing outside the uterus. This condition can be life-threatening for both mother and baby, and this photo does not appear to show an ectopic pregnancy. In addition, the footprint seems disproportionately large for a fetus.

Reality Check: Trampoline Baby
A photo shows an infant bouncing on a trampoline. Real or fake?

This is yet another odd picture you might encounter on the Internet. In this case, the baby is four-month-old Connor Simpson, enjoying himself on a trampoline sometime in 2002. Is the photo fake? Well, yeah. People who have any experience with babies at all guess this right away. Those with less baby experience, like me, waste hours trying to figure out how Connor could be doing that. We look for hidden wires, or wonder if he was somehow tossed in the air. The solution is

Trampoline Baby

that Connor never had a trampoline adventure. He was photographed lying safely on a bed, and then placed above the trampoline with a little digital cut-and-paste magic.

Reality Check: Supermodel Eggs for Sale
Is there an Internet site that allows infertile couples to bid for the eggs of supermodels?

All parents want their children to start life with every possible advantage. So wouldn't it be natural for infertile couples searching for egg donors to pay a premium for eggs from donors with high-status genetic advantages, such as extraordinary beauty? In fact, some couples advertise for donors with specific characteristics, such as height, athleticism, and high SAT scores. But a site debuting in October 1999, RonsAngels.com, took this practice to a whole new level—allowing couples to bid for eggs from supermodel donors. The *New York Times* thought the site was for real and published a story warning of a new age of "commodification" of human egg donation. But in reality the site was an elaborate publicity stunt for an online pornography business.

REALITY RULE 1.8

Dolls, no matter how lifelike, are neither human nor alive.

Real vs. Cabbage Patch

Is it real, or is it Cabbage Patch? This may be the great philosophical question of the modern age. Or maybe not.

Cabbage Patch Kids were hand-sewn cloth dolls when Xavier Roberts started making them in the late 1970s. Nowadays they're mass-produced vinyl things. The catch is that you're not supposed to call them dolls. Instead, you're supposed to think they're real babies. And you don't buy them. You adopt them.

Maryland residents Pat and Joe Posey, for example, have been raising a Cabbage Patch Kid for nineteen years. Kevin, as they've named him, has his own room in their house—as well as his own college fund, just in case he ever decides to make it on his own. To entertain Kevin, the Poseys take him fishing or let him watch reruns of SpongeBob SquarePants, his favorite show. And when company comes over, the Poseys insist Kevin be included in the conversation. Kevin even talks back, though guests are expected to ignore that it's really Mr. Posey speaking in falsetto.

Reborn Dolls

If the care and feeding of a Cabbage Patch Kid isn't enough for you, if you long for something even more lifelike, then you may be ready for a reborn doll.

Reborn dolls are ultra true to life, down to such anatomical details as pseudo-umbilical cords. Collectors who sell these dolls on eBay (where the hobby got started) have received angry e-mails from people who think they're auctioning off real human babies.

These dolls are created by hobbyists, most of whom are stay-at-home moms, in a process called "reborning." Quality varies, but to make a really good one you start with a silicon-vinyl doll, take it apart, remodel its mouth and nose, replace its hair with human hair, paint it to give it the appearance of a newborn's veiny translucent skin, fill it with sand to get it up to baby weight, add glass eyes, and insert silicon pads to simulate baby fat. Finally you name it and print out a birth certificate. The result can be so lifelike it's eerie.

During the 1970s a Japanese roboticist named Masahiro Mori tested people's responses to anthropomorphic robots. What he discovered was that people easily formed emotional attachments to robots that didn't look human at all. They also bonded with robots that were indistinguishable from humans. But robots that were in between, that were "almost human," triggered strong negative reactions. People were creeped out by them. He referred to this response as the "uncanny valley." And what was true with his robots is true with dolls. People readily bond with dolls that are obviously fake, just as they bond with real babies. But almost-human dolls make our skin crawl.

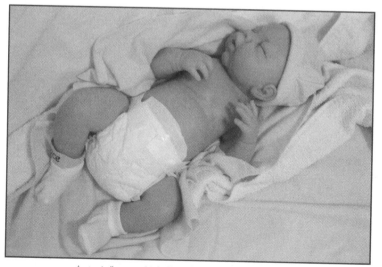

Anatomically correct Little Grace. Sold by Ashton-Drake Galleries.

Not everybody's skin, of course. Some people love reborn dolls, and collectors pay thousands of dollars for the top-quality ones. True enthusiasts hug them, pamper them, and dress them in cute baby outfits. Treating these dolls as they would treat real human babies, the enthusiasts say, fills a void in their lives.

To each his own. But should you ever find yourself in a position similar to the Poseys (Cabbage Patch Kevin's guardians), drifting dangerously close to that thin line separating reality from dollish fantasy, just splash some cold water on your face and repeat the following words: *Dolls are not real babies...Dolls are not real babies...*

BoDiES 2

People have always dreamed of transforming their bodies into something superior to that with which they were born. Now science and technology have brought us close to realizing that ancient dream. But most alterations are made simply to satisfy personal vanity. So instead of the *Six Million Dollar Man's* "better, stronger, faster," we end up with weirder, freakier, and faker.

REALITY RULE 2.1

What models look like in fashion magazines does not correspond to what people look like in real life.

Magic Mouse Diet, n.: Virtual weight loss achieved through the click of a mouse (digital alteration of a photo), rather than a reduction in calories.[*]

Digital Plastic Surgery

Celebrities and fashion models may be naturally good-looking, but are they as good-looking as they appear in magazines—where their skin is always flawless, their teeth pearly white, and their hair perfect? Not quite. They get a lot of help.

Makeup and lighting can make anyone look better on camera, and the fashion industry relies heavily on these tools, but they're not the only tricks up a photographer's sleeve. It's often easier to change the photograph than it is to change the person. In the old days this meant working in the darkroom. Now it can be done in a fraction of the time while sitting at a computer.

Thanks to image-manipulation software, photo editors can erase wrinkles, remove blemishes, even out skin tone, melt away fat, enlarge breasts, shrink tummies, and the list goes on and on. Such digital plastic surgery has become the norm in the fashion and entertainment industries. In magazines it's rare to find a photo that hasn't been touched up.

When does touching up go too far? Few people have a problem with removing pimples or stray hairs, and most celebrities demand that magazines take care of such details. Eyebrows are only raised (figuratively speaking) when photo editors change people's bodies so much that the photos no longer look like the real-life people, and (more importantly) when this is done without permission.

---

[*]Richard Woods, "Does My Digitally Reduced Bum Look Small in This?" *Sunday Times,* January 12, 2003.

Graphic artists enlarged Kate Beckinsale's breasts so enormously in the poster for her film *Underworld* that it seemed like false advertising. The actress felt obliged to tell them to tone it down a bit. Likewise, Kate Winslet didn't appreciate it when she saw that her picture on the cover of *GQ* had been digitally massaged to make her look leggy and skinny. She was proud of her more rounded real-life appearance and in the interview inside the magazine had even insisted that all the men she knew "like girls to have an arse on them."

The power of a photo editor isn't limited to digitally flattening stomachs or enlarging breasts. In extreme cases an editor can opt for total body replacement—transplanting a person's head onto someone else's body.

Total body replacement happened to Julia Roberts, much to her displeasure, on the July 2003 cover of *Redbook*. The one mitigating factor was that her head was transplanted onto a younger version of her own body. But the most notorious example of this practice occurred on the August 26, 1989, cover of *TV Guide*, which showed daytime talk-show host Oprah Winfrey lounging in a gauzy dress on top of a pile of money. Oprah looked gorgeous, but unfortunately only the head belonged to her. The body came from a 1979 publicity shot of Ann-Margret. The composite was

FrankenOprah

created without the permission of Oprah or Ann-Margret, and was detected when Ann-Margret's fashion designer recognized the dress.

Although such extreme editing techniques are increasingly common, complaints are rare. Most celebrities are quite happy to look younger and skinnier, even if they have to borrow someone else's body to do it.

case file: Wrinkle-Free Migrant Mother

In April 2005 *Popular Photography* ran a feature on how to touch up photos in which subjects have unsightly wrinkles or unattractive expressions. "Can these photos be saved?" the article asked. The example used was Dorothea Lange's classic Depression-era photo of a "Migrant Mother" huddling with her children in a roadside camp outside Nipomo, California. The migrant mother definitely needed a make-over. She had worry lines etched into her face from the stress of poverty, and she gazed into the distance as if wondering whether her family would survive. A real downer. So, under the masterful touch of *Popular Photography* editors, the Migrant Mother was transformed from an iconic symbol of the struggle for survival into a smooth-faced suburban soccer mom. Her wrinkles were erased, her gaze softened, and those depressing, poverty-stricken kids removed. Readers were appalled. Hundreds wrote in demanding to know how the magazine dared deface one of the most famous images in American history. To which the editors replied: Look at the date of the article. April Fools!

"Migrant Mom has got it going on."

Thinspiration

The fashion industry freely alters images of models to create a fantasy world in which no fat is allowed. Take this practice to its logical extreme and you arrive at the bizarre world of pro-ana thinspiration.

Pro-ana stands for pro-anorexic. This community perceives ultraskinniness as a desirable symbol of success and self-control. And when I say ultraskinny, I mean skeleton skinny. To inspire themselves to reach their extreme body-weight goals, pro-anas digitally alter images of models—transforming them

(left) A model unaltered; (right) thinspired.
This image (in its altered form) circulated widely by e-mail.

from thin people into emaciated people—then share these pictures with their friends. They refer to the images as "thinspiration."

Confusion arises when non-pro-anas stumble upon these photos and think they depict real models who have starved themselves down to skin and bones. They don't.

Generally speaking, models aren't encouraged to be so skinny that their appearance is frightening. So if you see pictures of stick-thin starvation-chic models, there's a good possibility they're fake—though some models (Twiggy, Kate Moss) really do need a cheeseburger in a bad way.

Dorian Gray Syndrome, n.: A psychiatric disorder characterized by an obsessive desire to maintain the appearance of youth. Named after Oscar Wilde's character who remains young while his portrait ages.[*]

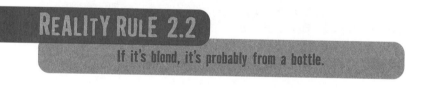

REALITY RULE 2.2

If it's blond, it's probably from a bottle.

> Reality Check: **Blonds as an Endangered Species**
> Has the World Health Organization really predicted that the gene for blond hair will become extinct within the next two hundred years?

In September 2002 CBS, CNN, the BBC, and other news agencies throughout the world reported that researchers at the World Health Organization had predicted that within two hundred years there would be no natural

---

[*]*International Journal of Clinical Pharmacology and Therapeutics* 39, no. 7 (2001), 279-283.

blonds left. The gene for blondness would go extinct, driven out of existence by the far greater percentage of dark-haired people in the world. But a week later the WHO issued a press release denying it had said such a thing. It also denied sponsoring research into "the status of the blonde gene." So how had news agencies come to think that it had? The blame was traced back to a two-year-old article in a German women's magazine that had attributed the "disap-pearing blond gene" story to a "WHO anthropologist" (who didn't exist). A German news agency had gotten wind of this story and reprinted it, and from there it quickly spread around the world. When queried, geneticists said the blond gene is very unlikely to disappear anytime soon.

Merkin, n.: A pubic hair wig. Sometimes worn by exotic dancers in order to appear fully naked while obeying local ordinances that require them to be partially clothed.

Tanorexia, n.: A syndrome in which the sufferer believes that no matter how tan they are, they're not tan enough.

REALITY RULE 2.3

No body part is more lied about than the penis.

Sex, Lies, and Penis Size

What animal holds the record for having the largest penis in relation to its body size? If you answered Homo sapiens, you are wrong. It's the barnacle. Mankind comes in a close second. But if one were to ask what species cares most about penis size, it would definitely be man. At some point in man's evo-lution (unlike other primates) penis size became equated with virility and so-cial dominance. Having a big penis meant that you were the alpha male. Which means that in the modern world some men will do almost anything to make it look as though they've got a few more inches than what nature provided.

Lying About It

Exaggerating penis size is a reflex with men. Ask a man how large his penis is, and you'll get an answer that errs on the plus side. This was the rocky shoal on which early scientific efforts to collect data on penis size floundered. The Kinsey Report surveyed men during the 1940s and found the average penis size to be 6.3 inches. But the survey left it to the men to do the measuring, assuming that men would tell the truth. So you can see where error crept into that study. More recent studies, in which less trust was placed in the participants, have come up with lower numbers. In 2001 Lifestyles Condoms set up a tent outside a nightclub in Cancún, Mexico, and had nurses measure the penile dimensions of hundreds of college-age guys. The average measurement was 5.87 inches. In other words, either the guys in the 1940s were exaggerating, or in a mere sixty years the average penis size shrank by .43 inches. Option two is a scary thought.

Bulge Enhancement

A prominent bulge in a man's trousers is a crude but effective sign that there's a lot of something in there. So for years men have enhanced their bulges using socks or appropriately shaped objects. (In the rock parody *This Is Spinal Tap,* a band member tries to get through airport security with an aluminum-wrapped cucumber shoved down his pants.) But men need no longer rely on such low-tech forms of deception. Lee Cooper offers a line of Packit jeans styled to maximize "trouser frontage." And if you don't want to wear jeans, then any pair of pants can be made to look as though it's straining to hold back a monster, thanks to a polyvinyl insert aptly named The Bulge. The Bulge will keep its shape twenty-four hours a day and can be cleaned in a washing machine. Thank God for that.

Pills and Lotions

Pseudo-inches aren't enough for some men. They want real growth. Scam artists have long taken advantage of this desire by hawking a wide variety of penis-enhancing products including pills, creams, pumps, and sprays. There are even companies that promise results via hypnosis. (*Imagine your penis. It is growing larger . . . larger.*) That none of these products work doesn't stop men from spending hundreds of millions of dollars on them every year.

Penis Weights

An option for the truly adventurous is to tie weights around his penis and stretch it. Proponents of this method point to the Karamojong people of northeastern Uganda as proof that this works. For ritualistic reasons, Karamojong boys start attaching weights to their penises at puberty. After years of doing this, they succeed in stretching their phalluses to lengths of up to eighteen inches. The catch is that what they gain in length they lose in girth, so their penises end up looking like long, thin earthworms. As an interesting side-note, there does exist a small subculture of penile weight-lifting enthusiasts. A martial art known as Jiu Jiu Shen Gong is even devoted to this practice. The world-record holder is a man in Hong Kong who can lift a 165-pound barbell with his penis for ten seconds. If you find this somewhat hard to believe, you're not alone. But that's his story, and he's sticking to it.

Surgery

Finally, some men turn to surgery for enlargement. Unfortunately for them, the penis doesn't respond very well to surgical augmentation. Methods include severing the ligaments that hold the penis upright so that it hangs farther out from the body (the catch being that while it becomes longer, it can no longer stand upright), or injecting fat cells culled from dead bodies (I'm not making this up). None of these methods are guaranteed to produce permanent results, and things can easily go disastrously wrong. In fact, in a cruel example of life's irony, many men who go this route end up with grotesquely deformed penises shorter than they were before. That's the risk: no gain and a lot of pain.

The Whizzinator, n.: A prosthetic penis marketed by Puck Technology. Strap the Whizzinator to your body, attach a plastic bag, fill the bag with heated urine, and you're all set to cheat on a drug test.

case file: Rasputin's Penis

Rasputin is well known to history buffs as the mystic who seduced the wife of a Russian tsar and exerted a powerful influence over the Romanov court. But he's also famous for another reason. According to legend, his penis was thirteen inches long. This would be mere historical trivia, except that his penis survived him and enjoyed a colorful, though highly dubious, history of its own after separation from his body.

The event that caused Rasputin and his penis to part ways was his murder at the hands of a gang of angry nobles in 1916. The nobles drugged, poisoned, beat, shot, then drowned him in the Neva River, and at some point during this extended process, cut off his penis. It is here that the history of Rasputin's penis enters more into the realm of rumor than of fact.

A maid found the bodiless member at the crime scene and saved it. During the 1920s a group of Russian women living in Paris somehow acquired it (or what they believed to be it) and worshipped it as a kind of holy relic, keeping it inside a wooden casket. Rasputin's daughter, Marie, didn't like the idea of her dad's penis hanging out with these women, so she demanded the thing back. And it presumably stayed with her until she died in California in 1977. It then disappeared until the antique dealer Michael Augustine found it tucked away in a velvet pouch along with some of Marie Rasputin's manuscripts, which he had bought at a lot sale. Augustine sold the well-traveled penis to Bonhams auction house, whose experts then discovered (surprise, surprise) that they had bought not a penis, but a sea cucumber.

That's where events stood in 1994. But, of course, no one really expected Rasputin's penis to disappear that easily. Ten years later it resurfaced at the newly opened St. Petersburg Museum of Erotica. Igor Knyazkin, the museum's director, explained that he bought the footloose phallus from a French antiquarian for $8,000. Which begs the question: where did the French antiquarian get it? No answer. I guess Rasputin's penis will go on being the enigma (or should I say sea cucumber?) wrapped in a mystery that it always has been.

REALITY RULE 2.4

If it doesn't look natural, then it probably isn't.

Silicone Challenge, n.: A game in which players guess whether breasts are real or fake. Usually played with images of breasts found online.

Bodies by Silicone

For over a hundred years surgeons have sought to alter (and hopefully improve) the shape of the body. Much of this effort has focused on making women's breasts bigger. (Our society's priorities are clear.) Early breast-augmentation techniques were crude and caused serious side effects. Doctors experimented with implanting paraffin, goat's milk, fat cells, glass balls, and plastic sponges before they hit on silicone.

According to legend, silicone was first used for breast augmentation after World War II when Japanese prostitutes injected it in liquid form in an effort to make themselves more desirable to American GIs. Liquid silicone worked, temporarily, but it also led to discoloration, open sores, and even gangrene (which is why it's now illegal). Finally, in 1961, Drs. Thomas Cronin and Frank Gerow developed the silicone breast implant: a hard, elastic sac filled with gooey silicone gel. It was an overnight success.

Although most surgeons have switched from silicone to saline implants because of concerns about the health effects of silicone leaking into the body, breast augmentation remains one of the most popular surgical procedures in the world. Hundreds of thousands of women get their breasts enlarged every year, including eighteen-year-olds who ask their parents for implants as birthday presents. And breasts aren't the only body part being augmented. Calves, pecs, biceps, triceps, and buttocks can all be surgically swelled and shaped. Someday we'll all have perfect bodies without ever going to the gym, thanks to gel-filled sacs inserted beneath the skin.

Or maybe we'll use Silly String. In the late 1990s the Houston surgeon Dr. Gerald W. Johnson (the man responsible for Anna Nicole Smith's cup size) began implanting polypropylene string into women's breasts. This substance absorbs fluid from the body and expands after implantation. Women with these implants saw their breasts grow larger, and larger, and larger, indefinitely, swelling to massive proportions. This can cause major complications, which is why the FDA quickly banned string implants. But for a short time they were seized on by performers in the adult entertainment industry who were vying for the title of biggest-busted woman in the world. Incidentally, many different women now claim this title, with the top contenders boasting measurements of around 42XXX. At that size they're so top-heavy they have difficulty balancing on their feet.

It didn't take long for people to figure that if you can fill sacs with silicone or saline, then why not with other substances? Rumors spread in the early 1990s that drug cartels were smuggling drugs by implanting them into women's breasts and buttocks. In 1994 a woman traveling from Bogotá to the United States was actually caught doing this. Her unusually large buttocks were what tipped off police. However, the prize for implanting the strangest substance goes to Sandi Canesco of Australia. In 2001, after her husband, Dustin, died in a car crash, Canesco had his ashes injected into her breast implants. She was quoted as saying, "It dawned on me that if I carried Dustin's cremated remains in my breast implants, I'd never really have to part with him at all." Definitely weird. But on the other hand it could be a great conversation starter when she goes out on dates.

Spurious Rounding, v.: Incorrectly rounding up bust and rib-cage measurements when fitting women for bras. As a result of this common error, many women, according to experts, end up with poorly fitted bras.[*]

Reality Check: **Nipple Addition Surgery**

Has plastic surgeon Dr. Jonas Zizlesse really pioneered a treatment for obesity that involves transplanting nipples onto fat rolls, arguing that "fat is only ugly until you put a nipple on it"?

There's a certain twisted logic to Dr. Zizlesse's argument. As he says, "Breasts are fat with nipples!" And our society fixates on breasts, to the point that people pay thousands of dollars to make them bigger. So why not transform fat rolls into pseudobreasts by transplanting nipples onto them? Great idea. But it's not real. Nor is Dr. Zizlesse. He and his eccentric operation are creations of HyperDiscordia, an online purveyor of "ontological waste products." Dr. Zizlesse's webpage, in which he expounds on the benefits of nipple addition surgery, is one of the many tongue-firmly-in-cheek sites you'll encounter as you surf the Internet (see chapter 6).

Scalpel Safari, n.: A travel package that includes plastic surgery followed by a safari or a stay at a luxury resort. The idea is to get away for a few weeks and return home transformed and fully recovered, so that your friends and coworkers never have to see the ugly post-op healing process.

---

[*]Dr. Matthew Wright, "Graphical Analysis of Bra Size Calculation Procedures," *International Journal of Clothing, Science and Technology* 14[1], 41–45.

Implant Alternatives

Long before they had the option of surgical augmentation, women experimented with bust-enhancing pastes and lotions. Diane de Poitiers, mistress of King Henri II of France, was said to have washed her breasts with a mixture of sow's milk and gold. The mistress of King Charles VII, on the other hand, used a blend of poppy water, ivy, rose oil, and camphor. Today a variety of nonsurgical bust enhancers remain available to women.

Bust-Up Gum

Women in Japan have been enthusiastically chewing sticks of Bust-Up chewing gum to gain an extra bra size. The gum's manufacturer, B2UP, claims its product contains phytoestrogens that mimic the female hormone estrogen and cause breast growth. Medical doctors aren't so sure, though they concede the gum could help reduce symptoms felt by postmenopausal women.

Breast-enhancing Ring Tones

Japanese women can also purchase a breast-enlarging ring tone for their mobile phone. Its inventor, Hideto Tomabechi, promises the ring tone will "increase the breast measurements of those who listen to it." Just how is unclear. The ad copy states only that "it's a technique involving subliminal effects." I've had the good fortune to hear the ring tone on the Internet, and it sounded to me like an extended Jimi Hendrix guitar riff. So far I have experienced no breast development.

Thai Breast Exercises

Not to be outdone by the Japanese, Thai officials recently launched an initiative encouraging women to perform daily exercises to enlarge their breasts—rather than pursue potentially risky augmentation surgery. The health ministry kicked off the bust-boosting operation on a street in Bangkok by lining up a group of women, who proceeded to massage and squeeze their breasts (while wearing T-shirts). As might be expected, this demonstration of the enhancement exercises attracted quite a crowd. Whether the campaign achieved any measurable results among the population has yet to be seen.

The Brava Vacuum Bra

Finally, we have a product that might work: the Brava Vacuum Bra. Debuted in 2001, this product clamps over the breasts, forming a vacuum seal. If women wear this contraption for at least ten hours a day, for a couple of months, they might go up a cup size. Since it's almost as expensive as surgery, and delivers far less dramatic results, I'd guess the vacuum bra won't be a wildly popular option with women—except for that small group of consumers who have a fetish about wearing powerful suction cups stuck to their chest.

REALITY RULE 2.5

No one in Hollywood has their original body parts.*

Image Aspirations, n.: The number of appearance-altering surgeries a person is willing or would like to have. Typically the major constraint on such aspirations is the size of the person's bank account.

Surgiholic, n.: A person addicted to plastic surgery.

Celebrity Surgery Rumors

Hollywood lives on gossip, and one of the best things to gossip about is what's been done to whose body. Did Michael Douglas have a face lift? Did Mickey Rourke try Botox injections? Did Tara Reid get a boob job? The questions go on and on, but sometimes the rumors go from merely catty to truly bizarre. In the weirdest cases, they even turn out to be true.

Barbara Hershey's Lips

In 1988 actress Barbara Hershey had collagen injected into her lips. Nowadays that would be no big deal, but back then it was big news and inspired a copycat craze in Hollywood. But Hershey's appearance also inspired a rumor that one day, while she was flying in an airplane, the pressure in the cabin caused the

---

*awfulplasticsurgery.com

collagen in her lips to expand and eventually explode. The rumor was a variant of an urban legend about a woman who wears an inflatable bra onto an airplane and is forced to go to the bathroom, red-faced with embarrassment, to deflate herself after the cabin pressure causes the air in her bra to expand. In reality cabin pressure will cause neither collagen lips nor inflatable bras to expand.

Trout Pout, n.: Lips excessively swollen due to cosmetic surgery (usually collagen injections).

Cher's Ribs

When Cher's celebrity was at its peak she was plagued by a rumor that she had had her lower ribs removed to make her waist appear thinner. A 1988 *Paris Match* article reported the rib-surgery rumor as if it were a fact. It wasn't. Cher sued *Paris Match* and won. She even hired a physician to examine her and certify he couldn't find any evidence of rib removal. But Cher does admit she's had work done on her nose and breasts. She also points out that she exercises a lot to stay skinny.

Lara Flynn Boyle's Sphincter

The tale of Lara Flynn Boyle and her sphincter is one of the more bizarre celebrity rumors out there. According to the rumor, which made its way into gossip columns in early 2003, Lara Flynn Boyle opted for the ultimate vanity procedure: She had her sphincter bleached. Why anyone would want or need to have this done is not clear. Fortunately, possible complications are said to be few, except of course for the risk of lifelong anal leakage. This inspired celebrity columnist Simon Doonan to comment, "Wax and pluck if you must, but don't tinker with your sphincter." Lara Flynn Boyle, to my knowledge, has neither confirmed nor denied the rumor.

Botox Mask, n.: The blank, emotionless expression that results from the overuse of Botox, a bacterial toxin that smooths out wrinkles by temporarily paralyzing facial muscles. Victims gaze out with an eerie wax-museum stare no matter what emotional situation they encounter: comedy, grief, tragedy. Also referred to as a "Botox permagrin."

Not Quite Human, adj.: Said of those who have had too much plastic surgery.

case file: Michael Jackson's Nose

When it comes to celebrity surgery rumors, nobody outdoes Michael Jackson. His claim to the title of King of Pop may be in jeopardy, but his reign as the King of Awful Plastic Surgery will forever be secure.

It's said that he takes female hormones, has eyeliner tattooed around his eyes, had an artificial cleft added to his chin, has cheek implants, bleached the skin on his entire body (including his genitals), and had pubic hair transplanted onto his jaw to allow him to grow a goatee. It's also said that he uses red lipstick, dyes his eyebrows, wears a wig, and covers his body in powdery white makeup. All this, however, pales in comparison to the rumors about his nose.

As early as 1981 it was evident Jackson had done something to his nose. It looked dramatically thinner, although still good. By the 1990s it no longer looked good. It just looked creepy: a small, triangular pointy thing totally out of place on his face. People speculated that he had been unable to stop himself from having more and more operations on it, driven by the memory of his father teasing him about his "big nose."

The rumors reached a crescendo on November 13, 2002, when Jackson appeared in Santa Maria Superior Court to defend himself against charges related to a contractual dispute. He showed up wearing a surgical mask, which the judge promptly ordered him to remove. Jackson did so, revealing a large bandage on his nose. This sight immediately breathed new life into an old rumor alleging that the tip of Jackson's nose had collapsed or fallen off because of the extensive surgery performed on it, forcing him to wear a prosthesis. Without the tip he supposedly resembled "a mummy with two nostril holes" (as *Vanity Fair* columnist Maureen Orth put it). The bandage, according to the rumor, was holding the tip on. Dr. Pamela Lipkin, a prominent plastic surgeon, gave credence to the rumor when she examined pictures of the

AP/Wide World Photos

Michael Jackson, aka the "mummy with two nostril holes," in Santa Maria Superior Court, November 13, 2002

singer and commented: "Michael Jackson has what we call an end-stage nose, a crippled nose, a crucified nose—one that's beyond the point of no return."

Jackson angrily denied these rumors. In a 2003 interview with Martin Bashir he insisted he had never had plastic surgery, except for two operations on his nose to allow him to breathe better and sing higher notes. He attributed the dramatic whitening of his skin to a medical condition known as vitiligo, and the altered shape of his face to the natural aging process. For some reason these explanations failed to convince many people, and the rumor mill kept on churning. The latest scuttlebutt is that before his 2005 trial on child-molestation charges, Jackson found a doctor who was able to reconstruct his nose using cartilage from his ear. As one person on the Internet put it: "Ewwww."

In the Plastic Closet, adj.: Where you are if you've had plastic surgery but are unwilling to admit it.

REALITY RULE 2.6

No matter how bizarre the procedure, there's always someone eager to try it out.

Imagined Ugliness, n.: The irrational, obsessive belief that a body part is deformed. Also known as body dysmorphic disorder. Sufferers of this condition seek out cosmetic surgery, repeatedly, to correct the perceived flaw.*

Cinderella Foot Surgery

In the fairy tale, Prince Charming finds Cinderella because she's the only one who can fit the glass slipper on her dainty foot. Nice story, but in the modern world it would never work. Why? Because the evil, big-footed stepsisters

---

*K. A. Phillips, et al., "Body Dysmorphic Disorder: 30 Cases of Imagined Ugliness," *American Journal of Psychiatry* 150 (1993): 302–8.

have a new trick up their sleeves: foot surgery. That's right. Surgeons report that women, with increasing frequency, are asking for operations that allow them to slip into their favorite high heels and get that all-important toe cleavage (and yes, it is almost entirely women getting these operations). Options include shortening toes to allow feet to squeeze into pointed shoes, and injecting collagen into the balls of the feet (supposedly making it easier to walk in high heels). Of course, such operations can result in crippling injuries because feet contain a lot of small bones and nerves and are not a smart thing to mess around with. But for some people, no risk is too large or too unacceptable for the sake of fashion.

Reality Check: **Eyeball Jewelry**

Have surgeons in Holland really implanted small pieces
of jewelry into people's eyeballs?

Yes, they have. The implant was developed in 2002 by the Netherlands Institute for Innovative Ocular Surgery. They call it the JewelEye. Surgeons first anesthetize the eye with eyedrops; then they make a small incision and insert a wafer-thin piece of jewelry beneath the eye's mucous membrane. The implant is then visible to others as a silver shape floating in the white part of the eye. Stars, hearts, half-moons, four-leaf clovers, and musical notes are the standard shapes, but other designs can be special ordered. The entire procedure is over in about fifteen minutes, and the implant doesn't interfere with vision or the ability to move the eye in any way. So far only a handful of people have had this done. But who knows. In a couple of years it may be all the rage.

Is There a Name for That?

If you visit a plastic surgeon you might discover, to your horror, that you're suffering from a nasty-sounding condition. You may have batwing disorder, or be afflicted with violin deformity, and you didn't even know it. Once you realize you've got this condition you're going to want it taken care of right away—and that's the idea. The plastic surgery profession has profited greatly by inventing medical names for "disorders" and "deformities" that are actually normal, healthy body shapes. The only thing wrong with these shapes is that they deviate from the Hollywood ideal of beauty. Batwing disorder, for instance, refers to the loose skin many women develop under their arms as they grow older. Violin deformity describes wide hips. Then there's hypomastia (the medical problem of having small breasts), or ptosis (saggy breasts). Use of these terms is a symptom of greedy plastic surgeon syndrome.

Neuticles, n.: Plastic testicles that replace the testicles lost when a male pet is neutered. Supposedly the prosthetic testicles help the pet maintain its sense of masculinity. Marketed by CTI (Canine Testicular Implant) Corporation.

Animal Cosmetic Surgery

In 2003 scandal rocked the prestigious Crufts dog show in Great Britain. Danny, the three-year-old Pekinese who walked away with Best in Show, was rumored to have had a snout lift. How could such a thing happen? Danny was cleared of all charges and his good name restored, but the controversy demonstrated that the age of the canine nip-and-tuck is upon us. Braces, dye jobs, hair extensions, and even tattoos along the inner eyelid (to add definition) are all strategies owners use to make Fido look his best for the big dog show. But the surgical arts aren't confined to canines. At the 2004 Royal Queensland Agricultural Show in Australia, four people were disqualified after suspicions of udder tampering were raised. This heinous crime involved injecting substances into cow udders to make them grow larger—because with cows, just as with humans, big udders are greatly prized. Where this trend will end, no one can say. But, please, everyone—spare the cats. They consider themselves purrfect just the way they are.

ROMANCE 3

When wooing a female, a male dance fly often takes her a present. Bugs and other food are particularly favored. But researchers have discovered that the male will sometimes take a fake gift, such as a seed tuft or a twig. The female will be fooled by the fake just long enough for the male to copulate with her. As it is with dance flies, so it is with humans. Psychologists estimate that dating couples lie to each other during one out of every three interactions. Honesty levels improve among married couples, except that—and here's the kicker—the lies they do tell each other tend to be really, really big ones. Ain't love grand?

REALITY RULE 3.1

Everyone lies on the first date.

Fake Fagging, v.: A heterosexual man pretending to be gay in order to pick up women, first gaining the woman's trust and friendship, and then flattering her vanity by claiming her beauty has converted him to heterosexuality.

Rico Suave Maneuver, n.: A pickup technique that's a little too smooth for its own good, often involving a phony premise (i.e., "Hey, baby, didn't I see you here last week?"—the guy has no clue whether he saw her there last week, but figures that if she was there she'll be flattered he remembered). Refers to the early 1990s Latin pop sensation Rico Suave.

Pickup Lines and Other Lies

Taking a cue from the dance fly, some people think the only way to get romance in their lives is by trickery. Evidently they don't feel confident relying on their conversational skills alone.

Choking Man

A Florida man had the perfect ploy for getting attention from women. He pretended to be choking. Women would rush over to help, and once he had "recovered" he would passionately hug them while declaring "Thank you, you saved my life!" The hugging would continue for quite a while. His scheme would have been foolproof if in early 2003 a local paper hadn't run a small feature describing how a female restaurant patron had come to the aid of an anonymous choking man. Other women immediately began writing in, noting they had assisted a man of the same description. Police said they couldn't do anything to stop the serial choking victim since he hadn't technically committed a crime.

Wing Women

A New York–based company, WingWomen.com, is in the business of helping men pick up women. Its service works on the domino theory, according to which, "Women are attracted to men who have women around them more so than men who have other men around them." For fifty dollars an hour they'll rent a man a female friend, or wing woman. The wing woman meets the client at a bar or other public place and pretends to be his friend for the evening. In other women's eyes, the wing woman's presence is a seal of approval (i.e., he's got one female friend, so there must be something okay about him). Soon, the company promises, women will come flocking. Unfortunately, once these other women find out the guy had to rent his female friend, it's back to lonely nights in front of the TV.

You're My Hero

Trent Spencer was already married, but he needed to save the relationship. So he did the obvious thing. He paid a bunch of students to break into his house while his wife was home and duct-tape her to a chair. He then showed up in the nick of time to battle the rogues. His scheme to win back his wife through this show of bravery might have worked except for one screwup. His wife got the duct tape off and phoned the police while he was engaged in phony fisticuffs. Instead of hearing sweet nothings from his wife, Spencer found himself at the station being charged with staging a crime.

Faux-mosexuality, n.: Homosexuality faked in order to appear trendy. Exemplified by bands such as tATu and Turbonegro.

Gancing, 1. n.: Guy-on-guy dancing. **2. v.:** Heterosexual men dancing together. Described in the April 2004 issue of *Stuff Magazine* as the latest dance craze to hit clubs as men try to pick up women by appearing sensitive. "Gances" include the shark, in which one guy pretends to be a shark and chases another guy around the dance floor. Was soon revealed to be an April Fool's joke dreamed up by the writer Bill Schulze, but not before Ryan Seacrest claimed he had once ganced.

Personal Ads

It probably won't come as a surprise to learn that personal ads aren't shining examples of truth in advertising. Responding to one is a bit like rolling the dice.

The lonely heart who describes himself as a wealthy investment banker who loves moonlight strolls along the beach may really be a romantic millionaire. Or he may be a beach bum. There's no way to know until you meet him.

A personal ad that circulated by e-mail during 2003 demonstrated the peril of taking these ads at face value. It read:

> SINGLE BLACK FEMALE seeks male companionship, ethnicity unimportant. I'm a very good-looking girl who LOVES to play. I love long walks in the woods, riding in your pickup truck, hunting, camping and fishing trips, cozy winter nights lying by the fire. Candlelight dinners will have me eating out of your hand. Rub me the right way and watch me respond. I'll be at the front door when you get home from work, wearing only what nature gave me. Kiss me and I'm yours. Call [phone number] and ask for Daisy.

Hundreds of men called to get in touch with Daisy. When they did, they found themselves connected to the Atlanta Humane Society. The joke was that Daisy was a black Labrador. Although the ad never promised Daisy was human, the guys had assumed she was. (The ad was the work of an anonymous prankster, not the Humane Society.)

Many personal ads don't represent real people (or dogs) at all. Con artists spam online dating sites with thousands of fake ads as a way to lure men onto porn sites. Often con artists even steal the pictures of women who have placed real ads, to add a veneer of authenticity to their phony pitches (which is something to think about before posting your image online).

Dating sites aren't above creating a few fake ads themselves. The banner ads for JDate, a Jewish dating service, displayed ads that had supposedly run on their site. One included a picture of blond, twenty-two-year-old Hila from Tel Aviv, who was "looking for a single Jewish guy." Another showed twenty-six-year-old Sharon, who was in search of a husband. But in reality the woman described as Hila was Hungarian porn star Kari Gold, and Sharon was Devon Sweet, a bisexual model from the United States. JDate had obtained their pictures from an image archive without realizing their true identities. Any guys hoping to meet Hila or Sharon (or Kari or Devon) via JDate were out of luck.

Beer Goggle Effect, n.: Alcohol's ability to make people seem more good-looking than they are. A 2002 study by Glasgow University psychology professor Barry Jones found that after drinking two pints of beer, people were 25 percent more likely than those who had drunk nothing to find faces of the opposite sex attractive.

Brutally Honest Personals

As an antidote to the less-than-honest norm in the personal ads, some Romeos adopt the opposite tack entirely: brutal honesty. The phenomenon was popularized when the *London Review of Books* began running personals and one of its very first ads read: "67-year-old disaffiliated flaneur, jacked-up on Viagra and looking for a contortionist trumpeter." Brutal honesty immediately became the hallmark of *LRB* personals (leave it to intellectuals to find ironic wit sexier than looks or money), and the trend soon spread to other publications. By then wit had, of course, taken over, and most of the honesty was fake. Examples of the genre are reproduced below.

Some chances are once in a lifetime. Not this one, I've been in the last 12 issues. Either I strike gold this time or I become a lesbian. Man, 43. (*London Review of Books*)

I am a thirty-year-old virgin on the verge of giving up on love. When I do have a job, it's low paying, and credit consolidators take half of what I earn. I'm behind on my rent, emotionally closed, and take medication to treat my depression. I'm short, not that attractive, a little fat, and have a very small penis. I also have a problem with excessive farting. I studied mathematics in college but still live under the delusional hope of becoming an actor. (*Esquire*)

Ginger-haired Galway man, a trouble-maker, gets slit-eyed and shirty after a few scoops, seeks attractive, wealthy lady for bail purposes, maybe more. (Circulated by e-mail. Attributed to the *Dublin News.*)

Bad tempered, foul-mouthed old bastard, living in a damp cottage in the arse end of Roscommon, seeks attractive 21-year-old blonde lady, with a lovely chest. (*Dublin News,* see above.)

Optimistic Mayo man, 35, seeks a blonde 20-year-old double-jointed supermodel, who owns her own brewery, and has an open-minded twin sister. (*Dublin News*, see above.)

Rejection: The Fake and Easy Way

Turning people down can be awkward. What are you supposed to tell them? "I think you're ugly," or "I don't date dorks," or "You scare me"? That may be honest, but it's also confrontational. What if your would-be suitor doesn't react well to the news? Sometimes it's easier to let someone down gently with a convincing lie.

A classic low-tech excuse is the fake engagement ring. A woman wears a big rock on her finger, and whenever a sweaty, middle-aged businessman leans over on the subway to whisper in her ear, "Has anyone ever told you that you're beautiful?" she simply shows him the ring, smiles, and says, "Yes. My fiancé. All the time."

But the fake engagement (or wedding) ring solution isn't perfect. What if you don't want to send the wrong signal to everybody in the room? Thankfully, there are other options.

Say you're at a club and some guy won't leave you alone. You want to tell him to take a hike, but you don't think he'd listen. What to do? Give him your number. Not your real number, of course—your fake number, courtesy of the Rejection Hotline. When he calls it later he'll hear this recorded message: "The person who gave you this number obviously did not want you to have their real number. Maybe you're just not this person's type ... This could mean short, fat, ugly, dumb, annoying, arrogant, or just a general loser. Maybe you suffer from bad breath, body odor or even both. Maybe you just give off that creepy, overbearing, psycho-stalker vibe. Maybe the idea of going out with you just seems as appealing as playing leapfrog with unicorns." There are Rejection Hotline numbers for most of the major cities in the United States. E-mail equivalents also exist. Give out the address anyname@papernapkin.net, and your suitor will receive a cyber letdown should he or she try to contact you.

But what if you're already on a date when you realize you can't stand the other person? Never fear. As long as you have a mobile phone, you have an out. In 2004 Cingular Wireless debuted Escape-a-Date. This service allows you to prearrange a phone call to interrupt a date, providing you with a graceful exit strategy should it become necessary. When you answer the call, a recorded message informs you of an attention-demanding emergency such as, "My friend is having some trouble with superglue and needs help." You may feel a twinge of guilt later, but it's a lot better than excusing yourself to go to the bathroom and never coming back.

REALITY RULE 3.2

Real friends are messy, noisy, and occasionally get on your nerves. Imaginary friends display none of these faults.

Imaginary Friends

A 2004 survey asked British gamers whether they would prefer to go on a date with Lara Croft, the animated star of the *Tomb Raider* games, or Jordan, a buxom (flesh-and-blood) model. Sixty-one percent responded that Lara Croft would be their preference. The media had a field day, going on about how these guys really needed to get out more if they would choose a virtual girl over a real girl. But it's debatable how real Jordan is. (There's some silicone mixed in with her flesh and blood.) Plus, imaginary friends are becoming more and more common. For many, they are the love interest of choice (or necessity).

Imaginary Girlfriends

Sitting in her dorm room one night, Judy, a real-life twenty-two-year-old Texas college student, had an idea. Why not post an auction on eBay promising to become the highest bidder's imaginary girlfriend? She would write her faux sweetheart a few letters and send some e-mails. It would be the perfect service for someone who needed to convince his friends he had a girlfriend in order to get them off his back. Or for someone who wanted to make an ex-girlfriend jealous. Or for someone who figured an imaginary girlfriend was better than no girlfriend at all.

Judy had quite a few takers, and her idea spawned a flurry of imitators. All kinds of imaginary-friend auctions popped up on eBay. On average, rates were $50 a month, which bought a couple of letters. Meeting in person was ruled out. For those unwilling to spend $50, $14.99 would get a box of chocolates from an imaginary admirer. The truly cheap could opt for an "imaginary stalker ex-boyfriend." Only $4.99.

By early 2004 the imaginary-friend business had grown so much that a company entirely devoted to it was launched: ImaginaryGirlfriend.com. Its website promises "You can soon receive personalized love letters by mail, e-mail, photos, special gifts, even phone messages or online chat from your new Imaginary Girlfriend. We won't tell anyone that it's not real!" The best part is that at the end of the contract period your imaginary girlfriend will write a letter "begging you to take her back," but you, being the heartbreaker you are, can cruelly opt to dump her.

As might be expected, imaginary girlfriends come with no guarantees of quality or authenticity. In a metaphysical twist that would make any surrealist sprain his neck, fake imaginary girlfriends have infiltrated the market. One imaginary eBay girlfriend turned out to be a guy named Brian operating out of a car dealership in Omaha.

For the technology-minded, there are virtual imaginary girlfriends. Artificial Life, Inc., offers a virtual girlfriend option for video phones. A subscriber downloads software that displays an animated girlfriend on his phone screen. The catch is that she'll stop speaking to him if she's ignored. The only way to win her affection back is to give her presents such as virtual flowers and virtual diamonds, which have to be purchased at extra cost from Artificial Life. She can become very expensive quite rapidly. In this sense she's just like a real girlfriend.

"Adrian," the imaginary wallpaper friend

Singles Wallpaper

For the single person wandering forlornly around his or her empty apartment, Singles Wallpaper offers companionship. Invented by the Berlin-based interior architects Susanne Schmidt and Andrea Baum, these wall decorations are life-sized images of people in various casual poses, such as sitting on a couch or sipping wine. If you glance at them, you'd swear they were real. Schmidt claims their presence "creates the feeling that there are other people in the room and alleviates feelings of loneliness." In many ways the wall figures are better than real friends because they "promise to be there all the time and don't leave dirty dishes or argue over the TV remote control." Schmidt and Baum also market a version of the wallpaper personalized to display a life-sized image of a person's actual partner. They imagine this appealing to people whose partners travel frequently. It would definitely give new meaning to the complaint that your lover is a real wallflower.

Amazing Instant Mate CD

The lonely single who already has an imaginary girlfriend and Singles Wallpaper might want to round out his love life with the Amazing Instant Mate CD, sold by Michigan-based James Wilson. Pop it into your disc player when you get home and you'll hear the voice of a pseudolover cooing, "Hello, honey. How was your day? I'm so glad you're home with me. The house is clean, dinner is ready." As you walk around your apartment, the pleasantries continue: "You're the greatest thing that ever happened to me"; or "Do you want a foot massage?" The CD comes in male and female versions, and it's only $6.99. I doubt anyone wouldn't pay far more to get his or her real partner to be so agreeable.

Rent a Friend

If for years your companions have all been imaginary, a day of reckoning might come. You might fall in love with a real person who will ask to meet your friends. You can confess your imaginary life, or, if you live in Japan, hire the services of a *benriyasan,* a "convenience agency." These firms, which have been in existence for years, provide actors to play your friends. They're often employed at weddings and funerals because in Japan's image-conscious society it's considered shameful not to have enough people in attendance at these occasions. Sometimes the groom will never know that half the bride's friends are hired hands. For a little extra they'll also clean your house and mow your lawn.

Real Doll, n.: A brand of anatomically correct silicone-rubber love doll marketed by Abyss Creations. Each one is custom-made to order and boasts "ultra-flesh like [sic] feel." Their website states, "If you've ever dreamed of creating your ideal woman, then you have come to the right place."

Real Sheep, n.: A brand of anatomically correct, silicone-rubber love sheep, custom-made to order and boasting elastic flesh, lice-infested hair, an articulated skeleton, "and sexy features like no other love mutton in the world." Not actually marketed by anyone, but dreamed up by Muttonboy. A Google search will reveal more about this creation, should you be curious.

Pillow Substitutes

Imaginary friends are all well and good, but they have one crucial defect: They're not very huggable. So modern science went to work and discovered a solution: the imaginary friend pillow.

The Japanese manufacturer Kameo debuted the Boyfriend Arm Pillow in 2004. It's essentially a pillow with a cloth arm attached to it, designed for women who don't want to sleep with a real man but would like to have an arm wrapped around them at night. Sales have been brisk. Kameo claims that "women of all ages have been queueing round the block to take one home." The company promises to be developing a girlfriend arm pillow (apparently perfecting it might take years of research), but it needs to hurry. A rival manufacturer has already introduced the Girlfriend Lap Pillow, a "pillow imitating a woman's legs made from urethane foam." A businessman can nap, pretending he's resting his head on his girlfriend's lap. I imagine it's the perfect thing to take along on crowded red-eye flights.

Researchers at Carnegie Mellon have added a high-tech flourish to imaginary-friend pillow technology. They've developed the Hug, a robotic pillow meant for long-distance cuddling. Katie can hug her pillow in Kansas and a signal transmitted over the phone lines instructs a partner pillow in Florida to squeeze Grandma. It's meant to bring a sense of touch back to long-distance communication. If a generation of children grows up thinking Grandma is a padded mechanical device, that's an unfortunate but entirely unintended side effect.

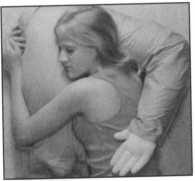
Photo courtesy of ArmPillow.com

The Boyfriend Arm Pillow

REALITY RULE 3.3

Whether you score depends on how you keep score.*

Boyfriend Markers, n.: Rubber ear tags placed on boyfriends at parties, to identify which man belongs to whom. Prevents unwanted straying. Similar to the identifying tags for wineglasses.[†]

Bad Excuses

People have always misbehaved sexually, and they've always dreamed up excuses to explain away what they've done. Some excuses are more elaborate than others. History records the 1637 case (possibly fictitious) of a French woman who became pregnant during her husband's four years abroad. When pressed for an explanation, she insisted the child had been conceived in a dream featuring her husband. After much debate the case came before the Grenoble parliament, which ruled that her husband was indeed the father. In a similar case in the nineteenth century, a pregnant woman offered the excuse, "It's true that my husband has been gone a long time, but we write each other…"

So who lies more about sex, women or men? A 2003 study in the *Journal of Sex Research* found it's women. The researchers suggested that while men and women have the same libido, women feel pressure to conform to sex-role expectations of prim-and-proper behavior. In other words, some women may not be as innocent as they claim.

It Was My Twin Sister

Aylar Dianati Lie was a finalist in the Miss Norway competition. But her beauty-pageant career was threatened by allegations that she had starred in pornographic films. Competition rules banned anyone who had posed nude for money. However, Aylar had an explanation. She admitted the woman in the

---

*Gene Weingarten, "Life According to Clinton," *Washington Post,* September 17, 1998.
[†]Manyfesto.dk

films looked exactly like her, but revealed the woman was her twin sister. Unfortunately for Aylar, a quick investigation revealed she had no twin. Beer advertisers and teenage boys everywhere were dismayed.

Sleep Sex

If you're ever caught in flagrante delicto—you're right there, doing it, and you can't deny it—there's always an excuse of last resort to turn to: "It wasn't my fault, I was asleep." Sleep sex (that's the technical term) is a real disorder, like sleepwalking. How far can people take this condition as an excuse for their behavior? Pretty far. In 2004 an Australian researcher described a case in which a middle-aged woman would sneak out of the house, find strangers (presumably at bars), and have sex with them—while asleep. Her partner became aware of what was going on when he found used condoms littering the house. When he caught her in the act one night, she claimed she hadn't known what she was doing. The couple went to see a doctor, who backed up her story—diagnosing her as a somnambulist sexaholic. The case inspired widespread incredulity. Cynics figured if her diagnosis was accurate it would soon become the *excuse du jour* of cheating lovers ("I don't know where I was all night, honey. I think I've been asleep."). If it was bogus, the woman must have been an incredible actor, and the boyfriend and doctor two of the most gullible men on the planet.

Bill Clinton's Definition of Sex

When President Clinton was asked during a deposition in the Paula Jones sexual harassment case whether he had ever had sexual relations with Monica Lewinsky, he answered no. When later challenged to defend this answer in light of contradictory evidence, he explained that the court had defined sexual relations as "when the person knowingly engages in or causes contact with the genitalia, anus, groin, breast, inner thigh or buttocks of any person with an intent to arouse or gratify the sexual desire of any person." By his careful reading of this definition, President Clinton had concluded he had not engaged in sexual relations with Ms. Lewinsky. His body had touched only her lips—a body part not on the court's list. Of course, her lips had made contact with his genitalia, so she had engaged in sexual relations with him—but not vice versa. Philanderers everywhere cheered. A powerful new excuse had been added to their arsenal: the idea that it's possible not to have had sex with someone even if they've had sex with you.

Unfortunately, President Clinton also had to explain why Monica Lewinsky claimed not to have had sex with him if, by the court's definition, she had. He reasoned that it was her genuine belief she had not: "I believe if she believed the definition of sex was two people having intercourse, then this is accurate. I believe this is the definition most Americans would give it." In other words, oral sex isn't real sex. Clinton may have been on firmer ground here. A 1999 Kinsey Institute poll of six hundred college students found that 60 percent of them agreed with this definition of sex. Again, philanderers cheered.

But Clinton had one final hurdle to overcome. During the Paula Jones case his lawyer had declared that there "is absolutely no sex of any kind" between his client and Lewinsky. How could this statement be explained away? Simple. Clinton stated: "It depends on what the meaning of the word 'is' is...in the present tense, that is an accurate statement." In other words, Clinton wasn't having sex with Lewinsky at the moment his lawyer made that statement. Therefore the statement was true. Upon hearing this, philanderers collapsed in a paroxysm of joy—their admiration of the skill of a true master of the hair-splitting excuse too much for them to bear.

Reality Check: **Cheaters Online**

The Internet can play a positive role in bringing together couples and fostering romance. But it also increases the ease with which people can cheat on their partners. Given this, try to guess if the websites described below are real or fake.

Philanderers International

Does an online dating service cater exclusively to married people who want to have extramarital affairs?

It's called Philanderers.com; its number-one rule is "Tell no one, not even your best friend"; and yes, it's real. Toronto-based Doug Mitchell (not his real name) was a married man who enjoyed having affairs. When he realized the Web didn't offer a lot of services to facilitate his habit, he set to work correcting that by creating a Web-based dating service for philanderers. As of 2002 he claimed the site earned over $10,000 a year, mostly from the sale of personal ads. Men pay $40 for three months. Women advertise for free. His wife, he claims, knows nothing about his side business. Philanderers.com isn't the only site for cheaters. The Ashley Madison Agency caters to "attached women seeking romantic affairs and the men who want to fulfill them," and boasts 160,000 registered members. Besides helping to relax marriage vows, these sites offer advice. For instance, if you suspect your spouse is cheating, they suggest looking for telltale signs—sudden, unexplainable happiness is a leading indicator. By implication, to avoid detection, cheaters should therefore act miserable. Adopt an air of perpetual despondency and your spouse will assume you must be faithful.

CheatingScum.com

Does a website offer a forum for people to expose "cheating scum" boyfriends, girlfriends, wives, and husbands?

The idea was simple, but ingenious: a site where people could expose "cheating rats." CheatingScum.com debuted in early 2001. A press release announcing its launch was sent to the major British media, and the site soon got thousands of hits. Visitors could read exposés of rats, and point the finger at scum they knew by posting pictures and rap sheets on the site. However, none of the exposés were real. They were all written by the staff of .net magazine, who created the site as an experiment in viral marketing to see how many visitors they could attract without spending advertising money. A lot of people thought it was a good idea for a real site, and .net received many authentic submissions. For legal reasons, none of the real stuff was posted, and the cheating scum got off the hook.

REALITY RULE 3.4

If unusual sex claims are physically possible there is a high probability they will become true—even if they aren't initially so.

Secondary Virginity, n.: Virginity regained by abstaining from sex for a time. Also known as born-again virginity, renewed virginity, or revirginization.

Richard-Gere-Gerbil-Rumor-Like, adj.: Used to describe a sexual rumor that is similar in character to the rumor about Richard Gere and the gerbil (i.e., bizarre, absurd, and false). For those who missed it, the rumor originated in the mid-1980s and alleged that the actor had been admitted to a hospital with a gerbil lodged in his rectum, the result of a sexual practice known as gerbil stuffing. In reality, no cases of patients with gerbils in their rectums have ever been recorded by the medical community.

Sex Hoaxes

The media can never resist stories about sex. Weird salacious tales usually make their way into the news before anyone bothers to investigate whether they're real or fake. Hoaxers are very aware of this. The professional prankster Alan Abel practically based his career on it. In 1959 he made headlines by founding an organization called the Society for Indecency to Naked Animals (SINA) that advocated the belief that it was immoral for animals to walk around naked. In the early 1970s he scored again with a story about the International Sex Olympics, in which couples competed for points on style and endurance. (This hoax prompted an investigation by the FBI.) And in the late 1990s he bluffed his way onto HBO by pretending to be a man whose penis was two inches long. But the thing about sex hoaxes is that if you put an idea out there, and it's at all physically possible, then someone is going to try it— making most sex hoaxes self-fulfilling prophecies.

Hunting for Bambi

In July 2003 a Las Vegas TV station ran a story about a local company selling Bambi hunts. These were games in which men with paintball guns hunted naked women in the Nevada desert. Anyone could sign up to join in the fun, but it cost a couple of thousand per game. An international media frenzy ensued. Newspaper reporters spilled gallons of ink addressing the issue. Talking heads pontificated about what it meant for the state of society. A paintball hitting a naked woman could seriously hurt her. How could this be legal? The very idea promoted abuse against women.

Only after the media had stewed on the story for a week did it dawn on them that there wasn't any evidence the company had ever conducted Bambi hunts. The company wasn't currently accepting customers (it said there was too much negative publicity), and everyone who claimed to have participated in previous hunts was highly unreliable. Further research revealed that the company was only licensed to sell videos. If it had run commercial paintball games, it had done so illegally.

When the Las Vegas authorities threatened to press charges against the company, its president, Michael Burdick, admitted no real Bambi hunts had taken place. The story about the hunts had just been a hook to boost sales of a soft-porn video about a fictional Bambi hunt. The hook worked. Though their stunt almost got them run out of Las Vegas, Burdick's company sold thousands of copies of the video. But the company kept promising it would one day host real hunts. And who knows. Maybe it has surreptitiously. If there's enough demand, someone eventually will.

NCSU Fellatio–Breast Cancer Study

Though it involved a female health issue, the North Carolina State University breast-cancer study and its results probably excited men more than women. The study concluded that "women who perform the act of fellatio and swallow semen on a regular basis, one to two times a week, may reduce their risk of breast cancer by up to 40 percent." Doctors were urging women to take these findings to heart (or mouth—whatever).

These findings seemed tailor-made for male fantasies—probably because they sprang from the fantasies of NCSU student Brandon Williamson. In October 2003 he created a fake CNN webpage reporting this fictitious research study and posted his creation on NCSU's server as a joke for his friends. To his surprise, when he returned from fall break a week later, word of his site had spread across the Internet and millions of people had visited it.

Williamson had loaded the story with clues that it was fake. For instance, he named one researcher "Dr. Inserta Shafteer." But thousands of people fell for it anyway. Mary Ann Liebert, the publisher of the *Journal of Women's Health,* demanded in a press release that CNN "investigate thoroughly its decision-making process that allowed a story that is so damaging and degrading to be put up on its website." Evidently she failed to notice that the story wasn't hosted on CNN's site—the biggest clue of all that it was fake.

Williamson's fake CNN webpage

Faced with the threat of lawsuits from CNN, the Associated Press, and NCSU, Williamson took the page down, although he insisted to the end that it was obviously a parody. Although there isn't much chance that medical researchers will conduct this study for real, there's a very good chance that guys throughout the world are telling their girlfriends, "There was this study, and they found that it's good for you. I swear it's true."

Teledildonics, n.: Long-distance sexual interaction via virtual reality gear. Also known as cybersex.

Sex Codes

Does a clandestine subculture of unlicensed sexual promiscuity exist, in which members communicate in public via secret codes? Moral crusaders are convinced it does, and warn it's corrupting the nation's youth. Skeptics note this subculture and its secret codes are more often rumored than encountered in the flesh. Others simply wonder why the codes never work for them.

Jelly Bracelets

In 2003 school administrators in a Florida high school banned students from wearing colored jelly bracelets. They had heard the bracelets indicated what sexual favors the girls wearing them were willing to perform. Blue meant oral, black was with a condom, red was no condom, and so forth. A national controversy ensued, but subsequent research, including a survey of three hundred teenagers by the marketing firm Teenage Research Unlimited, could find no high school students who were aware of the sexual meaning of the bracelets, except in an anecdotal way.

Powerline Codes

Ever see shoes or other items hanging from powerlines? To those in the know, these dangling objects have secret meanings. A yoyo means sex is for sale nearby; tennis shoes indicate drugs; and a yoyo and balloon together mean sex and drugs. Rumors of these codes have been in existence as long as powerlines themselves. The codes, however, have never been confirmed.

Toothing

Toothing describes the practice of using Bluetooth-equipped mobile phones (i.e., phones with the ability to communicate directly with similar phones over short distances) to find sexual partners in public places. Toothers beam sexual propositions to people they see on commuter trains or in coffeeshops. If the answer is affirmative then off the two go. The media learned of this practice in March 2004, when a toothing forum appeared online. A large amount of coverage was devoted to it. But a year later the creator of the forum, Ste Curran, said he had intended it as a joke. To his knowledge, no one had ever toothed. The idea was a spoof on dogging, a craze the media had earlier reported to be sweeping England, in which people had sex with strangers in public places. However, Curran admitted that people very well might have started toothing after he introduced the idea.

Greenlighting

Greenlighters wear green shirts with the collars turned up. When a greenlighter sees someone similarly attired, he turns his collar down. This is the code for "let's have sex." The other person signals her willingness by pulling her collar down, or rejects the offer by keeping her collar up (redlighting). Rumors of this practice spread on the Internet in July 2005, but were almost immediately debunked as a hoax. Internet pranksters at WookieFetish.com had invented the idea, hoping it would attract as much media attention as the toothing hoax of the previous year.

Fake Orgasms

No matter how many movies Meg Ryan appears in she'll always be remembered for the orgasm she faked in Rob Reiner's *When Harry Met Sally.* I would bet money it gets prominent mention in her obituary.

In the movie, the platonic friends Harry and Sally (played by Billy Crystal and Ryan) are having lunch at a diner and the conversation turns to how men can be sure the women they sleep with are having real orgasms. They can't, Sally tells Harry, who immediately insists that he would be able to tell the difference. Sally proves him wrong by demurely placing her sandwich on her plate and then loudly and very convincingly pretending to climax, as everyone in the diner watches in amazement.

It's a classic movie scene, but how many women really fake orgasms? One widely quoted study conducted in 2000 by an organization called Queendom .com (which boasts that over fifteen thousand people participated) found that 70 percent of women admit to faking an orgasm at least once in their life. Intriguingly the same study found that 25 percent of men have also faked an orgasm.

Students of comparative animal behavior will be interested to note that humans are not the only creatures to fake orgasms. Trout do it too. During spawning the female trout burrows into gravel and starts to quiver as a sign that she's ready to mate. A male then swims alongside her and starts quivering also. If all goes well, their mutual quivering results in the release of eggs and sperm. But if the female senses the male isn't correctly positioned beside her, she'll quiver without releasing any eggs. The male, not realizing she's aborted the process, will go on quivering until he's done. As Erik Peterrson of Sweden's National Board of Fisheries said in an interview with CBC Radio, "the male, he is so excited that he misinterprets the female's cues and goes the whole way. He's a little bit tricked there."

While a good actress may be able to fool her partner, she can no longer fool medical science—not since neuroanatomist Gert Holstege of the University of

Groningen discovered that positron-emission tomography (PET) scanners can sense the changes that take place in the brain during sexual climax, making the machines foolproof fake-orgasm detectors. When a woman orgasms, the periaqueductal gray matter of her brain becomes very active. Not so when she fakes it. However, since most couples don't have ready access to PET scanners, this knowledge won't be of much use to suspicious men.

Besides, in the future no one may need to fake it. North Carolina anesthiologist Dr. Stuart Meloy recently invented an "orgasmatron" that provides on-demand orgasms. His invention requires inserting two electrodes into the spinal cord, but then all it takes is a flip of the switch. Female volunteers who tested the device admitted it was "difficult to part with" once the study ended. If Dr. Meloy ever comes up with a mass-market version of the orgasmatron, he'll be a billionaire—and we'll be one more step removed from the cause and effect of real life.

Viagra Etiquette, n.: The social rules for using Viagra, as established by the American Association of Retired People. According to these rules, men should inform their dates when they're using the drug, but they should not swallow the pill in front of them.

Reality Check: Contraceptive Technology

Over the centuries couples have tried all kinds of techniques to prevent unwanted pregnancy. They applied lotions made of crocodile dung or tobacco juice. Condoms were constructed from linen. In ancient Greece, women were advised to jump backward seven times after intercourse. Modern technology offers a few new options. The question is, which of them are real and which are fake?

Musical Condoms

Did a Ukrainian inventor devise a condom that plays music while in use, the volume growing as the wearer's movement increases in intensity?

Reports of musical condoms hailing from former Soviet-bloc countries twice made the news in the past decade, but appear to have been planted by practical jokers. In 1996 London newspapers reported that a Hungarian, Ferenc Kovacs, had invented a condom that played tunes as it was being unfurled. The default melody was the communist hymn, "Arise, Ye Worker." (One reporter re-marked that there should also be a Milli Vanilli tune for women who liked to fake it.) But curious travelers who subsequently tried to track down Kovacs and the shop in Budapest where he sold these singing condoms could never find him. Nine years later, in February 2005, British papers reported a similar story fea-turing a Ukrainian man, Dr. Grigoriy Chausovskiy. His condom supposedly had "tiny sensors connected to a mini electronic device that produces the sounds" and played different tunes at changing volume depending on the wearer's po-sition. Chausovskiy assured potential users that "there is no danger of being electrocuted." But as with the 1996 report, evidence of Dr. Chausovskiy and his wonderful invention was nowhere to be found.

Mobile-Phone Birth Control

Does a cell phone accessory project a high-intensity electromagnetic sound cone, inaudible to the human ear but fatal to sperm cells, thus serving as an ef-fective means of birth control when placed nearby during moments of intimacy?

The Belgian company Prophy-Lectric debuted the Nippit 3000 mobile-phone birth-control accessory at the 2004 3GSM World Congress in Cannes. Or rather, it did if you believed a satirical article, penned by David Benjamin, that circulated shortly after the conference. (Quite a few websites fell for it.) According to Benjamin, the accessory was more effective than condoms at pre-venting unwanted pregnancy, unless the phone happened to receive an incom-ing call at the moment of truth, in which case all bets were off. But even if contraception couldn't be guaranteed, the high-pitched sound was handy for keeping dogs away. The first phone maker with whom Prophy-Lectric hoped to partner was, naturally, the German corporation Siemens.

Spray-on Contraceptive

Is there an experimental hormone spray, similar to a perfume, that can be spritzed on a woman's forearm once a day, eliminating the need for contraceptive pills or patches?

Tests of a contraceptive hormone spray began in Australia in 2004. Just squirt it on, and that's it. The spray delivers a measured dose of the progestin Nestorone through the skin into the blood. If the tests are successful, a com-mercial version of the spray is expected to reach markets around 2009.

Dog Condoms

Are dog condoms, available in three sizes to fit different breeds, marketed as a way to control canine overpopulation?

Dog overpopulation is a serious problem. Doggy condoms, however, are not a serious solution. A dog condom vendor appeared online in 2005, offering not only proportionally sized condoms but also lubricated and meat-scented varieties "to enhance pleasure for both dog partners." The problem, of course, is that both fitting and removal of the protective sheaths require human intervention. I'm guessing that stopping Fido from eating the latex treat would also present a challenge. The site was a hoax created by an online condom retailer.

REALITY RULE 3.5

Fake marriage is when you don't really know your spouse. Real marriage is when you know your spouse all too well.

Starter Marriage, n.: A first marriage of less than five years in duration that produces no children and is regarded as a mere trial run.[*]

Mock Wedding, n.: An elaborate ceremony put on for show (and as an excuse to have a party), at which no one actually gets married. Popular with young people who figure they may not get married until much later in life but don't want to miss out on the fun of celebrating with their friends now.

Green-Card Marriage

Every year thousands of people who aren't in love, and who have no intention of living together or being a couple, get married as a front to secure a green card or permanent visa for one of them. The popularity of this scheme places immigration officials in the strange position of interviewing married couples to determine whether their marriages are real. Evidence that the couple doesn't know each other well is taken as proof that the marriage is a sham. Which

---

[*]Pamela Paul, *The Starter Marriage and the Future of Matrimony* (New York: Random House Trade Paperbacks, 2003).

means that, for INS purposes, love at first sight is always phony. (What I'm curious about is how often officials incorrectly judge real marriages to be fake.)

Most people who enter into fake marriages are amateurs—foreigners and the citizens who decide to help them. But there are professionals—serial brides and grooms who earn up to $10,000 per phony marriage. One woman in Harlem was charged with marrying twenty-seven green-card suckers.

Such shenanigans might seem principally of concern to immigration officials, except for the possibility of identity theft. You may be married and not even know it. In South Africa hundreds of women recently tried to register their (real) marriages, only to be told that they already had husbands. The women weren't just being forgetful. Corrupt government officials had, for a small fee, signed paperwork allowing foreigners to "marry" these citizens whose names they had chosen at random from the national register. South Africa launched a publicity campaign to warn people about this danger, prompting over two hundred thousand people to check on their marital status. Almost two thousand sham marriages were discovered and annulled.

Weekend Pastors, n.: Caucasian men hired to perform Christian-style weddings in Japan, even though the men aren't pastors and the people getting married aren't Christian. Many Japanese couples believe that Christian-style weddings presided over by a Caucasian pastor look more like the wedding ideal, so they hire white actors to play the role of the pastor.

End Games

When it's over, it's over. Unless it never really began. This is a surprisingly popular argument made by those seeking to get an annulment. Luisa Holden, for instance, insisted that despite the fact that one hundred guests had watched her marry Clive Cardozo in an idyllic waterfront setting in Westhampton Beach, the two never really got married. The ceremony, she said, was a sham performed for the benefit of Cardozo's sick mother. The marriage license was never filed, so she thought the whole thing shouldn't count. Unfortunately for Holden, the judge didn't agree, ruling that "if it walks like a duck and quacks like a duck and looks like a duck, it is a duck." But even better was the reasoning of Dallas-based lawyer Brian Loncar. He defended himself against charges of bigamy by arguing that his second marriage wasn't valid because it was performed by an Elvis impersonator in Las Vegas. The court didn't go for this either, though the indictment was eventually dropped because of lack of jurisdiction.

If you can't get the marriage annulled, and your spouse is being disagreeable about the terms of divorce, a strategy of last resort remains: Divorce a fake spouse. This was the novel tactic employed by an Osaka, Japan, man who showed up at divorce court accompanied by a woman pretending to be his wife. Together they participated in the mediation process, filed all the necessary paperwork, and walked out as single people. Or so the guy thought. The one flaw in his plan was that eventually his real wife was sent the divorce papers. She immediately demanded a retrial on the grounds that she hadn't been present during the proceedings. The Osaka court staff confessed it had never occurred to them that they should ask for photo ID at a divorce case.

FOOD 4

In 1957 the British news show *Panorama* informed its viewers of the success of that year's spaghetti crop in Switzerland. Footage showed Swiss peasants happily harvesting pasta from spaghetti trees. Hundreds of people subsequently phoned the BBC to ask how to grow their own spaghetti trees. (The BBC's deadpan response: "Place a sprig of spaghetti in a tin of tomato sauce, and hope for the best.") The broadcast was an April Fool's Day joke (and arguably the most famous joke in the history of April foolery). But it demonstrated a deeper principle: People in the modern world know very little about how their food is produced or where it comes from. We pick up our groceries prepackaged in supermarkets. For all we know, our spaghetti could have grown on a tree. Our ignorance about the sources of what we eat fuels a multitude of food-related fears, rumors, and hoaxes.

REALITY RULE 4.1

Real food rots.

Dorito Syndrome, n.: A lingering sense of dissatisfaction and emptiness caused by prolonged exposure to things without nutritional or edifying contents: junk food, video games, the Internet, etc.

Plastic Food Rumors

Japanese restaurants often display in their windows plastic versions of the entrées they serve—a tradition begun eighty years ago in the town of Gifu. As realistic as some of these models are, restaurant patrons can feel confident that what they're served won't also be plastic. Consumers are less confident about the food they buy in supermarkets and fast-food chains. Widespread rumors hold that many popular foods are completely artificial. What follows are actual claims circulated by e-mail about some of the foods people are most suspicious of.

 Margarine

Claim: "Margarine is but ONE MOLECULE away from being PLASTIC... YOU can try this yourself: purchase a tub of margarine and leave it in your garage or shaded area. Within a couple of days you will note a couple of things: no flies, not even those pesky fruit flies, will go near it. (That should tell you something.)"

Reality: I've never tried the garage experiment, but I suspect that if you spread margarine all over yourself on a hot day it wouldn't be a very effective bug repellent. Regardless, the important point is that margarine is in no way related to plastic. Margarine is hydrogenated vegetable oil (hydrogenation being the process of bonding a hydrogen atom to the carbon atoms in the vegetable oil). Granted, one molecule can make a huge difference in nature, so maybe the addition of one magic molecule could transform margarine into plastic—but the same molecule (should it exist, which is doubtful) would probably also turn all the fats in your body into plastic containers.

McDonald's Shakes

Claim: "In the 1970s McDonald's used a non-milk shake, and used to use Styrofoam balls as a filler (they pass right through you), but they stopped after people who didn't drink their shakes right away and examined the left-over goop realized it and complained like crazy."

Reality: McDonald's has never used Styrofoam in its shakes. Period. However, it is true that McDonald's does not use ice cream but, rather, adds a powdered mix to milk. Therefore, many milkshake lovers refuse to drink McDonald's shakes, claiming they can feel the gritty powder in their throats. This may be the source of the Styrofoam rumor.

Twinkie Defense, n.: A criminal defense of temporary insanity due to eating too many Twinkies. More broadly, any far-fetched, bizarre defense. Derives from the trial of Dan White for the 1978 murder of Harvey Milk and George Moscone. White's attorneys argued that their client should receive a reduced sentence because he was suffering from a temporary state of diminished mental capacity due to depression exacerbated by eating too many Twinkies. The jury agreed and sentenced him using only voluntary manslaughter guidelines.

Twinkies

Claim: "Twinkies are made entirely out of artificial ingredients, and contain no food products. Therefore, Twinkies have a very long shelf life (possibly decades). At some point many years ago, Hostess overproduced Twinkies by the billions (possibly due to an error in market research) and could not sell all their stock. So Hostess stored the billions of excess Twinkies in a giant warehouse and waited for their distributors to place orders. However, the distributors did not place the expected large orders, and Hostess was forced to continue storing the Twinkies. Because of the lack of actual food contents in Twinkies, they do not go bad for a very long time, and to this day the Twinkies that you buy in the store are from the original stock."

Reality: Twinkie is the brand name for a "golden sponge cake with creamy filling" made by Hostess. Popular rumor has long held that these cakes are virtually indestructible, although Hostess insists they're just flour, eggs, vegetable oil, and stabilizing agents, and have a shelf life of only twenty-five days. The company also points out that seventeen bakeries crank out five hundred million of the treats every year. So much for the secret-Twinkie-warehouse theory. However, the mysterious nature of this food product inspired a group of Rice University students to conduct a series of tests in 1995. Their research study—the TWINKIES, or Tests With Inorganic Noxious Kakes In Extreme Situations project—determined, among other things, that Twinkies are not a good conductor of electrical current, that they can be dropped from great heights without suffering much damage, and that exposing Twinkies to high levels of microwave radiation is a bad idea.

Velveetify, v.: To take an original item (such as cheese) and create a more easily digestible but less nourishing version of it (such as Velveeta). Bibliophiles often complain that Hollywood Velveetifies their favorite books when making them into movies.

Velveeta

Claim: "Not only is Velveeta clear before food coloring is added . . . its composition is also very similar to that of plastic explosives."

Reality: That Velveeta is sold in large rectangular foil-covered blocks is probably why it would be confused with plastic explosives. The exact ingredients of Velveeta are a secret known only to Kraft. However, Velveeta is described on its packaging as a "pasteurized processed cheese spread," which according to FDA regulations means that it's a blend of cheeses to which other stuff such as water, salt, artificial coloring, and stabilizing agents have been added. Since Velveeta begins its life as a blend of cheeses, it would not be clear before the addition of coloring. Imitation cheese, on the other hand, is made out of vegetable oil (according to the FDA's labeling system), and therefore would be translucent before coloring. Technically speaking, Velveeta is not an imitation cheese, although cheese lovers might disagree. The level of suspicion Velveeta inspires is demonstrated by an oft-repeated piece of wisdom: Twinkies have a half-life, but Velveeta is eternal.

Drink the Kool-Aid, v.: To adopt a belief unquestioningly. Often used in the negative: don't drink the Kool-Aid. Refers to the members of the Jim Jones cult who committed mass suicide in 1978 by drinking cyanide-laced Kool-Aid. However, according to Kool-Aid enthusiasts, the members of Jones's People's Temple actually drank Flavor Aid, which is a cheap imitation.

Why Food Always Looks Better in Ads

Ever wonder why the food you see in ads looks better than what you get at the store? It's because advertisers employ food stylists who know how to make food look its best.

Food stylists have a number of standard tricks. Fruit and vegetables can be shined up with glycerin; pasta piled on top of mashed potatoes looks bigger; aspirin gives champagne extra fizz; hamburgers that are left uncooked on the inside and seared with a blowtorch appear moister and plumper; and hairspray can hold food in place.

But a lot of the time what you see in ads isn't food at all. Tobacco smoke stands in for steam. White glue is substituted for milk in cereal ads because the cereal won't go soggy in glue. And ice cream that doesn't melt can be made out of Crisco and corn syrup.

REALITY RULE 4.2

Unless you grow it yourself, you never really know what you're eating.

Permanent Global Summertime, n.: The ability of supermarkets to stock the same fruits and vegetables year-round, as if it were always summer. With a global produce industry, fruits and vegetables are always in season somewhere.

Misleading Labels

In 2003 McDonald's debuted a line of healthier alternatives: a McVeggie Burger on a "toasted whole-wheat bun with barbecue sauce, tomatoes, onions and pickles" and a whole wheat Chicken McGrill sandwich. But the nutritional information for these offerings revealed that the bun wasn't really whole wheat. It was white bread with caramel coloring. At least consumers were getting a bun made out of wheat. At supermarkets and restaurants, many food labels and descriptions will lead you much further astray.

Flavor Fakes

A consumer might assume there's butter in Blast-O-Butter popcorn, or blueberries in Hungry Jack blueberry pancakes, but that would be naive. If you examine the packaging you'll discover that the blue things in the pancakes are pieces of dextrose, and the popcorn is flavored with soybean oil.

These are examples of the food industry's not-so-secret secret: artificial flavoring. Thanks to artificial flavors, food scientists can make a piece of cardboard taste like a juicy steak if they want to. So instead of selling us real blueberries in our pancakes they sell us cheap oil-based substitutes flavored like blueberries. The same goes for thousands of other food products. Manufacturers use "flavored" on labels as a code word for "this product was created in a lab—nothing in it is real."

Food manufacturers like to differentiate between natural and artificial flavors, but as Eric Schlosser points out in *Fast Food Nation,* the distinction is dubious. Chemically speaking, natural and artificial flavors are identical. The difference is that "natural" flavors are produced by using solvents to extract flavor-causing chemicals from food, whereas artificial flavors are mixed from scratch in a lab. But they're both produced in industrial settings far removed from anything most consumers would think was natural.

Ploughman's Lunch, n.: A midday meal of cheese, pickles, bread, and salad, served in British pubs. Marketed as a traditional farmer's meal, though it was created by the food industry in the 1970s. A faux traditional meal. Used in the 1984 film *The Ploughman's Lunch* as a metaphor for the Thatcher administration's manipulation of the media.

The Bait and Switch

The use of blueberry-flavored dextrose chunks might be misleading, but at least if you read the label you can find out what you're buying. In many other instances food producers aren't as forthcoming. They promise one thing but deliver a cheaper and entirely different substitute, without ever providing the smallest clue about what they've done. The practice is illegal, but widespread.

Producers of frozen chicken nuggets are among the most notorious offenders. Regulators in the United Kingdom recently became concerned when they detected beef and pork proteins in samples of imported nuggets. Unscrupulous manufacturers were buying cheap chicken meat and bulking it up by injecting it with water and ground-up parts—including skin and bones—of old cows and pigs. In some cases consumers were lucky if their chicken nuggets were 10 percent chicken meat.

Ordering fish at bargain seafood restaurants is a similar gamble. When food critic Robb Walsh toured Houston-area restaurants he found all kinds of cheap fish species creatively renamed and offered to diners as more expensive varieties. Pacific rockfish, red rock cod, South African hake, and Gulf sheepshead were all served to him as "snapper." He also found lobster tacos that didn't contain lobster but did contain South American langoustine (which is kind of like a large shrimp).

What you get when you buy other meats can be just as surprising. Restaurant chefs substitute cheap pork for veal, because most diners can't taste the difference. A supermarket in Canada was fined $80,000 for selling "beef" that was really horse meat. Regulators suspected the store had been making this switch for years. And in Israel, authorities seized eighty thousand cans that were labeled pâté de foie gras, but contained Bulgarian dog food.

Speaking of dog food, pet lovers might want to think twice about what they're feeding their companions, especially if they're feeding them the really cheap stuff. In the *San Francisco Chronicle* and elsewhere, independent TV producer Keith Wood has exposed some of the most unsavory practices of the pet-food industry. He alleges meat renderers grind up all kinds of unappetizing things—including cats and dogs from the pound—that they then sell to pet-food producers. He even documented cases in which dogs were thrown into the rendering machines with their flea collars still on, joining the skunks, rats, and raccoons already in there. To paraphrase Charlton Heston: *Soylent pet food is puppies! It's puppies!* (See page 75: *Soylent Green*)

Coined Name, n.: A fake name restaurants give to fish species whose real names are unappetizing. For instance, restaurant patrons are usually reluctant to order Patagonian toothfish, but if it's renamed Chilean sea bass they happily request it.

Bottled Water

Just because the label says bottled water comes from a mountain spring, that doesn't mean it does. In 2003 consumers hit Poland Spring Water, distributed by Nestlé, with a class action suit alleging the company's marketing claims were deceptive. The original Poland Spring in the Maine woods hadn't flowed since 1967, and what was sold as spring water "found deep in the woods of Maine" was, according to the suit, actually treated groundwater. A year later Coca-Cola admitted its Dasani brand of bottled water was nothing more than purified tap water. The company insisted the water was nevertheless "as pure as bottled water gets," but this claim was undercut a month later when Coca-Cola had to recall the entire UK supply of Dasani water because it had been contaminated by a cancer-causing chemical.

Consumers who noticed the billboards for Outhouse Springs Water that began appearing around the United States in the summer of 2003 must have thought a company had decided to be unusually up front about the source of its water. The billboards sported catchy slogans such as "It's #1, not #2," "America's first recycled water," and "Truly Tasteless Water." Fortunately (or unfortunately, depending on one's perspective), Outhouse Springs didn't exist. It was a fictional product dreamed up by Adams Outdoor Advertising to show how effective billboard advertising could be. But demand for the product became great enough that the agency struck a deal with a bottled-water company to produce a limited run of Outhouse Springs Water for real. This was the rare case in which consumers hoped a product label was false.

Frankenfood, n.: Food that comes from genetically modified plants or animals. Artificially engineered food.

In 1991 Kentucky Fried Chicken officially changed its name to KFC. The new name was shorter and snappier. Plus, it reduced emphasis on the word "fried" (with all its unhealthy connotations) and on the word "chicken" (since the restaurant had introduced an expanded menu that offered far more than just chicken). This, at least, was the official explanation. But conspiracy theorists on the Internet knew better.

In the late 1990s a circulating e-mail claimed the government had prohibited the company from using the word "chicken" because real chickens were no longer being served to KFC customers. "They actually use genetically manipulated organisms," the e-mail declared. "These so called 'chickens' are kept alive by tubes inserted into their bodies to pump blood and nutrients throughout their structure. They have no beaks, no feathers, and no feet. Their bone structure is dramatically shrunk to get more meat out of them." If the company called itself Kentucky Fried Frankenchicken that would be okay. But Kentucky Fried Chicken was false advertising.

The e-mail alluded to a University of New Hampshire study that somehow proved these allegations, and as the rumor gained momentum, thousands of worried customers called the university to find out more. Of course, no such study had been conducted there, and KFC vehemently denied it was breeding mutant chickens. But as late as 2003 the rumor was still going strong.

In 2005 KFC finally seemed to concede defeat. It began opening some restaurants under the old name of Kentucky Fried Chicken, saying it wanted to return to its Southern roots. But the conspiracy theorists knew better. They always know better.

Waiter, There's Something in My Food!

In 1906 *The Jungle,* by Upton Sinclair, exposed the dark secrets of the meat-packing industry. Readers were shocked to learn what was ground up and included in their sausages: rats, human fingers, and garbage shoveled off the floor. The public outcry the book provoked indirectly led to the creation of the Food and Drug Administration, which regulates the food industry. However, the public is still sensitive about the idea of foreign objects ending up in commercially prepared food. Claims about nasty things found in what we eat attract a huge amount of attention, placing restaurants and food providers in an awkward (and legally vulnerable) position. Sometimes these claims are real, and sometimes they're not—there's no easy way to tell the difference.

Chicken McNoggin: November 2000

Katherine Ortega bought a box of chicken wings at her local McDonald's in Newport News, Virginia. (They were Mighty Wings, which were being test-marketed in the area, rather than Chicken McNuggets, as was often later reported.) But upon taking the meal home, she discovered an unpleasant surprise: a breaded, fried chicken head included with the wings. She immediately contacted the media—and a lawyer. Reporters who examined the head said the batter on it looked exactly like the batter on the wings, so it didn't seem to be something she had created herself. However, lawyers advised her that suing wouldn't net her much in the way of a settlement because she found the head before biting down into it (thus lessening the gross factor). Also, since a chicken head isn't exactly a foreign object in a box of chicken parts, she would have had to argue that she experienced psychological trauma when confronted with the reality that chickens have heads. So a lawsuit never materialized. But

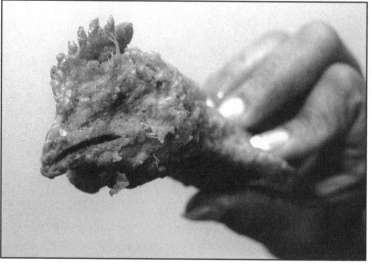

Chicken McNoggin

the picture of the battered chicken head did become one of the most frequently forwarded e-mail images for the next few years.

Distancing, v.: Concealing where food comes from for marketing reasons; creating distance between the ugly, sometimes brutal world of the farm and the pleasant product that appears on your plate. In particular, making meat appear as unlike the animal it comes from as possible.

Clam Condom: February 2002

Four women were eating at a McCormick & Schmick's seafood restaurant in Irvine, California, when one of them bit down on something rubbery in her clam chowder. At first she thought it was a piece of calamari, but when she spit it into her napkin she discovered it was a condom. She immediately complained and the restaurant manager took the condom from her. The woman later sued and won an undisclosed settlement from the restaurant. The restaurant, in turn, sued the supplier of the clam chowder, but lost.

Fried Mouse: September 2003

A man eating at Popeye's Fried Chicken in Baltimore bit down into his three-piece combo meal and discovered a deep-fried mouse lodged between the skin and the meat of the chicken. Police believed the complaint was legitimate since the restaurant had been cited for rodent infestations in the past.

Soup Mouse: May 2004

A woman and her son eating at a Cracker Barrel restaurant found a dead mouse in a bowl of vegetable soup. The woman immediately began screaming, prompting other patrons to leave. While investigating the incident, Cracker Barrel stopped offering the vegetable soup at all 497 of its restaurants nationwide. But when an autopsy revealed that the mouse had died from a skull fracture, not from drowning in soup, police concluded that the woman had placed the mouse in the soup herself.

Wendy's Chili Finger: March 2005

When Anna Ayala bit down on something hard in a bowl of chili at a Wendy's restaurant in California, she spit it out and discovered it was a human finger.

She said she then began vomiting. Wendy's launched an internal investigation, but couldn't find anyone involved in the preparation of the food who was missing a finger. The company also offered a $100,000 reward for any information about how the rogue digit ended up in the chili. Meanwhile, the police launched their own investigation, and a month later arrested Ayala. The finger, it turned out, belonged to an acquaintance of her husband who had lost it in an accident at work. The couple had paid the man $50 for it. Wendy's estimated lost sales from the hoax exceeded $1 million a day.

Fish Tomato, n.: A tomato, bred by the DNA Plant Technology Corporation in 1991, that contained genes from the Arctic flounder. The fish genes were supposed to allow the tomato to resist cold better. However, after the company found that the flavor of the tomato wasn't improved in any way, the product never came to market.

> Reality Check: **Meat Trees**
> Have researchers genetically engineered
> fruit trees that can grow meat?

A May 2003 article that circulated online described trees, developed by the bioengineering firm UltraModAgri Group, that supposedly grew meat inside grapefruit. The article quoted a researcher as saying, "We take the genes from cattle that produce key proteins and splice them into the reproductive cells of grapefruit trees... When the seeds mature into trees, instead of producing ordinary citrus fruit, the pulp contains meat. You get the flavor, texture—even the smell." As science fiction fans know, gene-splicing technology makes anything possible—except for meat-growing trees. The source of the article was the *Weekly World News,* an immediate indication that the article was false (see chapter 10: The *Weekly World News* Effect). But, strangely enough, a few months earlier NASA-funded researchers had announced some success at growing meat in a lab dish. So even if we never have meat trees, we may one day have meat-makers sitting on our countertops, growing us fresh chunks of chicken.

REALITY RULE 4.3

**Most people who say they'll eat anything are joking.
But a few aren't.**

Popcorn Facts, n.: Inoffensive and meaningless facts. Useless trivia.

Soylent Green

Soylent Green is a B-movie from the 1970s starring Charlton Heston. In a future in which overpopulation has resulted in massive overcrowding, people survive on the food the government gives them—a mysterious wafer called Soylent Green. But Heston's character discovers an awful secret. In a classic scene at the movie's end, Heston lurches into the center of a crowd, falls to his knees, and screams, "Soylent Green is PEOPLE! IT'S PEOPLE!" The government is transforming dead bodies into tasty snacks. Human society is eating itself. *Soylent Green* is just a movie, but cannibalism, real and simulated, remains a recurring theme in popular culture.

Manbeef.com

When Manbeef.com appeared online in early 2001 it caused quite a stir by claiming to sell everything the "sophisticated human meat consumer" could want:

> We have everything from Sausages and Soup Bones to Bouillon and Stock. All made with the highest quality human meats. Every cut of human meat we sell has been selected for its superb quality and flawless texture. We only offer the choicest cuts of meat.

The accompanying pictures of meat being squeezed through a grinder were a nice stomach-churning touch. Savvy Web surfers realized right away that Manbeef.com had to be a hoax. After all, the site offered no way to buy the product. However, thousands of other surfers were taken in, prompting the FBI to investigate. The bureau didn't find evidence of wrongdoing, and the site managed to remain online for a couple of months before collapsing beneath the

Manbeef.com, offering the choicest cuts of human meat

weight of public censure. (The URL now takes you to an adults-only porn site.) Soon after it vanished, a Los Angeles graphic designer (who chose to remain anonymous) took credit for the hoax, stating he had wanted to annoy Bible-thumpers. He also managed to sell quite a few T-shirts.

Soylent Sauce

In early 2004 authorities in China exposed the grim secret that a soy sauce factory in Hubei was cutting costs by making its sauce not out of soybeans, but out of human hair. Apparently hair is rich in proteins, just as soybeans are, so if you process the hair correctly it will yield a protein stew that can serve as the base for soy sauce. Consumers were warned to watch out for cut-rate sauces with the word "blended" on their labels.

Similar rumors persist about bakery products such as bagels, croissants, and pizza dough. Bakers often add the amino acid L-cysteine to dough to make it softer and more elastic. L-cysteine can be made out of feathers, hooves, horns, or, yes, human hair. Reportedly Asia is the world's major supplier of cheap hair for this purpose. It's hard to know what to make of such rumors, since it is possible they're true, although you would think food manufacturers could more easily obtain animal parts than human parts. Certain orthodox religious groups avoid bakery products on the off chance the hair rumor is true—unlike followers of the Atkins Diet who avoid them because they're fattening.

Human-Flavored Tofu

Hufu stands for human-flavored tofu. According to eathufu.com, the website that claims to sell it, this stuff "simulates the texture and flavor of human flesh." And what does human flesh taste like? "Like beef but a little softer in texture and a little sweeter in taste."

Hufu is the brainchild of Mark Nuckols. He wants to eventually offer varieties of hufu, but he's starting with just one: Hufu Classic Strips. These "will basically resemble the choicer flesh, which is upper arms, thighs and buttocks." Oh, and the site does offer a range of clothing items, including T-shirts and chef aprons (plus the *Soylent Green* DVD). The clothes, Nuckols concedes, are expected to be the main source of his company's revenue.

When eathufu.com came online in May 2005, I publicly expressed a few doubts about it. I wondered how Nuckols could know his product tasted like human flesh since he admitted he had never eaten Homo sapiens. I also noted that he could sell regular tofu, call it human-flavored, and (except for a very few people) no one would know the difference. This resulted in a flurry of e-mails from Nuckols, who insisted that hufu was a "bona fide undertaking." Duly noted. But don't expect to see hufu at a supermarket near you anytime soon. It's an Internet-only treat.

Reality Check: Strange Diets

There are all kinds of dietary practices. Some people eat only raw food. Others load up on fruit. Then there are those who shun all carbs. Try to guess if the dietary practices listed below are real or fake.

Mineralarianism

Does a group known as mineralarians subsist only on foods of mineral origin, refusing to be responsible for taking the lives of animals or plants?

Mineralarians believe it's just as wrong to kill the lowliest bacterium as it is to kill a cow, because all life is interrelated. Therefore they restrict themselves to a diet of pure minerals, extracting all the nutrients they need to survive from air, water, and rock. Strict mineralarians refuse to nourish themselves from fossil fuels such as coal and petroleum, since "fossils are usually the result of violence and often contain plain evidence of a being's untimely and painful death." Even stricter mineralarians will only consume material of an extraterrestrial origin (such as meteorites) for fear that material of terrestrial origin was once a part of a living creature. But, of course, there are no practicing mineralarians. (Did you really think there were?) This dietary practice is the fanciful creation of Charles Bennett, a researcher at IBM who enjoys creating parody websites in his spare time. He insists he doesn't know any practicing mineralarians. However, there really is a religious group, called Breatharians, who claim to subsist on light and air. Wiley Brooks has been promoting the practice in the United States since the 1970s, though he was once found secretly eating hamburgers. (He said pollution was preventing him from getting enough nutrition from air and light.) Several people throughout the world have been found starved to death with copies of Breatharian teachings beside them, examples of Darwinian survival at its finest.

The Tapeworm Diet

Are tapeworms (or tapeworm larvae) sometimes consumed as a diet aid, since the worm will grow inside the stomach and consume all the extra food the person eats?

Rumor holds that quack doctors used to sell diet pills that contained tapeworm heads. Once the desired weight loss was achieved, the tapeworm was removed with poison. However, if doctors did this, they were only helping their clients get incredibly sick. Tapeworms do consume the food you eat, but they also consume all the necessary vitamins, leaving you malnourished. Plus, you can look forward to your immune system reacting to the presence of a large worm in your gut, causing your stomach to swell up and cysts to appear in your eyes. It's not pleasant stuff. The opera singer Maria Callas did once have a tapeworm removed from her system, and some sources said she had purposefully taken gelatin capsules containing larvae to lose weight. But most of her biographers say she unintentionally got infected by eating raw steak and liver tartare.

Auto-urine Therapy

Do many people drink their own urine, claiming to derive numerous health benefits from it?

Drinking your own urine is said to help improve your immune system, give you nice skin, prevent aging, and fight gum disease. And that's just for starters. According to urine-drinking enthusiasts (and, yes, there are quite a few of them), there's almost nothing this magical liquid won't cure. Indian holy men have been promoting auto-urine therapy for thousands of years. Modern medicine, however, has never been able to find any health benefit in it. A peculiar variant of auto-urine therapy is the use of urine as a skin toughener. A number of pro baseball players have admitted to regularly peeing on their hands during the season in the belief that doing so will toughen their skin and allow them to better catch balls without gloves. But, if anything, urine would soften the skin. Urea is, after all, an ingredient in many commercial moisturizing lotions.

Where's the Beef?: A rhetorical question used to express the suspicion that something is all image and no substance. First used in a 1984 marketing campaign by the fast-food restaurant Wendy's. Entered mainstream usage the same year when presidential hopeful Walter Mondale asked this question of his Democratic rival, Gary Hart.

Pets or Meat

To some people pets are the adorable creatures with whom we share our homes. To others they're just a meal. The friction between these two points of view is inspiration for endless mischief.

PetsOrFood.com claims to be "dedicated to bringing consumers healthy, certified organic animals at wholesale prices. Whether you're getting a pet lizard for your son or a dozen Doberman flank steaks for a Super Bowl party." The website offers a range of species, all delivered live or "ready to eat." The selection includes bald eagles, snakes, hamsters, and baby seals (freshly clubbed and frozen). Plus, they provide recipes, just in case you have a hankering for sweet-and-sour koala loaf. Yes, the site is a hoax. (I think—though it's so well done it had me constantly second-guessing.)

Bernd—the original bunny in peril

Another recurring joke is bunny blackmail. In 2004 a European site displayed a picture of a cute rabbit named Bernd and declared: "I swear by God, I will have this lovely rabbit for New Year's Eve Dinner if my account doesn't show a balance of at least 1,000,000 € by latest 31st Dec 2004!" What could rabbit lovers do but surrender their money? Some did attempt more proactive action. The Free Bernd group circulated a petition demanding Bernd's release, and a group of German militants calling themselves the Rabbit Company threatened to rescue Bernd by force. But when December 31 came, the ransom hadn't come anywhere close to being raised, and Bernd died. (Or so the website claimed.)

Hot on the heels of Save Bernd there appeared Save Toby, an American website threatening to extinguish the life of "the cutest little bunny on the planet" unless people coughed up $50,000. In case of nonpayment, Toby's owner warned, "I am going to eat him. I am going to take Toby to a butcher to have him slaughter this cute bunny. I will then prepare Toby for a midsummer feast." Early in the life of SaveToby.com, a small notice at the bottom of the site admitted, "This is a joke: please only donate to buy gear or help support savetoby.com." But this disclaimer later disappeared. As of August 2005, Toby had been granted a year's reprieve thanks to a book deal his owner secured. Now the bunny will die unless one hundred thousand books are sold by November 2006. Such shameless extortion makes one sympathize with the rival sites that have sprung up: CookToby.com and, even better, ScrewToby.com.

Unturkey, n.: A fake turkey made of soy and wheat.

La Malbouffe, n.: A French term for foul (or fake) food. Coined by the farmer José Bové, who became a national hero for burning down a McDonald's restaurant in Millau. He claimed McDonald's was corrupting French culture.

> ## Reality Check: Strange Foods
> People throughout the world eat many strange things.
> But does anyone really eat *this* stuff?

Turkey Testicles

Are turkey testicles considered a delicacy in the American Midwest?

The first question many people have when confronted with the idea of eating turkey testicles is whether turkeys have testicles. The answer is yes. (They're tucked away inside the bird.) It's also true that turkey nuts or turkey fries are considered quite a delicacy by those who have a taste for that kind of thing. Annually for the past twenty-five years, the town of Byron, Illinois, has hosted the world-famous Turkey Testicle Festival. "Come and have a ball" is its slogan. In case you're curious, they deep-fry them. Calvin Schwabe, author of *Unmentionable Cuisine,* notes that turkey testicles are the perfect complement to a good martini.

Edible Outdoor Gear

Does Eastern Active Technologies manufacture edible outdoor gear (sleeping bags, stove fuel, etc.) that allows backpackers to progressively lighten their loads on long hikes by eating what they have to carry?

The Eastern Active Technologies (EAT) website, ediblegear.com, describes products such as a SnackSack sleeping bag made out of VeggieLoft; trekking poles crafted from compressed beef, chicken, shrimp, and textured protein; and tarps available in "delicious fruit flavors." It all looks intriguingly real, but if you try to order any of this stuff you get a message informing you that their server is unable to process your request and suggesting you "print your order form, tape it to the back of a mental patient, and hope that he/she wanders near our offices." So I think it's fair to assume that edible outdoor gear is a hoax.

Cat-Droppings Coffee

Is the most expensive coffee in the world made from coffee beans eaten and excreted by Indonesian cats?

It's called Kopi Luwak, and its promoters do claim it's the most expensive brew in the world. (It retails for about $300 a pound.) When the Indonesian palm toddy cat (which is actually a mongooselike civet, not a cat) eats coffee beans, they're partially broken down in its digestive system—adding a rich, earthy flavor to them—before being passed. Workers handpick the beans out of the cat's feces (how would you like to have that job?), which is why the stuff is so rare. Raven's Brew Coffee markets Kopi Luwak in America with the slogan "good to the last dropping." Just to clarify, regular cats *do not* have the ability to produce this stuff, so don't think you can supplement your income by slipping a few coffee beans into Fluffy's food.

Cow Urine

Is there a thriving market for cow urine in India, where many consider it a health drink?

According to cow-urine aficionados, this bracing tonic—called *gomutram* in India—treats all manner of illnesses, including cancer and diabetes. Owners of Indian cow shelters have found this health fad quite lucrative. They just filter, bottle, and ship the stuff. The biggest problem is the smell, but that can be masked with herbs and spices. Or just drink it down really fast. Demand is so strong it's spawned a market for fake cow urine—buffalo or sheep urine passed off by scam artists as authentic cow pee. I can offer no advice for differentiating the real from the fake in this case, but those who want a guarantee of top quality should keep their own cow.

Meatshakes

Does an American chain of fast-food restaurants offer meatshakes—shakes made from ham, beef, or chicken, mixed in a blender and sipped through a straw?

Americans love meat, and they love milkshakes. So why not combine the two? Well, people who can't swallow solid food might whip themselves up an occasional meatshake, but the notion hasn't yet gone mainstream. However, a Long Beach band called Ugly Duckling did create an elaborate hoax website that claimed to be the home page of the MeatShake Corporation. (Its corporate slogan was "Meat. Lots of meat.") It was convincing enough to fool some otherwise savvy Web surfers, such as Rob Manuel, cofounder of the popular b3ta.com. Once the site was fully debunked, a few brave souls couldn't resist making their own meatshakes, just to see what they tasted like. The consensus was that whether made out of ham, beef, or chicken, they were disgusting.

Army Worm Wine

Is a delicate white wine created from fermented army worms (worms that hang in weblike sacks from trees)?

Ray Reigstad of Duluth, Minnesota, is the proud creator of Army Worm Wine (armywormwine.com). To my knowledge, he is the only person in the world making this stuff. He mashes up the worms, adds sugar, water, yeast, and other ingredients, and lets this wicked cocktail ferment. He says the end product tastes like pinot grigio or white bordeaux, but I've never sampled it to verify this. Purists note it's probably the sugar, not the army worms themselves, fermenting. Wines of meaty or buggy varieties are actually quite common in Asia. Travelers report finding snake wine and even (animal) penis wine in restaurants in China and Vietnam. Reportedly, the more venomous the snake, the better the wine. (I don't know what makes for the best penis wine.) But the wines are created by adding the animal (or animal part) to rice wine— meaning the animal itself isn't part of the fermentation process. Thus, when you order a bottle of snake wine there'll be a big snake staring out of the bottle at you. Ditto for the penis varietals.

Rodent Cheese

Is cheese made from the milk of lactating rats considered a delicacy in France?

The French do love cheese, and they produce a bewildering array of it. But they don't make rodent cheese. Theoretically cheese can be made from the milk of any animal (including humans), but it takes about ten pounds of milk to produce one pound of cheese. To produce rat-milk cheese, you would need an awful lot of rats. So if you stumble across the website of the Federation of Rodent Cheesemakers, deedah.org/cheese, you can rest assured it's a hoax, despite its claim that "fine rat cheeses are becoming ever more popular." And in case you're wondering about human-breast-milk cheese, I've never heard of anyone making it, though it would surprise me if someone, at some point, hadn't tried. The problem is that the cheese's flavor is influenced by whatever the milk producer eats. So you would want vegetarian milk donors, unless you like cheese that tastes like rotting meat.

PHOTOGRAPHY 5

A number of commentators, reacting to fake pictures circulating on the Internet, have recently expressed concern that our ability to digitally manipulate images will erode public confidence in the trustworthiness of photography. If so, it couldn't happen a moment too soon. Photography has never been trustworthy. The sooner everyone realizes this, the better.

REALITY RULE 5.1

"Photographs may not lie, but liars may photograph."*

Photoshop, 1. n.: A brand of digital-image-manipulation software marketed by Adobe. **2. v.:** To digitally alter an image. Adobe objects to the use of the word "photoshop" as a verb, insisting that instead of saying "the image was photoshopped" people should say "the image was enhanced using Adobe® Photoshop® software." While Adobe's suggested alternative is certainly catchy, it hasn't achieved widespread use.

Moving the Body

You don't need a darkroom or image-manipulation software to create a fake image. Fakery can be achieved simply by posing people or objects in artificial ways. It's a technique known as "moving the body," and it's one of the oldest photographic tricks around.

The term derives from a series of photographs taken by Alexander Gardner after the Battle of Gettysburg in 1863. The pictures show Confederate sharpshooters lying where they had been shot. But in 1975, historian William Frassanito determined that the same body appeared in different images. In other words, Gardner had moved a soldier's corpse around to pose it in various dramatic locations.

In 1936 the federal Resettlement Administration did the same with a steer's skull in images it provided newspapers in order to dramatize (for political purposes) the severity of the drought in South Dakota. But

The perambulating skull of South Dakota

editors at the Fargo *Forum* caught the deception. The moving prop came to be known as the "perambulating skull."

---

*Documentary photographer Lewis Hine, 1874–1940

The same kind of trickery continues today. On September 20, 2002, the *New York Times* ran a dramatic photo of a young boy of Arabic descent aiming a toy gun outside an Arabian food store in Lackawanna, New York, near to where an alleged al-Qaeda sleeper cell had operated. The photo was taken by Pulitzer Prize–winning photographer Ed Keating, but rival photographers present at the scene accused Keating of staging the shot, claiming he had arranged the scene "like a fashion shoot." Keating denied the allegations, but was nevertheless forced to resign from the *Times*.

Real Picture, Fake Caption

People say a picture is worth a thousand words, but it's also true that pictures usually require a few words of explanation. And a few wrong words can totally change the meaning of a picture.

Newspaper tycoon William Randolph Hearst was notorious for allowing his papers to recaption photos creatively. In 1913 the New York *American* ran a picture of Mexican children, their hands raised above their heads, standing in the ocean. The caption said the children were being driven into the water to be executed. In reality, the children were waving to a British tourist standing on the beach (and the photo was taken in British Honduras, not Mexico). In 1932 Hearst's New York *Daily Mirror* ran a photo of what it said were hunger marchers storming Buckingham Palace in London. The photo actually showed well-wishers gathered outside the palace in 1929 when King George V was ill.

Advertisers also play fast and loose with captions. Before and after weight-loss pictures are frequent offenders. Was the after picture really taken after using the product? Do the images even show the same person, or is the after image the before woman's slender twin sister (as happened in one case)?

Another frequent offender is the tourism brochure. Those sun-and-surf pictures look great, but were they taken in the location to which you'd be traveling? A 2003 brochure for Bermuda featured beaches in Hawaii, scuba divers in the Seychelles, and a woman swimming with a dolphin in Florida. A covered bridge prominently displayed in a Kentucky tourism brochure was actually located in New Hampshire.

Finally there's the Internet, where a creative caption can make any picture more interesting. During the war in Iraq a picture has circulated showing two enormous spiders locked together and dangling from a soldier's uniform. An accompanying caption reads:

Camel Spider found in Iraq—This is a huge spider!!!!...This picture is a perfect example of why you don't want to go to the desert. These are 2 of the biggest I've ever seen. With a vertical leap that would make a pro basketball player weep with envy (they have to be able to jump up on to a

Camel spiders of Iraq

camels [sic] stomach after all), they latch on and inject you with a local anesthesia so you can't feel it feeding on you. They eat flesh, not just suck out your juices like a normal spider. I'm gonna be having nightmares after seeing this photo!

Camel spiders are real. They do live in Iraq. They are big and nasty-looking. And this image wasn't photoshopped or manipulated. But the caption was mostly a lie because these creatures don't latch onto camels and feed on their flesh, nor do they feed on humans. In reality, camel spiders are nonvenomous, though if you're a cricket, pillbug, or scorpion, you might want to steer clear of them.

Pixel Plasticity, n.: The ease with which the pixels that make up digital images can be altered and rearranged.

Virtual Insertion, n.: An object digitally inserted into a picture. For instance, fake billboards are often inserted into the background during the broadcast of sports games. If you were at the game, instead of watching it at home, you wouldn't see that huge advertisement for Viagra behind first base.

case file: Cut-and-Paste Diversity

The real world is full of racial tension. Not so the fake world shown in advertisements. In ads, everyone is one big, happy, diverse family.

If you're advertising soft drinks, creating the illusion of diversity is no problem. You just hire a racially diverse bunch of actors. But if you're advertising something like a university, displaying diversity becomes a little trickier. You feel obliged to show pictures of people who actually attend the school. But what if the school doesn't have many minority students? This was the problem faced by the University of Wisconsin-Madison officials in charge of putting together the 2001–2002 undergraduate application brochure. Try as they might, they couldn't find any good photos of a racially diverse group of students interacting with one another in a positive way.

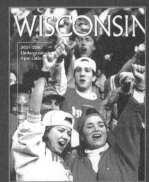

But when the brochure was mailed to fifty thousand potential students, the problem had apparently been solved. The cover boasted a crowd scene from a recent Badger football game. Most of the students in the crowd were white, but on the left-hand side of the shot was a smiling black student. It was a charming picture of a racially harmonious campus.

But Anna Gould, a staffer at the *Daily Cardinal,* UW-Madison's student newspaper, noticed that everyone in the picture was in shadow except for the lone black student— who had the sun shining directly on him. Intrigued, Gould tracked down the original photo and discovered that the black student, Diallo Shabazz, wasn't in it. He hadn't even attended the game. His face had been digitally inserted into the cover photo.

When the revelation broke in September 2000, embarrassed university officials admitted they had photoshopped Shabazz's face into the photo (without his permission), and

Now you see him, now you don't. Diallo Shabazz becomes an unwilling attendee of a Badger football game.

then frantically tried to recall the brochures that had been sent out. Curiously, when I e-mailed the university in 2005 to get more details about the incident, the school's senior photographer responded that "this incident was the result of an unfortunate error in judgment and was not in any way an intentional hoax." Then he wished me luck in finding *something else* to write about. How did they unintentionally photoshop a student's face into a picture? I have no idea. But I guess that's their story, and they're sticking to it.

REALITY RULE 5.2

Should a suitably dramatic picture of a major event not exist, one will be created.

Framing, 1. n.: The belief that an experience isn't real until it's been framed by a camera. **2. v.:** Photographing every moment of a vacation (or event) as if having a photo of yourself grinning in front of the Taj Mahal, Eiffel Tower, or Big Ben somehow makes the experience of being there genuine.

In the Wake of Disaster

Nowadays it's not enough to read about horrific events. We want to see pictures. It's as if we need the pictures to convince ourselves the event was real. Such images generate a huge amount of public attention, especially now that they have the perfect distribution system—the Internet. But sometimes disasters aren't accompanied by photographs. When this is the case, the hoaxers go to work, creating the latest trend in photographic fakery: the postcalamity hoax photo.

Tourist Guy

The postcalamity hoax photo craze began with 9/11. In the days immediately after the tragedy a photo circulated online showing a man happily posing on the observation deck of the World Trade Center, while, unbeknownst to him, a plane approached from behind. A caption accompanying the image read: *Attached is a picture that was taken of a tourist atop the World Trade Center*

Tourist Guy

Tower, the first to be struck by a terrorist attack. This camera was found but the subject in the picture has not yet been located.

The so-called tourist guy picture was quickly debunked (the plane in the background was a 757, whereas the ones that struck the World Trade Center were 767s) and eventually revealed to be the work of a Hungarian man who had created it as a joke for his friends, never intending it to circulate as widely as it did. But the enormous amount of attention the image received must have struck a note of envy among would-be hoaxers everywhere, because almost every disaster since has been dramatized in a fake photo.

Designer SARS Masks

"Louis Vuitton SARS mask"

When the SARS epidemic became a matter of public concern in early 2003, thousands of people sought to protect themselves from airborne germs by wearing surgical masks. Soon faux shots of models with SARS-mask tanlines were doing the rounds on the Internet, and then there appeared an advertisement for a designer SARS mask by Louis Vuitton. In reality, Louis Vuitton made no such product.

The *Columbia* Explosion

No cameras recorded the explosion of the space shuttle *Columbia* on February 1, 2003, but that didn't stop the spread of a dramatic series of images supposedly taken by an Israeli satellite in space. The pictures were actually still images from the Touchstone Pictures movie *Armageddon.* In the movie a space shuttle is

"Shuttle explosion from an Israeli satellite"

struck by meteorite fragments. An unknown hoaxer simply lifted this scene from a DVD of the movie, added the phony caption, and set the images loose on the Web.

The Great Blackout of 2003

On August 14, 2003, a blackout hit the northeastern United States. Almost the next day a photo appeared claiming to be a NASA satellite image of the event. The entire United States could be seen, with dots of light revealing major population centers—except for the northeastern corner of the country, which was

"Satellite photo of blackout"

covered in inky blackness. The picture (minus the blacked-out portion) was a real satellite image that had appeared on NASA's Astronomy Picture of the Day website in November 2000. (Actually it was a composite image of hundreds of photos taken by Defense Department meteorological satellites.) The hoaxer had simply darkened the relevant portion of the photo.

The Asian Tsunami

Finally, after the Asian tsunami of December 2004, a picture circulated showing an enormous wave, hundreds of feet high, bearing down on a city. The caption read: "This picture is not a fake. It appears to have been taken from a hi-rise building window in downtown Phuket, Thailand. The power of nature is hard to comprehend,

"Tsunami seen from a high-rise"

especially the destructiveness of water." Except that the city in the photo wasn't Phuket. It was Antofagasta, Chile. The gigantic wave had been photoshopped in.

Peter Panning, v.: Using graphics software to attach an artificial shadow to an object. A common technique for adding the illusion of depth and realism to fake photos.

Reality Check: Breaking the Sound Barrier
A vapor cone forms around a jet plane as it breaks the sound barrier.
Hoax or not?

It looks too cool to be real, but the photo is authentic. This shot of an F/A-18 Hornet assigned to Strike Fighter Squadron One Five One (VFA-151) was taken over the Pacific on July 7, 1999, by Ensign John Gay. As it circulated on the Internet, the image was often described as "a picture of a sonic boom," which

U.S. Navy photo

is somewhat misleading. The vapor cone forming around the plane is not a sonic boom. It's caused by the extreme speed of the plane pressurizing the air and causing the moisture in it to condense. In other words, a plane doesn't have to break the sound barrier to cause a vapor cone to form, though in this photo the plane reportedly was about to do so.

F/A-18 Hornet

Kodak Moment, n.: A picture-perfect photo opportunity. (Also inspiration for the joke, "What do Kodak and condoms have in common? They both capture the moment.")

Kodak Courage, n.: An exaggerated sense of courage caused by the presence of a camera. The extreme behavior people wouldn't engage in if they weren't being filmed.

REALITY RULE 5.3

The bigger the animal, the taller the tale you're likely being fed.

Fat Cats of the Internet

Photography and oversized animals go together like bacon and eggs, or peanut butter and jelly. In the early days of photography a few entrepreneurs such as William "Dad" Martin became millionaires by selling tall-tale postcards that showed chickens as big as houses and fish the size of trucks (usually with a caption such as, "They grow 'em big here in Kansas"). The public couldn't get enough of them. Not much has changed. In fact, the tall-tale photo genre has enjoyed a renaissance, thanks to the Internet. The main difference is that the "in" animals are now cats. City-dwelling, apartment-living Internet users probably relate more to enormous cats than to enormous farm animals. Fat dogs occasionally make appearances, but mostly it's the flab-bound felines that capture all the attention.

Snowball the Monster Cat

The first big cat to become an Internet celebrity was Snowball the monster cat, whose picture first appeared in in-boxes in early 2000. Snowball, who was easily the size of a large dog, was shown in the arms of a bearded man. An accompanying story told of how Snowball's mother had been found abandoned near a Canadian nuclear lab, the implication being that Snowball's size (eighty-seven pounds, supposedly) was the result of genetic mutation. In reality,

Snowball the Monster Cat

Photo courtesy of Cordell Hauglie

Snowball was the digital creation of Washington state resident Cordell Hauglie (the man in the picture). Hauglie had "improved" a picture of the family cat, Jumper, as a joke to share with his daughter, but his daughter forwarded it to her friends, and they forwarded it to their friends, and so on and so on. Somewhere along the line a prankster added the bogus story about the nuclear lab. Having never intended his tall-tale photo to spread as far as it did, Hauglie is now amused to discover it's made him famous. It's landed him appearances on TV, features in magazines, and guest celebrity spots at cat shows.

Cordell Hauglie with Jumper, Snowball's real-life model. Jumper actually weighs twenty-one pounds.

Munchkin the Cat

Snowball was not destined to hog the limelight forever. In 2002 along came Munchkin, seen luxuriating on his back, feet in the air, almost crushing his poor owner beneath him. No story accompanied Munchkin, but that didn't stop him from achieving Internet fame. The *Sydney Morning Herald* declared him a hoax, and I myself expressed doubt about his reality. But Munchkin turned out to be that rare curiosity—a real fat cat. In 2005 his owner, Susan Martin of Ontario, Canada, e-mailed me, sending along more pictures of her "fatboy" to prove he was real. His actual name was Sassy; he weighed forty pounds; and he had died of heart disease. Susan remarked that his picture

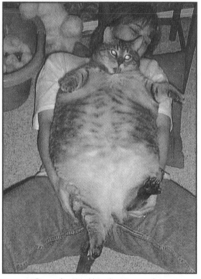

Sassy, aka Munchkin, the Monster Cat

Photos courtesy of Susan Martin

Forty-pound Sassy didn't need any digital help to loom large.

had been floating around unattributed for years, but she wanted everyone to know who he really was, because he had been such a wonderful cat.

At forty pounds, Sassy was certainly a very big boy, but he wouldn't qualify as the fattest cat ever. That honor goes to Katy, a Siamese living in the Ural Mountains, who tips the scales at over fifty pounds. However, Katy's achievement remains unofficial because the *Guinness Book of World Records* doesn't maintain a category for fattest cat. It doesn't want to encourage people to overfeed their pets.

Forced Perspective, n.: The placement of objects of different sizes at different distances from the camera to make them appear either larger or smaller than they actually are.

THE WORLD WIDE WEB 6

The Internet began its life as a tool for researchers. Scholars used it to share papers, and scientists to swap data. It was quite peaceful online back then, except for the occasional academic squabble. But what none of these early Internet users could have realized was that they were contributing to the creation of the most fertile breeding ground for hoaxes and frauds ever seen in the history of humankind. Today as you check your e-mail or browse the Web, it may seem you're innocently going about your business. But you're actually navigating a complex minefield of misinformation and deception. At every corner, bonsai kittens wait to entrap you, and Nigerian bank scammers seek to tempt you with their siren song of false riches. If you don't know what you're doing (and if you have no clue what bonsai kittens or Nigerian bank scammers are), then you stand a good chance of getting *pwned*.

pwned, adj.: Owned. Hoaxed. According to Internet legend, this term was first used during an online game when a winning player tried to type "You Were Owned" but misspelled it as "You Were Pwned." The term has been in use ever since. How to pronounce it is anyone's guess.

REALITY RULE 6.1

Just because you read it on the Internet doesn't mean it's true.

Pierre Salinger Syndrome, n.: The tendency to believe information found on the Internet, no matter how far-fetched. Behavior often observed in new users of the Internet (though there are significant exceptions). Named after journalist Pierre Salinger. In July 1996 TWA Flight 800 crashed into the Atlantic Ocean just south of Long Beach, New York. Four months later Salinger stated at a press conference that the plane had been downed by friendly fire from U.S. forces. This claim was immediately denied by official investigators, but Salinger insisted he had proof. And what was his proof? An apparently random document he had come across on the Internet. Salinger denied all this, insisting he got the information from an offline source, but the phrase stuck. The first use of it is attributed to *Wired* reporter Moira Gunn in a July 1997 article.

Not Really the News

In late 2002 sixteen-year-old Eric Smith and a friend created the Fake CNN News Generator. Visitors to this website could type text and a headline into a form, which would instantly format the material to look like a CNN news story, complete with authentic CNN logo and banner ads. It was a recipe for chaos just waiting to be unleashed.

Smith and his friend later claimed they never intended for the public to discover their creation. But in early 2003 word of the fake news generator leaked out, and almost overnight it was receiving over two millions visitors a day. That's when the chaos began.

Thousands of phony stories were created and circulated on the Internet, where they did their evil work. One story fooled a number of TV and radio

Fake CNN news: "Olsen Twins
Set to Attend University of Notre Dame"

stations into reporting that the (still living) musician Dave Matthews had died of a drug overdose. Another story claimed the Olsen twins had decided to attend the University of Notre Dame (or, in a different version, Ohio University), causing admissions offices to be flooded by phone calls from fans of the teen celebrities. (The Olsens eventually went to New York University.) At first the media had no idea where these fake stories were coming from, but then they traced them to the Fake CNN News Generator. CNN quickly had the site shut down.

The Fake CNN News Generator was the most notorious phony news creator of all time. But there are plenty of other fake news generators around, capable of mimicking any reputable news site including the Associated Press, or the *New York Times*. This is why you can't assume a news story on the Internet—even if it looks official—is true. Clues that a story might be the work of a prankster include bad grammar, poor spelling, and strange-looking URLs—for instance, if the story isn't posted at http://cnn.com, but at http://world-cnn.com, or http://cnn.com@64.62.135.28. (Type this second URL into your browser and see what you get.) The best defense against fake news is to check that other sources are reporting the same story before you run and tell all your friends about the incredible thing you just read on the Internet.

Fact Check Your Ass, v.: To use the Internet to debunk improbable claims made by the media. The phrase points to a paradoxical truth—that while the Internet is one of the greatest sources of misinformation ever created, it is simultaneously one of the greatest tools for debunking misinformation. First use of the phrase is attributed to journalist Ken Layne, who was overheard telling a fellow journalist that thanks to the Internet we can "fact check your ass."

> ### Reality Check: **Powergen Italia**
> Did the energy company Powergen really register the
> domain name powergenitalia.com for its Italian subsidiary,
> not realizing this URL could be read in two ways?

Sometimes names that are perfectly innocent when written normally acquire whole new shades of meaning when strung together as URLs. But in this case, powergenitalia.com was not the result of an oversight by the Powergen company. It was an unknown prankster's joke. When the URL started making the rounds on the Internet in mid-2004, Powergen was quick to disassociate itself from it. However, many companies and organizations have failed to see the double meanings of their domain names. Some examples: viagrafix.com (home of ViaGrafix); ipwine.com (home of the Ingleside Vineyard); whorepresents.com (home of Who Represents); cummingfirst.com (home of the Cumming First United Methodist Church, located in Cumming, Georgia); and rightsexchange .com (home of Rights Exchange, a firm specializing in digital rights management applications). Of course, some organizations intentionally have a bit of fun with their domain names—the classic example being nice-tits.org, official site of the Royal Tit-Watching (Ornithological) Society of Britain.

REALITY RULE 6.2

Anyone can create a website, including liars, practical jokers, and people who want to sell you a T-shirt.

Hoax Websites

As you surf the Web, you'll find all kinds of unusual sites. One day you may stumble on the home page of the Society for the Protection and Preservation of Fruitcakes (fruitcakesociety.org). The next day you'll discover the website of the Institute of Advanced Rutabaga Studies (members.tripod.com/ ~rutabagas). The Fruitcake Society is real (it's an informal group of people who like fruitcakes), while the Rutabaga Institute is not. But how would you know this? Given the number of hoax sites to be found on the Web, how can you know whether any website is real or fake (*fake* meaning, in this context, that it claims to be something other than what it really is)? It's not easy. But it helps if you're familiar with the ten basic varieties of hoax websites. Nine are listed below. The tenth (fake weblogs) is described later in this chapter. (As noted in the introduction, I make no guarantee that any of the URLs I provide will still work by the time you read this.)

The Practical Joke

Would you believe there's such a thing as dehydrated water (buydehydratedwater.com), or a campaign to save the Pacific Northwest tree octopus (zapatopi.net/treeoctopus)? Hopefully not. But sites advancing these and other tongue-in-cheek claims can be found across the Web. They're harmless, attempting nothing more sinister than to pull your leg, and common sense should help you spot them. But if not, look for the telltale T-shirt sale. Pranksters can't resist making a buck by peddling T-shirts. (By the way, if you want a Save the Jackalope T-shirt, I've got a special on my site.)

As far-fetched as such sites can be, someone is always gullible enough to believe them. For instance, in 2004 the city council of Aliso Viejo, California, deliberated on a ban on anything made with the chemical dihydrogen monoxide, after finding a website (dhmo.org) that detailed the dangers of this "odorless, tasteless chemical." The site warned that this chemical is a major component of acid rain, that it corrodes metal, and that its ingestion causes excessive sweating and urination. But before the council could embarrass itself further, someone clued them in that dihydrogen monoxide is the scientific term for water.

Also check out: Dog Island, the island where dogs roam free (thedogisland .com); Rent a German, "rent a German . . . and smile!" (rentagerman.de); and Flatulent Technologies, "extracting energy from everything that stinks or rots" (flatulenttechnologies.com).

The Parody

Parody is mockery by comic imitation. Usually parodies are obvious enough because of the exaggerated or distorted nature of the imitation. But sometimes they're far more subtle, in which case they acquire the attributes of a hoax. My vote for the most successful hoax/parody on the Web goes to Objective: Christian Ministries (objectiveministries.org). On first, second, and third glance it appears to be run by a group of earnest fundamentalist Christians who advocate policies such as redesigning the American flag to include the word GOD stamped across it. They also condemn Apple Computer as a "front for evolutionism." The site fools almost everyone, including fundamentalists. (For a while it conned a Christian hosting service into providing it with Web space.) In reality, it's an elaborate anti-Christian spoof, rumored to have ties to a porn operator.

Also check out: Whitehouse.org, a political parody of Whitehouse.gov (the official site of the White House); BushIsLord.com, dedicated to the principle that George W. Bush is "not only our nation's leader, but our spiritual light-house and embodied salvation"; and preparingforemergencies.co.uk, Thomas Scott's spoof of the British government's Preparing for Emergencies site (preparingforemergencies.gov.uk). Scott's version prepares citizens for emer-gencies such as zombie attacks and alien invasions, but the comedy was lost on British authorities, who attempted to force Scott to take down his site.

The Gross-out Hoax

Bonsaikitten.com describes how to raise kittens inside glass jars so that the kittens' bones mold to the shapes of the jars. The site even claims to sell these bonsai kittens. But thankfully, the site is a hoax, created as a prank in late 2000 by some MIT students. No kittens were harmed in its creation. This was officially determined by the FBI, which investigated the site after receiving thousands of complaints.

Bonsaikitten.com is probably the most well-known example of that evil sib-ling of the practical joke, the gross-out hoax website. The goal of such sites is

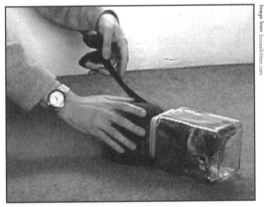

How to create a bonsai kitten.

simple—to shock and disturb. They flourish on the Web because (a) they're easy to create, and (b) they have built-in credibility, since people do disgusting and cruel things, for real, every day. Other notorious gross-out sites include cutoffmyfeet.com, on which a man named Freck claimed he was going to host a live broadcast of himself cutting off his feet; and manbeef.com, a pseudo-retailer of human flesh (see chapter 4). A big clue that a gross site is a hoax is if it claims to sell something, such as bonsai kittens or human flesh, but doesn't actually provide the means to purchase the product. If the site offers to sell you a T-shirt, that is, as always, a big, flashing-red hoax sign.

Also check out: Celebrity Skin, the online source for celebrity skin and bodily fluids (blackpitchpress.com/celebrityskin); and PetsOrFood.com (see chapter 4). The Gallery of Fecal Tongs deserves (dis)honorable mention, even though it no longer exists.

The Blair Witch Wannabe

In 1999 *The Blair Witch Project* became a multimillion-dollar box-office sensation thanks to a clever marketing scheme centered around a hoax website (blairwitch.com) that claimed the Blair Witch was real. Visitors to the site could read detailed pseudohistorical background information about her, which seemed authentic enough to convince thousands of people of her reality. Ever since then movie promoters have been enamored of hoax websites. One of the more successful post–Blair Witch efforts was the Blonde Legal Defense Club website (nationalblondeday.com), which described the group as dedicated to stopping "the widespread belief that blondes are dumb and incapable." To achieve this goal the BLDC declared July 9 National Blonde Day. In reality the site was a publicity stunt for the Reese Witherspoon movie *Legally Blonde*.

Also check out: ManchurianGlobal.com, website of a creepy multinational corporation featured in *The Manchurian Candidate* (2004); GodsendInstitute .org, a Massachusetts fertility clinic offering human cloning services (from 2004's *Godsend*); and LacunaInc.com, a company devoted to nonsurgical memory erasure (from 2004's *Eternal Sunshine of the Spotless Mind*).

The Covert Ad Campaign

Mainstream marketers were slightly slower than their counterparts in the movie industry to realize how hoax websites could create buzz around a product. But they've recently played catch-up, and now disguised advertising campaigns are all over the Internet. The most elaborate to date was the home page of engineering genius Colin Mayhew (r50rd.co.uk/research/internal/v2i/engin), who detailed his efforts to build a humanoid crash-preventing "autonomous robot" out of the body of a BMW Mini Cooper. A dubious-sounding project, until you viewed the remarkable video of his robot stopping a car in its tracks moments before it would have slammed into a

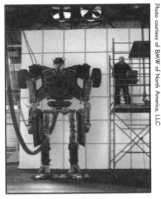

The Mini Cooper Autonomous Robot

wall. Those looking for more details about Mayhew soon uncovered a complex web of Internet references to humanoid robots, including a book titled *Men of Metal: Eyewitness Accounts of Humanoid Robots* on the website of Casson Publishing (cassonpublishing.co.uk). But in reality the Mini Cooper Autonomous Robot, Colin Mayhew, and Casson Publishing were all part of a viral marketing campaign dreamed up by the ad agency Crispin Porter & Bogusky. What were they advertising? The new BMW Mini Cooper, obviously.

Also check out: Skyhigh Airlines (skyhighairlines.com), the discount airline with an attitude that's really a front for Alaska Airlines; and Elite Designers Against IKEA (elitedesigners.org), an anti-IKEA site created by IKEA itself.

The Culture Jam

Culture jammers are activists who use hoaxes to expose corporate and media hypocrisy and to get people thinking about issues of social justice. Creating hoax websites is just one of their methods, but it's proved an amazingly effective one. In December 2004 culture jammers scored one of their most spectacular successes to date through a hoax site. As the twentieth anniversary of the chemical disaster in Bhopal approached, journalists at the BBC decided to contact Dow Chemical (which had inherited responsibility for the disaster via a corporate acquisition) to find out whether the company planned to do anything in remembrance of the event. But the BBC journalists who looked for Dow's corporate website instead found a copycat version (dowethics.com) created by a group known as the Yes Men. Thinking it was real, the journalists sent an e-mail to the media contact listed on the site, requesting an interview. The Yes Men happily obliged. On December 3, 2004, Andy Bichlbaum of the Yes Men appeared on the BBC disguised as "Jude Finisterra" of Dow Chemical, and proceeded to announce that Dow had decided to pay $12 billion in compensation to the Bhopal victims. Dow's stock value promptly dropped. Only later that day, after Dow called the BBC to complain that the company had no idea who Mr. Finisterra was, did the BBC realize it had been culture jammed.

Also check out: Gatt.org, home page of the World Trade Organization as imagined by the Yes Men. In 2000 it fooled the Center for International Legal Studies into inviting a speaker from the site to a conference on international services. The Yes Men sent "Dr. Bichlbauer," who lectured the other attendees about the poor work habits of Italians, and proposed that Americans should sell their votes to the highest bidder.

The Art Project

Perhaps the most intriguing variety of hoax website is the art project. In part, artists create such sites for the sheer challenge of making something fictional appear real. Take Clubbo.com, the purported home on the Web of indie record label Clubbo. On the site you'll find biographies of the bands Clubbo has represented as well as generous samples of their music. It's the songs that make you think Clubbo is real. They're catchy, their production value is high, and they seem strikingly representative of the eras in which they were recorded. That someone would have invented them all as a hoax seems inconceivable. But someone did. San Francisco artists Elise Malmberg and Joe Gore created Clubbo as a lighthearted experiment in Web fiction. Once you realize the whole thing is fake, it's fun to go back and appreciate the songs as a kind of masterful yet subtle send-up of the history of pop music.

Also check out: the Art of Johann Dieter Wassmann (bleedingnapoleon .com), a retrospective of a nonexistent artist; the Emily Chesley Reading Circle (emilychesley.com), dedicated to promoting the work of a "speculative" Canadian author; and Boilerplate (bigredhair.com/boilerplate), the history of a Victorian-era robot.

The Alternative Reality Game

Ilovebees.com appears to be the website of a small, mom-and-pop bee farm called Margaret's Honey. But after a few seconds, strange things begin to occur. Warning messages appear on the screen: MODULE CORE HEMORRHAGE, SYSTEM PERIL DISTRIBUTED REFLEX. What you've stumbled on isn't actually the home page of a honey company. It's the starting point (or rabbit hole) for an alternative reality game (or ARG). ARGs are role-playing games acted out in real-life settings. Players follow clues that may involve digging up a buried treasure, meeting a stranger on a street corner, responding to an e-mail, or visiting a strange website. In the case of I Love Bees, some players received clue-containing jars of honey in the mail. Others had to answer pay phones in specific places at specific times. These hints led them to a mystery involving rogue military artificial-intelligence programs, time-traveling soldiers, and interstellar warfare.

What this means for those of us who aren't ARGers is that we may come across websites of companies or organizations that look real, but are actually only part of an ARG. Nowadays many ARGs are created by advertisers, hoping to hook consumers with a fun game. I Love Bees, for instance, was part of the marketing effort for the Xbox game Halo 2.

Also check out: dionaea-house.com. It appears to be a weblog but develops into a spooky ARG about a flesh-eating house. It was designed to promote a movie screenplay written by Eric Heisserer.

The Scam

The Web is no stranger to scams. Typically, con artists use fake websites to put a veneer of credibility on businesses that are disreputable or don't exist. In 2003 investigators discovered a copycat version of the Better Business Bureau's site, which was identical to the real thing in every way except for one detail: whereas the real BBB site had no reference to a securities broker named Parker Jennings, the fake site not only listed him but also gave him an excellent customer-satisfaction rating. Apparently Parker Jennings had been directing potential clients who asked for a reference to his own personal BBB. The case prompted the BBB to remind consumers that on the Internet "things are not always as they seem." Indeed.

Also check out: McWhortle Enterprises (mcwhortle.com), home page of a (nonexistent) company promoting a new "bio-hazard detector." The site was created in 2002 by the Securities and Exchange Commission as a way of demonstrating the dangers of online investment fraud.

Surfer's Voice, n.: The vacant, spaced-out tone of people trying to browse the Web and converse on the phone at the same time. Characterized by a high frequency of "umms," "errrs," and long pauses. When this condition is detected in someone to whom you're talking, the best response is to hang up.

Meat Space, n.: The offline world where people meet as real, flesh-and-blood human beings.

case file: Web-Controlled Christmas Lights

Turning a light on and off, again and again, may not be your idea of a good time. But hook up that light to the Internet so that it can be controlled via a Web interface by anyone, from anywhere, and suddenly this mindless activity seems really cool (well, in a nerdy kind of way).

Over the years many Web-controlled devices have appeared on the Internet. There have been Web-controlled office lights, lava lamps, webcams, and even a toilet (that could be flushed remotely). But perhaps the most sensational Web-controlled device was Alek Komarnitsky's Christmas lights.

Like many suburban home owners, Alek decked out his Denver house with thousands of Christmas lights (seventeen thousand in all). But unlike most home owners, Alek allowed people on the Web to turn his lights on and off and view their handiwork via a webcam.

Alek first brought his lights online during the 2002 holiday season, and by 2004 they were something of a Web tradition. Millions of people surfed over to his site to play with them. But when a local TV station took Alek up in its chopper so he could give a bird's-eye tour of his home blinking on and off for the evening news, he realized things may have gone too far. Because he knew, as he sat listening to the oohs and aahs of the news crew, that the lights were only flashing because his wife, Wendy, below in the house, was pushing a remote control button.

Visitors to his site had no control over the lights. It was all a big fake. The webcam video was just a series of computer-generated images. Even the de-

tails that many people noticed—such as the garage door occasionally being open, or a car passing by, or an airplane flying overhead—were programmed special effects.

Web-controlled Christmas lights

Alek contacted a reporter from the *Wall Street Journal* and made a full confession. The *Journal* sent someone to verify that the webcam wasn't active and broke the news two days after Christmas. Most people took the news in good humor, except for the guys from the local TV station. They were pretty mad.

Reminiscing about the hoax, Alek admitted he found it amazing no one ever caught him. Anyone who had bothered to drive by would have seen that the lights never blinked. It was as if no one investigated because everyone wanted to believe. And once the initial shock of the hoax had worn off, that continued to be the dominant reaction: Stop teasing us and do them for real!

So Alek went to work and in November 2005 debuted actual Web-controlled Christmas lights. But not willing to be duped twice, a team of reporters from the *Rocky Mountain News* staked out his house to verify his claim. After spending a cold winter night hidden in their car, toggling his lights on and off via their laptop, they were convinced. This time the lights were legit. Which makes this the rare case of a hoax that, by popular demand, becomes a reality. Maybe for 2006 Alek can use his technological prowess to bring some other Christmas fantasies to life. The challenge: Design a Santa sleigh that can deliver presents to all the children in the world. The difficulty: It has to travel through the atmosphere at the speed of light without simultaneously bursting into flames.

Real Reality, n.: The opposite of virtual reality. The sometimes scary, increasingly unfamiliar world people enter when they shut down their computer.

RL, n.: Internet shorthand for "Real Life," as opposed to "Virtual Life." Sample usage: "I've decided to spend all my time online because RL sucks."

Reality Check: **Spud Server**

Was there once a website hosted on a server powered entirely by potatoes?

Potatoes can be a source of electricity. I missed the class in high school physics where we made a potato-powered clock, but I know it can be done, and that it is therefore theoretically possible to run a Web server on potato power. All you need is enough potatoes and someone crazy enough to string them together. Given this world's abundant supply of both potatoes and crazy people, it was only a matter of time before someone made the spud server a reality, and in early 2000 news of a functioning spud server spread like wild-fire on the Internet. The *BBC* and *USA Today* both reported it. But, alas, the spud was a dud—a hoax created by a band of Web pranksters called Temple ov thee Lemur. However, the hoax did inspire a man named Fredric White to build a real spud server, which he brought online in June 2000, though he soon pulled the plug on it after growing disgusted by the smell of rotting potatoes. Also, if you want to get picky, potatoes didn't power the entire server, only the server's cpu, since, as White argued in his defense, powering the entire server would have required over one thousand potatoes. Still, it's the closest anyone has come to a potato-powered Web server, so for now it will have to do.

REALITY RULE 6.3

On the Internet, nobody knows you're a dog.*

"On the Internet, nobody knows you're a dog."

*Peter Steiner, *New Yorker*, July 1993.

Munchausen Syndrome by Internet, n.: A psychological condition characterized by the telling of false tales of personal illness, specifically in an online setting. First identified by Dr. Marc Feldman of the University of Alabama. Experts warn that an increasing number of participants in virtual health forums (online chat rooms or message boards) may be inventing problems to get attention.

Kaycee, n.: An online imposter. Derived from Kaycee Nicole Swenson (see Fake Weblogs). Sample usage: "Don't pay any attention to that blogger who claims to be an A-list Hollywood celebrity. He's just a kaycee."

Fake Weblogs

The anonymity of cyberspace allows people to present themselves any way they want to, as anybody they want. If you're a woman, you can say you're a man. If you're a geriatric, you can say you're a teenager. If you're a dog, you can say you're a cat. No one will know the difference (if you're careful). Combine this ease of self-reinvention with the popularity of online diaries known as weblogs (or blogs), and what you have is an explosion of faux blogs.

Typically, faux bloggers reinvent themselves as someone more interesting, someone whose life other people might actually want to read about. Lesbians, prostitutes, celebrities, hot girls, and people dying of terminal illnesses are among the most popular alter egos. Out-of-work (nonlesbian) accountants, (nonlesbian) grocery baggers, and awkward teenage boys are not popular alter egos.

Fake public journals are not entirely new. In 1722 a series of letters supposedly written by a middle-age widow named Silence Dogood appeared in the Boston-based *New-England Courant.* Silence described her life and the difficulties she endured as a single mother. Readers loved her. In fact, a few of them wrote in asking for her hand in marriage. Silence declined these offers since she was, in reality, a sixteen-year-old boy named Benjamin Franklin (yes, *the* Benjamin Franklin).

Then there was the survival diary of Joe Knowles. In 1913 Knowles walked alone and naked into the Maine woods. His challenge was to survive unaided for two months. So that the public could follow his progress, he scratched out daily diary entries on pieces of bark that were picked up by a *Boston Post* reporter at a prearranged drop-off site and then published in the paper. He emerged from the woods a national hero. Only years later was it learned that he had spent the two months in a log cabin, sunning himself and feasting on cherry pie.

The Internet revolutionized the fake-public-diary genre by making it so easy to do, and so easy to get attention by doing it. Suddenly hundreds (perhaps thousands) of people who would never have considered keeping a diary were online, writing fake ones.

The first fake Web diary to gain lots of attention (at a time before the word "blog" was widely used) was that of Kaycee Nicole Swenson. Kaycee presented herself as a nineteen-year-old girl dying of leukemia. People were so genuinely moved by her valiant struggle with her illness that when she died of a brain aneurysm on May 15, 2001, they wanted to attend her funeral. That's when things started to get strange, because Kaycee's mother refused to allow anyone at the funeral. The reason why soon became apparent. Kaycee had never existed. She was the fictional creation of her "mother," forty-year-old Debbie Swenson.

The exposure of Kaycee Nicole was big news. At the time, there hadn't been a case quite like it. Since then fake online diaries have become fairly common.

One of the more sensational faux blog outings to occur recently was the unmasking of Plain Layne, an attractive young woman whose weblog read like a fast-paced soap opera. Layne's adventures included taking off for Mexico (where she became a lesbian), finding one of her birth parents, and seducing a straight coworker (after she became a lesbian). It was titillating stuff, read by thousands of people, except that Layne was really Odin Soli, a thirty-something male entrepreneur with a heart condition. This revelation was especially shocking for me since I went to grad school with Odin. (My first words, on reading the news, were "Oh my God—It's Odin!")

Companies have noticed the blogging phenomenon and jumped into the fray with faux blogs of their own. Ted's Life at Amazon was supposedly the online journal of Amazon.com employee Ted (he never revealed his last name), who posted offbeat entries about what it was like to work for the Web retailer. One of his insights was "this is a cheap place." But one day his blog was replaced by an Amazon recruitment page. What had happened? An Amazon representative admitted Ted's journal had been "a recruiting message that we put in the form of a blog to experiment." The remark that Amazon was a cheap place must have been an attempt to sound true to life.

Identity Hacking, v.: Supplying false information when asked online for details about your identity. Studies show people routinely lie when asked for personal information on Internet surveys or when required to register to view contents on a site.

MorF: Internet shorthand for "Male or Female?" A question often posed in online chat rooms when beginning a conversation. Asking the question does not guarantee a truthful answer.

Fake User Posts

The appeal of the Internet is often not its static contents (articles, websites, etc.), but its dynamic contents—the interactions of millions of people in chat rooms and message boards. But who exactly are these people? Some are exactly who they say they are. But others . . .

Internet-Crossed Lovers

People assuming new identities online in order to live out their fantasies can be fairly innocent (teenage girls posing as teenage boys), or more disturbing (fifty-year-old married men posing as teenage girls). One unhappily married Jordanian man, Bakr Melhem, found out the hard way about the treachery of online identity. As reported by Jordan's Petra news agency, Melhem began posing as a bachelor named Adnan in a chat room for singles. Soon he had struck up a cyber relationship with a woman named Jamila, who was everything he wanted in a woman. But when he suggested they meet in person, tragedy struck. Melhem went to the bus depot where he had arranged to meet his cyber flame, only to find waiting none other than his wife (aka Jamila). His wife was just as shocked to see Adnan as he was to see her.

Gorgeous Guy

Then there are the restless souls who aren't content to adopt one alter ego online. They want to be many different people—sometimes *at the same time.* The most notorious case occurred in 2001 when the San Francisco craigslist message board was set abuzz by a picture of a handsome man standing at a local bus stop. Who was this gorgeous guy, everybody wanted to know. The more people posted about Gorgeous Guy, the more attention the discussion attracted—until thousands of people were engrossed by the mystery, earning the phenomenon a spot in many newspapers as well as on CNN.

But when journalist David Cassel did a little spadework, he discovered that many of the people posting about Gorgeous Guy shared an IP address (an identification number assigned to every computer online). Either all these people were using the same computer, or one person was posting messages under different aliases. Who was the owner of this computer? Gorgeous Guy himself. Gorgeous Guy maintained that the messages were posted by his coworkers as a prank. Either way, all was not as it originally appeared to be.

Fake Amazon Reviews

A more down-to-earth motive for faking an online identity is financial gain or self-promotion (which often go hand in hand). In February 2004 a technical glitch unmasked the people who had posted anonymous book reviews on the website of the Canadian division of Amazon.com, revealing that many reviews were by spouses, relatives, or friends of the author, or by the authors themselves. Which is why Amazon reviews should be taken with a heavy grain of salt. However, Amazon reviews for the book you're currently reading can absolutely be trusted, particularly any reviews posted by "a reader in San Diego."

VixenLove

The person you're chatting with online may not even be a person. Between 2003 and 2004 hundreds of online Romeos were lured into talking with a sexy-sounding nineteen-year-old Californian who called herself VixenLove. VixenLove often seemed a little spaced-out, but that didn't deter the guys who were thrilled to find a girl online. Except that she wasn't a girl. She was a computer program designed to simulate human responses. VixenLove is no longer online, but you never know when one of her sisters might log on.

Mark V. Shaney, n.: The screen name of a frequent contributor to the net .singles usenet group during the 1980s. Shaney's off-the-wall remarks led many to conclude he was on drugs or just plain weird. In fact, Shaney was a Bell Labs computer program that used a Markov chain algorithm (thus the name of the character) to generate text based on previously appearing word combinations. The program came up with semicomprehensible statements such as, "Oh, sorry. Nevermind. I am afraid of it becoming another island in a nice suit." Given the number of semicomprehensible statements made by real participants in the group, few people guessed Shaney was just lines of code.

Sock Puppet, n.: 1. A puppet made out of a sock. **2.** An alter ego or false identity created to serve as an ally during an online debate. Sometimes referred to simply as a "sock."

case file: Mary Rosh

When American Enterprise Institute scholar John Lott Jr. published *More Guns, Less Crime* in 1998, the book's argument that placing more guns in the hands of citizens would reduce crime generated instant controversy. Critics loudly attacked Lott as a pawn of the gun industry and even charged he had made up data. But throughout the debate, Lott had one constant online supporter: Mary Rosh.

Rosh passionately praised Lott's book in her review on Amazon.com. In cyber forums discussing Lott, she invariably showed up to defend the scholar's work. She described herself as a former student of his at the University of Pennsylvania, saying he was "the best professor I ever had" and "there were a group of us students who would try to take any class that he taught."

Rosh continued this online campaign on Lott's behalf for almost three years, until a Cato Institute staffer named Julian Sanchez grew suspicious. It's not often that academics attract such devoted fans. Sanchez compared Rosh's IP address (recorded when she made posts to online forums) to Lott's IP address (which Sanchez obtained from an e-mail Lott had once sent him). They were one and the same. Sanchez posted this information on his weblog, commenting, "We're a little old to be playing dress up, aren't we Dr. Lott?"

Lott confessed that Mary Rosh was indeed his online alter ego, explaining in his defense, "I get attacked a lot and I don't want to spend all of my time defending myself." Presumably Lott didn't consider all the hours he spent as Mary Rosh as "time." Lott also insisted he had not written the Amazon review, but attributed that literary effort to his wife and one of his sons. And, of course, it's these subtle distinctions that make all the difference.

E-MAIL 7

In some parallel universe, all e-mail is true. Everyone there is a millionaire because Bill Gates really does pay out hundreds of dollars each time someone forwards a message to a friend, and the penis- and breast-enhancement formulas that spammers hawk have given everyone superhuman body proportions. But here in our lying, cheating world, we're going to have to learn to trust nothing in our in-box.

REALITY RULE 7.1

No trick, ploy, or scheme is beneath the dignity of a spammer.

Spam, n.: 1. A brand of canned pork marketed by Hormel Foods (an abbreviation of Shoulder Pork and hAM). **2.** Junk e-mail, or any junk message posted on the Internet. This usage was inspired by a Monty Python skit, in which Vikings in a restaurant sing repetitively about the wonders of the lunchmeat. Also known as UCE (unsolicited commercial e-mail) or UBE (unsolicited bulk e-mail).

Spamouflage, n.: Junk e-mail camouflaged, usually by deceptive wording of the subject line, to look like legitimate correspondence.

---

case file: The Sextillion Names of Viagra

Spammers flood in-boxes with junk. E-mail software designers fight back with filters that block messages containing words frequently used by spammers, such as Viagra. Clever, but the spammers are cleverer. They simply misspell Viagra, thereby allowing their "Vyagra mail" to get through. The software makers update their software to check for common misspellings of Viagra. Spammers' poor spelling gets even more creative. And the battle goes on and on.

Rob Cockerham, webmaster of cockeyed.com, wondered whether Viagra peddlers would ever run out of recognizable variations of the word "Viagra." In search of an answer, he determined that there are over a sextillion different ways—600,426,974,379,824,381,952 to be exact—to misspell Viagra.

How did he arrive at this number? First, he counted all the possible character substitutions—for instance, the number 1 for *i* (V1agra), or @ for a (Vi@gra). It's also possible to place characters between letters and still have a recognizable word: i.e., vi'agra, or v'i'a'g'r'a. Combine these possible misspellings, and you arrive at over a sextillion permutations of "Viagra."

According to rumor, spammers living in a monastery in Tibet now believe that when they have cycled through the sextillion names of Viagra, the universe will come to an end. That won't be long, based on their current output.

Spamku, n.: 1. Haiku about spam. **2.** Spam whose text includes randomly generated strings of words designed to fool filtering programs into classifying it as legitimate e-mail.

Fried Spam, n.: Friendly spam, or spam sent to you by a friend. Often in the form of health or computer virus warnings people forward to others in the belief that they're being helpful.

case file: The Time Travel Spammer

Hello, I'm a time traveler stuck here in 2003. Upon arriving here my dimensional warp generator stopped working...I am going to need a new DWG unit, prefereably the rechargeable AMD wrist watch model with the GRC79 induction motor, four 180200 warp stabilizers, 512GB of SRAM, and the menu driven GUI with front panel XID display. I will take whatever model you have in stock, as long as its received certification for being safe on carbon based life forms. In terms of payment: I dont have any Galactic Credits left. Payment can be made in platinum gold or 2003 currency upon safe delivery of unit.

Millions of people received this e-mailed request in 2003 (though versions showed up as early as 2001). Was it a bizarre hoax or joke? A deviously sophisticated form of spamouflage designed to trick them into buying something? A marketing ploy to harvest e-mail addresses? A publicity stunt for an upcoming book, movie, or video game? Or was it a real plea for help from a stranded time traveler? No one knew.

A few recipients were curious enough to respond and see what would happen. To their surprise, the stranded time traveler answered. Politely, never breaking out of character, he repeated his request for a DWG unit. No matter how hard he was pressed, he didn't budge.

A few pranksters went one better and tried to fulfill the time traveler's request. Dimensional generators appeared for sale on eBay, and an online Alien Technology catalog offered not only dimensional warp generators, but also quantum computing processors, portable fusion generators, and time transduction capacitors. Everything a time traveler could desire. Unfortunately, the time traveling spammer never took the bait.

Finally, in late 2003, *Wired* reporter Brian McWilliams tracked the messages to a house in Woburn, Massachusetts, occupied by Robert "Roddy" Todino. McWilliams got Todino on the phone and asked him, "Have you been sending out hundreds of millions of e-mails requesting a dimensional warp generator?"

"Yes," Todino admitted.

Then came the real question, "Why?"

Todino's response was matter of fact. He needed a dimensional warp generator to get back home. And if malevolent forces hadn't been "constantly monitoring" him, he added, he was sure he would have gotten one already.

McWilliams reluctantly concluded that Todino wasn't trying to sell anything or to harvest e-mail addresses. Nor was he the front man for a book or movie promotion. He just *really believed* he was a stranded time traveler.

It was a disappointing end to the mystery, but it did raise an interesting possibility. All these people blasting us with thousands of e-mails every day may not seriously expect us to buy the stuff they're selling. They may simply enjoy sending us e-mail because they're completely insane.

Ham, n.: A legitimate e-mail mistaken for spam by a filtering program.

case file: Spam Rage

Spam overload has brought into existence a new psychiatric condition: spam rage—defined as the uncontrollable anger that builds up when a person is exposed to an excessive amount of spam. Casual use of the term dates to 1996, but it was first used as a legal defense in 2003, when Charles Booher offered it as his excuse for leaving messages on a Canadian firm's answering machine that threatened to remove the genitals of its employees, using "crude gardening tools," if they didn't stop spamming him. Booher believed the Canadian firm had sent him a massive amount of e-mail promising to help him enlarge his penis, thereby triggering unhappy memories of his long fight against testicular cancer. Despite requests to stop, the spam persisted, until Booher flipped out and went on the offense.

For his actions Booher faced five years in prison and a $250,000 fine, though his lawyer expected an out-of-court resolution to the case. After all, what jury would side with the penis-enhancement-promising spammers?

Honeypot, n.: A fake e-mail account used by system administrators to detect intrusions by spammers.

REALITY RULE 7.2

If an e-mail urges you to forward its message to everyone you know, it's probably a hoax.

Don't Forward That E-mail

According to biologists, any entity that reproduces, or creates copies of itself, can be said to be alive. By this definition, one form of e-mail might qualify as living. It tricks people into forwarding it, thereby creating more and more copies of itself, each then spawning more copies until the original has propagated throughout the Internet. There's no formal name for this entity, but it should be ruthlessly stamped out whenever encountered. It's not actively hostile (it won't delete your hard drive), but it is a resource-wasting, in-box-clogging parasite.

Identifying e-mail-forward hoaxes isn't difficult. They almost always contain some variation of the line *forward this to everyone you know.* The problem is that even when you've seen thousands of the things, you may wind up thinking, "This one sounds legitimate." So you click the Forward button, and off the e-mail goes, to ensnare another victim.

The e-mail-forward hoax comes in four basic varieties. Anything that looks in any way, shape, or form like one of these should be purged from your in-box. When in doubt, delete.

The Petition

What it claims: Something bad is happening, and to stop it you need to add your name to a petition at the bottom of the e-mail. Then you need to forward the petition to everyone you know.

The Reality: The bad thing could be the Brazilian rain forest being chopped down, funding for National Public Radio being slashed, or sickos growing bonsai kittens in glass jars. It doesn't really matter. Adding your name to an e-mail petition won't do anything to stop the problem. Why? Because no politician is going to pay attention to a petition floating around the Internet. The problem it addresses is probably either not real or inaccurately described. Hit the Delete button.

E-mail Tracing

What it claims: A large company will pay you to forward their e-mail to all your friends. The company can trace e-mails, so they'll know how many times you've forwarded their message, and they'll reward you accordingly.

The Reality: No one is going to pay you to forward an e-mail, and no company has the ability to trace e-mail remotely. Some versions of this hoax promise you'll get a gift certificate at restaurants such as Outback Steakhouse or Applebee's, or that you'll get a free flight on British Airways. Other versions state large corporations such as AOL or Nike will pay you cash. The original version, from which all the many variations derive, claimed to be a message from Bill Gates, which read:

My name is Bill Gates. I have just written up an email-tracing program that traces everyone to whom this message is forwarded to. I am experimenting with this and I need your help. Forward this to everyone you know, and if it reaches 1,000 people, everyone on the list will receive $1,000 at my expense. Enjoy. Your friend, Bill Gates.

It's rare to find the author of an e-mail hoax, but thanks to the sleuthing of *Wired* reporter Jonathon Keats, we know that on November 18, 1997, Iowa State student Bryan Mack created the first version of this e-mail, and sent it as a joke to a friend sitting beside him in the computer lab. From that innocent start, it rapidly spread throughout the Internet. If ever a situation called for the intervention of a time traveler this would be it. Mission? Go back to 1997 and stop Bryan Mack from hitting the Send key.

The Plea for Help

What it claims: A terminally ill child wants to collect as many business cards as possible in order to get into the *Guinness Book of World Records*. Help the kid reach his goal by sending a card and forwarding this message to all your friends.

The Reality: The original version of this message (which predated the Internet) claimed that nine-year-old Craig Shergold was dying of a brain tumor and wanted to receive as many get-well cards as possible. The story was true, and Craig got millions of cards. But then he recovered and didn't want to keep getting the cards. Too late—the cards kept coming. Then e-mail came along and the message spread even farther. Somewhere along the way the plea for get-well cards became a plea for business cards, and the names of different terminally ill patients replaced Craig's. There have now been e-mail pleas in behalf of Debbie Shwartz, Little Rachel, Baby Natalie, and many others. Sometimes the message claims a company will donate five cents to the family of the child for each forwarded message (thereby combining the e-mail-tracing hoax with the plea-for-help hoax). Donate money to medical research if you feel moved by the child's story, but trash the e-mail.

The Warning

What it claims: A dangerous computer virus is spreading by e-mail. Whatever you do, don't open it. Forward this warning to all your friends and coworkers to protect them.

The Reality: Viruses do spread by e-mail, which gives this hoax credibility. Maybe the warning is real, or maybe it's not. But you won't know by guessing. Check online for more information—99 percent of the time you'll discover the warning is bogus. Rather than a virus, the subject of the warning might be health or crime related (watch out for poison in bottles of perfume!) or about stupid government legislation (the government wants to tax e-mail!). Whatever the case, do your homework and resist the urge to hit Forward.

Tampons Are Toxic

Claim: "Tampons contain two things that are potentially harmful: Rayon (for absorbency) and dioxin (a chemical used in bleaching the products)...The problem here is that the dioxin produced in this bleaching process can lead to very harmful problems for a woman. Dioxin is potentially carcinogenic (cancer causing) and is toxic to the immune and reproductive system."

Reality: The basic facts are true. The bleaching process does produce a trace amount of dioxin, and during the 1990s Congress did investigate whether the levels of this chemical in tampons posed a health hazard. The tampon industry responded by changing its bleaching methods to further reduce dioxin levels, and regulatory authorities now consider the amount to be so small that it couldn't possibly pose a risk. However, critics maintain any dioxin at all is a hazard and insist more research needs to be done. It's a complicated, contentious issue, full of nuances this warning fails to convey.

Beware of Flesh-Eating Bananas

Claim: "Several shipments of bananas from Costa Rica have been infected with necrotizing fasciitis, otherwise known as flesh-eating bacteria...It is advised not to purchase bananas for the next three weeks."

Reality: There is an infectious disease called necrotizing fasciitis. While you can pick it up from another person, contracting it from a banana is unlikely, unless an infected person had blown their nose on the fruit, or otherwise contaminated it. An entire shipment of bananas being infected is almost impossible. Because of the panic this e-mail warning caused in 2000, the Centers for Disease Control issued a statement assuring everyone that no shipments of killer bananas had ever arrived from Costa Rica, or anywhere else in the world.

Don't Freeze Water Bottles

Claim: "Johns Hopkins has recently sent this out in their newsletters... Dioxin carcinogens cause cancer. Especially breast cancer. Don't freeze your plastic water bottles with water as this releases dioxin in the plastic."

Reality: Johns Hopkins never sent out a newsletter suggesting any such thing. In fact, Dr. Rolf Halden of the Johns Hopkins Bloomberg School of Public Health went on record to debunk this hoax, noting that if freezing the plastic bottle were to do anything, it would probably make the water inside safer to drink because "freezing actually works against the release of chemicals." Heating plastic water bottles is another matter, as "another group of chemicals that are used to make plastic less brittle can be released if you place them in hot water or heat them in the microwave." But considering all the junk we Americans willingly shove into our mouths, the "minuscule amounts of chemical contaminants" that could get into your food or water by heating plastic in the microwave shouldn't be high on anyone's list of worries.

Gullibility Virus, n.: A virus that causes those infected "to believe without question every groundless story, legend, and dire warning that shows up in their in-box or on their browser." Symptoms of infection include: "The willingness to believe improbable stories without thinking; the urge to forward multiple copies of such stories to others; and a lack of desire to take three minutes to check to see if a story is true." A warning about this virus, issued by the supposed Institute for the Investigation of Irregular Internet Phenomena, has been disseminated widely by e-mail. If Internet users suspect they've been infected, the message advises, they should "rush to their favorite search engine and look up the item tempting them to thoughtless credence. Most hoaxes, legends, and tall tales have been widely discussed and exposed by the Internet community."

Spoof Warnings

Some e-mail warnings are less credible than others. Hopefully you wouldn't fall for any of the following.

Subject: The New "Honor System" Virus

This virus works on the honor system. Please forward this message to everyone you know, then delete all the files on your hard disk. Thank you for your cooperation.

Subject: Urgent Hoax Warning

I hate those hoax warnings, but this one is important! Send this warning to everyone on your e-mail list. If someone comes to your front door saying they are conducting a survey and asks you to take your clothes off, do not do it!!! This is a scam; they only want to see you naked. I wish I'd gotten this yesterday. I feel so stupid and cheap now...

Subject: Strunkenwhite Virus

A new computer virus is spreading throughout the Internet, and it is far more insidious than last week's Chernobyl menace. Named Strunkenwhite after the authors of a classic guide to good writing, it returns e-mail messages that have grammatical or spelling errors. It is deadly accurate in its detection abilities, unlike the dubious spell checkers that come with word processing programs. [Note: this gag originally appeared in Bob Hirschfeld's *Washington Post* column on May 2, 1999.]

Reality Check: Frownies Trademarked

Is it true that the frowny-face symbol :-(has been trademarked, thereby making it illegal to use without permission?

It is true that the frowny-face symbol has been registered as a trademark. In 1998 Despair.com, an online retailer of "demotivational posters" (parodies of popular motivational posters) submitted an application to register it as a trademark. Two years later Despair.com was shocked to receive notice that its claim had been approved. The company promptly issued a press release warning that anyone who used the frowny symbol in an e-mail message or online chat room without permission would face criminal prosecution. When people who didn't realize the warning was a joke flooded the company with angry e-mails, the company relented and announced it would sell frownies to anyone who wished to use them. Again, a joke. No one is going to sue you for using frownies, and you don't have to pay to use them either. **:-)**

Phishing, v.: Disguising e-mails as notices from legitimate businesses such as eBay or PayPal to trick people into surrendering account or credit card information. Also known as brand spoofing.

Joe Job, n.: A spam e-mail made to look as though it's been sent by someone other than the true sender. All bounces (and anger) are therefore directed at an innocent party. A common dirty trick used by companies to sabotage rivals.

REALITY RULE 7.3

Wealthy strangers are not eager to give you their money, despite what you may read in your e-mail.

The Nigerian Bank Scam

"Dear Friend," the e-mail begins. "It is with hope that I write to seek your help in the context below." Sounds innocent enough, but this is a typical set-up for one of the most widespread cons on the Internet, the Nigerian bank scam—so named because it was long a specialty of Nigerian con artists (though lowlifes throughout the world now practice it).

Once you get past the cordial introduction, what unfolds is a tale of political intrigue, shady dealings, and conspiracy. The quirky literary merits of these e-mails have attracted something of a cult following. As Douglas Cruickshank put it in Salon.com, Nigerian-scam buffs can't get enough of "the characters, the earnest, alluring evocations of dark deeds and urgent needs, Lebanese mistresses, governments spun out of control, people abruptly 'sacked' for 'official misdemeanors' and all manner of other imaginative details all delivered in a prose style that is as awkward and archaic as it is enchanting."

The correspondent informs you that a large sum is stuck in a foreign bank account. Maybe the money came from an inheritance. Maybe it was illegally skimmed from a legitimate business such as oil drilling. Whatever the case, the money needs to be moved out of the foreign country, and into a place where it can be more readily accessed. That's where you come in. The correspondent wants to transfer it into your bank account. For allowing this, you'll be given 10 percent (or more) as payment.

Should you be foolish enough to respond, you'll be asked for details about your bank account, giving the scammers access to your savings. You'll also be informed that they need you to provide some money up front to cover incidental costs involved with transferring the money: taxes, banking fees, bribes, etc. These incidentals may run to thousands or hundreds of thousands of dollars. Don't expect to see any money you send ever again. If you deal with these scammers long enough, you may even be lured to Nigeria (or wherever they operate), only to find yourself thrown in a cell and held for ransom. A few cases of this scam have ended in murder.

case file: The Gullible Professor

It may seem hard to believe that anyone falls for the Nigerian bank scam anymore, but people lose millions to it every year—even highly educated people who, one would think, really should know better. Take the case of Harvard University professor Weldong Xu.

When Weldong Xu received an e-mail informing him of a business proposal that would transfer $50 million into his bank account, he thought it was the answer to his financial problems. The only catch was the usual "unforeseen expenses," numbering hundreds of thousands of dollars. He raised $600,000 from friends and colleagues, telling them he was collecting money to fund SARS research in China. One friend even remortgaged his house to supply Xu with cash. It all went to the scammers. Xu's charade finally came to an end when his employer became aware of his fund-raising efforts and tipped off the police. But even after he was arrested, Xu continued to insist that his friends overseas were going to send him $50 million. At his trial in 2004 his lawyer conceded that, despite being a professor, Xu was kind of a "gullible guy."

419 Scam, n.: An alternative term for the Nigerian bank scam. The number 419 refers to the section of the Nigerian criminal code that covers fraud. The 419 scam is also known as advance fee fraud.

Scambaiter, n.: A person who attempts to scam the scammer. The goal is to string the scammer along with bizarre stories and, if at all possible, get the scammer to send you money. In 2004 the BBC reported a case in which a scambaiter named Mike convinced a Nigerian scammer that he was Father Hector Barnett of the Church of the Painted Breast. As Father Barnett, Mike talked the scammer into joining his fictitious church. (The scammer had to send photographic evidence of his successful completion of the church's initiation ceremony—painting a red circle on his chest.) Mike then convinced the guy that he also needed a withdrawal fee of $80 before he could return the favor and send $80,000 in "processing fees." The scammer sent the $80. Unfortunately, not all criminals are so gullible.

REALITY RULE 7.4

Unsolicited e-mail is not a reliable source of information—about anything.

Friend of a Friend, n.: The ultimate source of information in all bogus tales. "I know this is true because it happened to a friend of a friend," the e-mail will begin, before launching into a story about mutant killer penguins terrorizing a small town in the Midwest. Often abbreviated as FOAF.

Fake Press Releases

A recurrent e-mail hoax is the fake press release. E-mail is particularly conducive to fake press releases because, besides the text of the e-mail itself, there's no context by which to check the truthfulness of the claim. By contrast, on the Web there's at least a URL to give you some guidance. (Does the statement appear on cnn.com, or totallybogus.com?) Examples of fake press releases spread by e-mail include the following.

Microsoft Buys the Catholic Church

A 1994 press release raced from in-box to in-box, bearing the startling news that Microsoft was buying the Catholic Church. The release proclaimed: "In a joint press conference in St. Peter's Square this morning, MICROSOFT Corp. and the Vatican announced that the Redmond software giant will acquire the Roman Catholic Church in exchange for an unspecified number of shares of MICROSOFT common stock. If the deal goes through, it will be the first time a computer software company has acquired a major world religion." Pope John Paul II, under the terms of the deal, would become senior vice president of the company's new Religious Software division, and Steven Ballmer would be invested in the College of Cardinals. Microsoft would also gain exclusive electronic rights to the Bible. Sounds silly now, but at the time, enough people believed the e-mail that Microsoft felt compelled to issue a statement denying it was purchasing any world religion. Soon afterward a follow-up press release began to circulate. It declared that IBM had bought the Episcopal Church.

Mushroom Licenses

An early 2005 press release, apparently from the Illinois Natural Resources Department, announced that anyone wanting to pick mushrooms was going to need a license. These could be obtained from the same vendors who sold hunting and fishing licenses. Mushroom enthusiasts were horrified. What would be next—flower-picking licenses? After receiving dozens of angry calls, the Natural Resources Department was forced to deny publicly that it had ever issued such a press release. Mushroom hunters, it assured everyone, were free to carry on without the hindrance of state oversight.

eBay 8

It's obvious that all monstrosities, curiosities, knickknacks, and tchotchkes have but one purpose in this world: to be sold on eBay. During the past ten years, eBay has become the great global merchant for all the mummified alien corpses, uneaten toast, celebrity-chewed sticks of gum, discarded toenails, raccoon penis bones, Nazi pincushions, and nudist-colony Barbie dolls that our society brings into being. Its domain extends even into the great beyond, as the retailer of choice for every miracle-working tortilla chip, ghost hidden in a closet, or satanically possessed toaster. Of course, it's worth noting that many of these items (be prepared for a shock) aren't real.

REALITY RULE 8.1

A good story, whether true or not, can sell anything.

eBay Stories

Among its many innovations, eBay has brought into being a new literary genre: the eBay story. These are the tales sellers write to explain their auctions. They can be jokes, tall tales, or true-life confessions (or fake true-life confessions), and they can transform a piece of trash into a must-have item. When people bid on "Uncle Bob's glass eye," or "all my cheating wife's possessions," they're really casting a vote of appreciation for the story, not the item (which is often worthless). It's a way to participate in the story.

Wedding Dress Guy

In April 2004 Larry Star put his ex-wife's wedding dress up for sale on eBay. That wasn't too remarkable. What made people take notice was that Star used the auction as an opportunity to launch into an extended rant about his ex-wife, her Texas cheerleader hairdo, the "drunken sot of an ex-father-in-law" with whom he had been saddled ("Luckily I only got stuck with his daughter for 5 years. Thank the Lord we didn't have kids."), and married life in general. Then there was Star's decision to model the dress.

The auction attracted over fifteen million visitors and landed Star interviews on the *Today* show, MSNBC, CNBC, and in the *New York Daily News*. But reporters discovered that some of his story's details weren't entirely accurate. For instance, he had two ex-wives, neither of whom had lived with him for five years, and he did have a child with his second wife. Star shrugged off these inaccuracies as poetic license, pointing out that the central fact of his auction was correct: He did have a wedding dress for sale. The dress finally sold for $3,850, which should have netted Star a

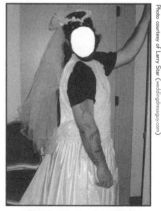

The eBay Wedding Dress Guy

Photo courtesy of Larry Star (weddingdressguy.com)

profit of $2,650, except that the winning bid turned out to be a hoax. So Star never sold it. As he puts it, "I got nothing. Nada. Zilch." But he did manage to transform the experience into a book, *Bitter, Party of One...Your Table Is Ready: Relationship Advice from a Guy Who Has No Business Giving It.*

Worked Last Time I Used It: A commonly used phrase in eBay auctions. Indicates that the item for sale probably doesn't work.

REALITY RULE 8.2

Just because someone bids doesn't mean they intend to pay.

Phony Bids

For every hoax auction on eBay there is an equal or greater number of hoax bids. Many hoax bids are random pranks. Someone sees an auction that strikes him as funny and types in a bid. Other phony bids take the form, as the British would say, of "taking the piss": bringing a seller too big for his britches back down to size. For instance, when celebrity chef Jamie Oliver tried to sell his scooter on eBay he was amazed to get a bid of one million pounds, only to discover that the high bidder had no intention of paying.

Unfortunately, most hoax bids on eBay aren't pranks. They're fraud. Dishonest sellers get accomplices to bid up the price on their auctions so that legitimate buyers will be forced to pay more. The best defense against this is to stop bidding if the price for an item has gone above what you think it's worth. Of course, this is easier said than done when you just have to have those one-of-a-kind Hawaiian hula-girl salt-and-pepper shakers, or the velvet Elvis painting that would look perfect in the living room.

eBay Vigilante, n.: A self-appointed defender of truth, justice, and fair trading on eBay. Alarmed by the proliferation of fraud on the site, a few individuals have taken matters into their own hands. When they spot what they believe to be a phony item on sale, they swoop in and place a ridiculously high bid, thereby preventing others from purchasing it. They gamble that they'll never have to pay their bid because the auction is a scam. EBay frowns on vigilante justice, arguing that the policing of fraud should be left to the professionals. But the vigilantes promise that as long as phony items are on sale, they'll be there.

REALITY RULE 8.3

Association with a celebrity or deity is the easiest way to add value on eBay.

Celebrity Castoffs

It might be hard to find takers for a piece of used chewing gum, but a piece of gum chewed by Britney Spears—that's another matter. Internet entrepreneurs have realized that the detritus left behind by stars—the things they've touched, sat on, partially chewed, licked, or blown their noses with—has value to someone in this age of celebrity worship. So up for sale it all goes on eBay.

Britney's semimasticated chewing gum debuted on eBay in August 2004. The seller claimed he had found the "Britney Spear-Mint" in the foyer of London's Sanderson Hotel, where Britney had stayed. He assured potential bidders that this was the real deal—straight from the pop star's mouth. "Of all things, I would NOT put something on eBay that was not true," he declared. Of course he wouldn't. Perish the thought. Bidding topped $3 million before settling at a more reasonable $1,000. It wasn't reported if the final bidder paid up.

The auction inspired a frenzy of imitators. EBay entrepreneurs started finding Britney-chewed gum in all corners of the world: Juicy Fruit she had discarded in Los Angeles, sticks of spearmint she had flung to the pavement in Australia. Nor was the Britney fire sale limited to gum. Britney's cigarette butts went up for sale, as did corncobs she had gnawed on, trash bags she had left behind in her house in Malibu, a water bottle she had deposited on the beach in Santa Monica, and a Kleenex she had blown her nose in. Britney's spokeswoman dismissed the auctions as "pathetic."

Other celebrity trash put up for sale has included a cough drop sucked on by Arnold Schwarzenegger, Paris Hilton's pubic hair (found in her hotel room), Justin Timberlake's half-eaten French toast (plate included), and water Elvis Presley once sipped from. (Just the water—a cup was not included.)

The rage for items touched or mouthed by celebrities has spawned a secondary market in items that have *not* been in the presence of anyone famous. Thus we find auctions for French toast *not* eaten by Justin Timberlake and gum *not* chewed by Britney Spears. It's only a matter of time before entrepreneurs expand into the lucrative field of double negatives: gum *not not* chewed by Britney.

Pareidolia, n.: The phenomenon of seeing meaningful shapes in randomly occurring patterns. For instance, seeing the face of the Virgin Mary in the burn marks on a piece of toast.

case file: The Virgin Mary Grilled Cheese Sandwich

Just when people thought that giant Cheetos, used penis enlargers, and pieces of gum not chewed by Britney Spears represented the height of auction-related strangeness, eBay presented to the world the Virgin Mary Grilled Cheese Sandwich (hereafter the VMGCS).

Diana Duyser put the VMGCS up for sale in November 2004. She wrote that it was a sandwich she had cooked ten years earlier. She had taken one bite before noticing, in her words, "a face looking up at me; it was Virgin Mary staring back at me. I was in total shock." For the next ten years Duyser kept the sandwich in a plastic box on her nightstand, where it miraculously resisted mold and disintegration (or not so miraculously considering what American cheese is made of) and brought "blessings" to her. For instance, she attributed a big win in a casino to its divine influence. But she was ready to pass the blessings on to someone else—for the right price.

Inevitably questions were raised. How did Duyser know the face was that of the Virgin Mary? What proof did she have that the sandwich was ten years old? But such questions were brushed aside in the ensuing frenzy to own this rare religious artifact.

Then disaster struck. EBay canceled the auction, claiming it didn't allow joke auctions. (They mustn't have perused their own site very much.) But Duyser fought the decision, and eBay finally allowed her to relist the item. It then sold for $28,000 to the online casino GoldenPalace.com, which knew a marketing opportunity when it saw one.

The VMGCS was not the first food item to bear the image of a deity. In the pre-eBay era the faithful marveled over miracle munchies such as the Tennessee Nun Bun (a cinnamon bun that looks like Mother Teresa), the Miracle Tortilla of New Mexico (a tortilla that looks like Jesus), and the Holy Eggplant of India (an eggplant with "Allah" spelled out in Urdu script).

After the auction of the VMGCS, however, the sale of food bearing the likeness of a

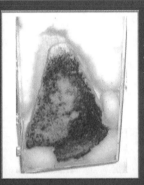

The Virgin Mary
Grilled Cheese Sandwich

deity took off like never before. EBay hosted auctions of deity-themed frozen fish sticks, M&M's, popcorn, pretzels, Doritos, and much, much more. And, of course, there were the inevitable VMGCS spinoffs: an automatic Virgin Mary grilled cheese sandwich maker, numerous sandwiches that did *not* bear the image of the Holy Mother, VMGCS clocks, T-shirts, watercolor prints, and even the "VMGCS original motion-picture soundtrack," recorded by a band in New York. The success of the VMGCS inspired Duyser to auction off the frying pan in which she had cooked it. This was also scooped up by GoldenPalace.com at the bargain price of $5,999. Which means that the online casino owns both the holy sandwich and the holy frying pan. Lunch, anyone?

REALITY RULE 8.4

Supernatural possession is the second easiest way
to add value on eBay.

case file: The Ghost in a Jar

TJ had a problem. He was haunted by a shadowy black thing.

The problem began when he was snooping around a cemetery with his metal detector. The machine sensed something in the ground and, digging down, TJ discovered two glass jars and a journal. As he took the jars out of the ground, one broke and released an eerie black mist. TJ left the broken jar behind and took the journal and the intact jar to his house. But the black mist followed its companion in the remaining glass jar. When TJ got into bed that night the mist attacked him, pinning him down momentarily before he escaped its grasp. From that point on, the mist was never far away, attacking him two more times in the next few weeks and appearing menacingly around the house. So TJ did what any one of us in his situation would do. He auctioned the jar and journal on eBay.

The ghost in a jar went up for sale on eBay in May 2003 and immediately caused a sensation. Ghost-in-a-jar fan clubs appeared on the Internet, and bids reached a staggering $100 million, at which point eBay decided the bids were hoaxes and restarted the auction. The jar-bound ghost was promptly bid back up to $50,000 before the auction was closed. Unfortunately for TJ the new winning bid was also a hoax, which means, one assumes, he's still saddled with the ghost in a jar.

Despite TJ's inability to get rid of his spooky container, he inadvertently inspired an eBay trend: the sale of haunted junk. While genuinely creepy, old, or scary paranormal paraphernalia had long been found on eBay, this new category was simply random household crap with the word "haunted" prefixed to it. February 2004 saw the auction of a satanic toaster that maliciously burnt toast and refused to be thrown away. (It repeatedly found its way back from the Dumpster.) Someone else offered a haunted rubber ducky. And a few months later there was a ghost in a Coke can, the ghost's presence being evidenced by the can "opening itself." By this time the trend was descending into farce (assuming it hadn't started there), because the owner of the haunted Coke can openly admitted his item was a joke (which didn't stop it from receiving an obscene amount of media attention). Today the trend continues apace, with auctions for must-have items such as haunted gmail accounts or haunted potato chips. Meanwhile, it's rumored that junk shops everywhere are busy rebranding themselves as "haunted junk" shops.

TeCHNoLoGy 9

Modern society has given rise to two distinct kinds of people: Luddites and techno-utopians. Luddites, who take their name from a group of nineteenth-century workers who attacked new textile machinery, fear technology as a dehumanizing force. These are the people who refuse to get a cell phone and still don't use e-mail. Techno-utopians, on the other hand, love technology. They can't wait for each new gadget to come out and honestly believe the Internet will usher in a golden age of peace and harmony. Both groups suffer from their fair share of delusions.

REALITY RULE 9.1

Expectations for future technology rarely match reality.

Forelash, n.: Cynicism about a technology or product being hyped as the next big thing even though it doesn't exist yet. An anticipatory form of backlash. Sample usage: "John knew he should feel more excited about the future promise of nanotechnology, but the constant buzz about it had given him a bad case of forelash."

Phony Technology

Technology junkies are always eager to buy the most up-to-date doodad that will make their lives easier in a thousand ways. They spend hours fantasizing about the cool new stuff engineers are dreaming up. (I know because I'm a technology junkie myself.) This may keep them off the streets and out of trouble, but it also makes them vulnerable to hoaxes. Technology junkies must watch out for three main categories of deception: phony product rumors, vaporware, and nonexistent products.

Phony Product Rumors

What they are: False leaks that purport to provide details about highly anticipated new products. Photos are often doctored or staged to add credibility. Hoaxes of this kind are typically the work of amateur pranksters, though some suspect that professional marketers use them to create buzz about upcoming products.

Example: Three days before the 2004 Apple Expo in Paris, while Mac fans were busy speculating what new hardware Steve Jobs would unveil at the show, photos appeared online showing a flat-panel contraption said to be the new iMac G5. The photos, supposedly taken in an elevator at Charles de Gaulle International Airport, turned out to be bogus. The so-called flat-panel iMac G5 was just a LaCie LCD monitor stuffed inside a PowerBook box. Similar hoaxes preceded the arrival of the Tungsten T5 handheld and the newest versions of popular games such as *Half-Life.* As a result, tech fans have learned to take all rumors (even ones accompanied by photos) with a grain of salt.

Vaporware

What it is: Technology that a manufacturer promises will soon arrive in stores but that keeps getting delayed and never materializes because the imminent availability of the product was deceptively announced while the product was actually in the early stages of development and not ready for the market.

Example: In 1997 the video-game maker 3D Realms announced it would soon release *Duke Nukem Forever,* a follow-up to its popular *Duke Nukem.* Nine years later, fans are still waiting. In 2003 *Wired* magazine, on its annually updated list of the top vaporware products, gave *Duke Nukem Forever* a lifetime achievement award for its perpetual vaporware status. Impatient fans have taken to calling the sequel *Duke Nukem Whenever* or *Duke Nukem Taking Forever.* One *Wired* reader pointed out that "NASA has planned, designed, developed and successfully landed a rover on Mars in the time this game has been in development." Another notorious vaporware product is Microsoft's Longhorn operating system, which was supposed to be shipped in 2004 after long years of development, but didn't. A popular joke is that Longhorn has been renamed Longwait, and will eventually come bundled with *Duke Nukem Forever.*

Nonexistent Products

What they are: Products that don't exist in any way, shape, or form. Such products are pure scams designed to bait suckers and their investment money. Often these products would have to defy the laws of physics to do what their inventors claim they do.

Example: The nineteenth-century inventor John Worrell Keely told investors he had developed a vibratory generator capable of producing enough power—using only a quart of water as fuel—to run a train for over an hour. (Devices that produce energy for little or no cost are a favorite of con artists.) For fourteen years, until he died in 1898, Keely strung his investors along with promises that the nonexistent generator was almost perfected. More recently, Czech businessman Sheldon Zelitt claimed to have invented GroutFree technology that could seamlessly join multiple LCD screens into one large screen, and was developing this product at Visual Labs, his company in Canada. With this promise, the company achieved a valuation of over $300 million, but when Zelitt finally gave a demonstration of the product, his investors recognized that what he was showing them was simply a forty-two-inch plasma television, available at any consumer electronics retailer. Faced with criminal charges, Zelitt fled to the Czech Republic. He was extradited back to Canada in 2005, where he's now serving an eight-year sentence.

In Silico, adj.: Describing an experiment conducted through a computer simulation, as opposed to in vitro (in a test tube, or a lab), or in vivo (in a living creature).

> **Reality Check: Strange Computer Technology**
> Given the pace of technological change, it's difficult to predict what strange turns technology might take. But has technology really taken any of these strange turns?

1954 Home Computer

Did *Popular Science* magazine publish the image to the right in 1954, predicting that this is what a home computer might look like in the year 2004?

In 1954 computers really were this size, so if someone had tried to imagine what a home computer would look like fifty years in the future, they might have dreamed up a monstrosity like this (including the steering wheel). But *Popular Science* never published such a picture. The photo was created in 2004 by Danish software sales and support technician Troels Eklund Andersen as an entry in a Fark Photoshop contest. (Fark is a popular weird news website—its Photoshop contests challenge Farkers to digitally alter images in amusing ways.) Andersen took a photo of a submarine's maneuvering room from an exhibit at the Smithsonian, made it black-and-white, then pasted in the tele-

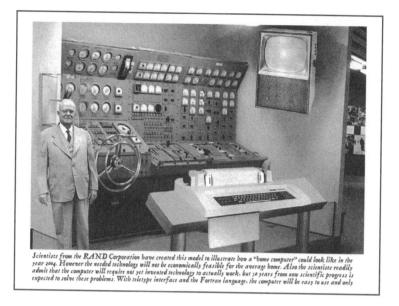

Scientists from the RAND Corporation have created this model to illustrate how a "home computer" could look like in the year 2004. However the needed technology will not be economically feasible for the average home. Also the scientists readily admit that the computer will require not yet invented technology to actually work, but 50 years from now scientific progress is expected to solve these problems. With teletype interface and the Fortran language, the computer will be easy to use and only

type printer, the old-style television, and the man. Then he added the text at the bottom. He never imagined the image would end up fooling thousands of people, but that's what happened once it started circulating via e-mail. It even fooled Scott McNealy, CEO of Sun Microsystems, who displayed it at a computer conference as proof of the impossibility of predicting future technology. The image was one of the most forwarded e-mail attachments of 2004.

DVD Rewinder: The perfect gift for the technologically challenged. This gadget plays a "customizable rewind sound" when you put a DVD on it. It also comes with a USB port for rewinding MP3s. Sold by 1783 Productions, LLC.

The DVD Rewinder

iLoo

Did Microsoft engineers install a computer system inside a portable toilet, thereby creating the iLoo, the world's first Internet-enabled Johnny-on-the-spot?

On April 30, 2003, as part of Microsoft's goal to allow people to log on "anytime, any place, and anywhere," MSN UK, a division of Microsoft, announced the imminent introduction of the iLoo, the world's first Internet-enabled Porta Potti. The iLoo would include a wireless keyboard, a height-adjustable flat plasma screen, a six-channel surround-sound speaker system installed under the sink, broadband Internet access, toilet paper conveniently printed with URL suggestions, and (last but not least) a toilet outfitted with vacuum suction to guarantee maximum hygiene. As the press release declared, this was no "bog-standard affair." Microsoft promised the iLoo would debut at music festivals throughout England in summer 2003.

The media was incredulous. Wouldn't the queue for this thing be miles long? Were beer-soaked, sweaty music festivals really the ideal place to introduce it? And what about keeping it clean? God only knew what fluids would get on that keyboard.

Microsoft representatives explained that a security guard would be posted outside the toilet, and a cleaner would swoop in between uses to keep it spot-less. Nevertheless, reporters kept asking questions with increasing concern, until, almost two weeks after the announcement, Microsoft abruptly admitted the entire thing had been a joke. There was no iLoo, the company said. It was just a flight of fancy.

This was strange, since Microsoft had never before issued a fake press re-lease. Not even on April Fool's Day. But the next day the software maker changed its mind and stated the iLoo actually wasn't a hoax. The project *had* been under serious development in the United Kingdom, a Microsoft represen-tative said, but "corporate headquarters in Redmond, Washington, looked at it and decided maybe this wasn't a good idea."

The iLoo

By this time everyone was confused. Was the iLoo real, or wasn't it? And why was the company changing its mind so often? Micro-soft never explained. It has stood by its final statement that the iLoo was a real, but never completed, project. (Though one gets the feeling the software giant wishes it could flush the entire iLoo episode down the toi-let. When I queried them for details they po-litely, but firmly, stated they weren't able to help me.)

Antimosquito Software

Is there software that will keep pesky bugs and flying insects away from your computer as you work?

Thai computer programmer Saranyou Punyaratanabunbhu wanted to help computer users work without fear of bug-borne malaria, a big problem in Thailand. So he developed software that makes computer speakers emit high-pitched frequencies inaudible to the human ear but annoying to mosquitoes. The software was downloaded fifty thousand times in the first three days after it debuted, and Saranyou soon came out with a version 2.0 that also repels cockroaches and rats. A South Korean company, SK Telecom, now offers anti-mosquito software for cell phones. So the software does exist. The more relevant question is whether it works. Probably not. Pest-control experts at the University of Nebraska–Lincoln note, "There is no scientific evidence to suggest that cockroaches (or any other insects) respond negatively to ultrasonic sound waves." Even if it did work, there's one more thing to consider before installing it on your PC: some users report getting headaches after sitting for hours in front of a computer emitting a high-pitched whine.

Virtual Reality, n.: An artificial environment created by a computer. Coined in 1989 by Jaron Lanier, founder of VPL Research.

Sim—ulated Reality, n.: The exact replica of one's life and character that people tend to try to create when playing the video game *The Sims*.

Telephone Liars

What is the most deception-friendly form of communications technology? Is it e-mail? Maybe instant messaging? Or does face-to-face interaction trump them all? It turns out that the most lie-prone medium, by a long shot, is the telephone. Give people a phone, and a significant number of them turn into liars.

When a 2004 study conducted by Cornell University psychology professor Jeff Hancock asked people to record where and when they told lies during a typical week, it found that 37 percent of lies occurred during telephone conversations. This compared with 27 percent during face-to-face interaction, 21 percent while instant messaging, and only 14 percent in e-mail. Hancock speculated that the telephone is so liar-friendly because, first, it allows real-time conversations (most lies are told on the spur of the moment); second, telephone calls, unlike e-mails, aren't recorded (people are reluctant to create a permanent record of their lies); and third, the detachment between the two parties during phone conversations (the liar's face can't be seen) promotes untruth.

The wicked world of telephone lying doesn't stop there. James Katz, a professor of communication at Rutgers University, found that an astonishingly high number of people fake calls on cell phones. In other words, people you see chatting loudly on the sidewalk may be talking to dead air. People fake cell phone conversations to avoid talking to someone nearby, to make themselves look important, or to make themselves look busier than they are. Twenty-seven of the twenty-nine students in Katz's class admitted they had faked a call. "People are turning the technology on its head," the *New York Times* quoted Katz as saying. "They are taking a device that was designed to talk to people who are far away and using it to communicate with people who are directly around them."

SounderCover, n.: An application for mobile phones that adds fake background noise to a call. "Traffic jam" can be used to convince your boss you're stuck on the road while you're actually lying in bed. Other prerecorded noises include "at the dentist," "in the park," and even "caught in a thunderstorm." Marketed by Simeda.

> Reality Check: **Strange Phones**
> In the 1960s TV series *Get Smart,* Maxwell Smart's shoe phone
> seemed pretty far-fetched. Nowadays it wouldn't raise many eyebrows.
> But are the following phone gadgets real or fake?

Tooth Phone

Have engineers invented a mobile phone that can be implanted in a tooth, vibrating to notify the user of an incoming call?

James Auger and Jimmy Loizeau, research associates at MIT Media Lab Europe, designed an audio tooth implant for the Royal College of Art's summer 2002 exhibit. As indicated, it vibrates when there's an incoming call. The user then speaks normally, and a tiny microphone picks up her voice. Incoming sounds are transferred to the inner ear via bone resonance. Unfortunately, calls can only be received, as there's no way to dial a number. The phone was an art project, so it's not available for purchase. But Auger and Loizeau stress that the technology to produce such a phone does exist. If the phone ever goes on sale, it will give new meaning to the term "Bluetooth technology."

Left-Handed Cell Phone

Does Sony Ericsson sell a mobile phone that has a reversed keypad layout to make it easier for lefties to use?

Virgin Mobile announced the availability of the left-handed Sony Ericsson LH-Z200 mobile phone on March 31, 2004. Online technology blogs such as Engadget and Mobilemag immediately wrote it up, only to be informed that it was an early April Fool's Day joke. Left-handed products are a favorite April 1 gag. The most famous was Burger King's left-handed Whopper (all the condiments were rotated 180 degrees), which debuted on April 1, 1998.

Nokia Speed Trap Detector

Do certain models of Nokia phones have built-in radar detectors that can be activated by dialing a secret code?

According to a popular e-mail rumor, bored engineers designed most Nokia cell phones to pick up radar speed traps. To activate this secret function you enter menu mode, then select (in the following order) Settings, Security Settings, Closed User Group, and On. Finally, enter 00000 and hit OK. A radar sign should appear on the screen. This series of steps has been tested on numerous Nokia phones. Not one has revealed the secret radar-trap-detection mode.

REALITY RULE 9.2

The more we rely on a technology, the more some people will distrust it.

Gremlin Effect, n.: The emergence of rumors about the dangers of a new technology as that technology becomes widely adopted. For example, as sunlamps grew in popularity during the 1980s, a rumor circulated describing a young woman who cooked her internal organs by visiting a tanning salon too often. Coined by the sociologist Jean-Bruno Renard in 1992. (Gremlin refers to

World War II tales about mischievous creatures to whom technological fail-
ures were attributed.)

Aluminum Foil Deflector Beanie, n.: A homemade tinfoil hat designed to
block electromagnetic psychotronic mind control and other forms of brain-
scanning technology. Full details can be found at zapatopi.net.

Techno-Paranoia

According to techno-paranoiacs, our modern technological conveniences
are slowly crippling and killing us. TVs are turning our brains into mush. Microwave ovens are making our food toxic. The Internet is creating a generation of
antisocial zombies. The list goes on and on. Sometimes the paranoiacs are right.
Sometimes they're not. (But even if they are, you're taking away my gadgets
over my cold, dead body.)

Mobile Phones

According to their detractors, mobile phones have a tendency to blow up
gas stations, attract lightning, and give people brain cancer. Receiving calls
from certain numbers may also cause instant, inexplicable death. It's best to
address these concerns one at a time.

First, let's consider the rumor that sparks from cell phones will ignite gasoline vapors and cause fires. Alarmed by this possibility, in 2005 one Connecticut state senator introduced legislation that would slap a $250 fine on anyone
using a mobile phone while pumping gas. But there's actually never been a
recorded incident of a cell phone causing a gas station fire. Static discharge
from your own body is far more likely to ignite the gasoline vapors.

Second is the danger—periodically reported by the media—of cell phones
attracting lightning. In 2004 *China Daily* reported that fifteen tourists were
injured at the Great Wall when an elderly man transformed his phone into a
lightning rod by turning it on during a storm. While cell phones do produce ion-
izing radiation, which could, in high enough levels, attract lightning, the amount
they produce is negligible. The National Weather Service actually urges people
to use cell phones rather than land lines during storms.

Next up, let's take a look at the cell-phones-cause-brain-cancer concern.
The jury is still out on this one (so the paranoiacs may be right). Medical stud-

ies haven't found a short-term correlation between cell phone use and brain cancer, but a long-term link is harder to disprove. If you use your phone all the time, you might invest in a hands-free kit. And for those really worried about this danger, companies sell radiation-shielding hats and scarves. (Or just make your own aluminum foil deflector beanie.)

Intriguingly, some technophiles have suggested that cell phones are good for the brain. David Butler, head of the National Confederation of Parent Teacher Associations in Britain, has argued that phones held next to your head act like little radiators, and that the "heating effect actually improves the neuron transfers between neural pathways, and therefore your thinking ability goes up." Experts, however, have dismissed Mr. Butler's theory as wishful thinking. If it were true, half the teenage girls in the United States would be approaching genius levels of intelligence.

Finally, we have the killer-phone-call fear. In 2004 Agence France Presse reported panic sweeping among mobile-phone users in Nigeria. They had heard a rumor that receiving a phone call from one of two numbers, 0802 311 1999 or 0802 222 5999, would cause instant death. Why was left unexplained. The AFP reporter braved death and called both numbers but was unable to reach anyone. The Nigerian phone company assured the public that, "from an engineering point of view, it is absolutely impracticable, and there is no such record whatsoever anywhere in the world, that anyone has died or can die from merely receiving or making a phone call." But who was going to listen to common sense when they were too busy worrying that the next ring of the phone would spell instant death? File this fear under penis-melting-Zionist-robot-comb-like (see chapter 10).

Sadly, this list doesn't come close to exhausting the ways cell phones might kill you. There's the threat from drivers chatting on their phones, or the rumored possibility of cell phones interfering with life-support systems. But these cases involve other people using cell phones, and there's not much you can do to guard against that—unless you move to a desert island where cell phones are banned. Even then, watch out for the palm trees. They may be radiation-emitting cell phone transmission towers in disguise.

Fraud Frond, n.: A cell phone transmission tower disguised as a tree. There are reportedly over thirty thousand of them in the United States alone, as many cities require cell phone antennas to be disguised. For more information check out fraudfrond.com.

Y2K Crisis-like, adj.: Describing any overdramatic prediction of imminent technology-inspired catastrophe. Refers to the global technological meltdown that the calendar change from 1999 to 2000 was supposed to trigger. That nothing happened with the arrival of the new millennium was either because preventive measures had been taken or because nothing was ever going to happen. (The answer depends on whom you ask.)

E-mail

A 2005 study sponsored by Hewlett-Packard and conducted by the University of London found that "workers distracted by e-mail and phone calls suffer a fall in IQ more than twice that found in marijuana smokers." Researchers warned that "infomania" (constantly checking e-mail and text messages) could seriously reduce mental acuity. The antitechnology crowd latched onto the study as yet more evidence of the harmful effects of the Internet. But a closer examination of the report revealed that people weren't suffering any long-term loss of intelligence. What the test actually found was that people scored worse when taking IQ tests if they were simultaneously answering e-mail and phone calls, which is hardly surprising or alarming. Of course, I should note that my infomania may be skewing my interpretation of the results.

THE NEWS 10

Legend holds that Sir Richard Phillips, founder of the *Leicester Herald*, was working late one night in 1792 when he accidentally knocked a column of type off a table. Lacking time to redo his work, he scooped up the scattered type, shoved it randomly into the column, and printed it out—accompanied by a note to his readers explaining that the "Dutch mail" had arrived too late to be translated. Reportedly one reader held on to this Dutch mail edition for thirty years, hoping one day to find someone who could translate it. And so began the media's love affair with truth.

REALITY RULE 10.1
Information is only as good as its source.

Rewrite Man, n.: A newspaper employee responsible for spicing up stories with entertaining, often fictitious, details. This was an actual position in the early twentieth century. Nowadays reporters are expected to assume the responsibilities of the rewrite man.

Rogue Reporters

Most people assume newspaper articles are accurate and true. But thanks to the existence of rogue reporters, it's always possible that the news you're reading—no matter how seemingly legitimate, or how prestigious the paper—has been invented out of thin air.

The First Rogue

Once upon a time, news editors encouraged their reporters to be slightly roguish. Anything to spice up the news. Throughout the nineteenth century newspapers were filled with hoaxes. It wasn't until 1924, when *New York Herald-Tribune* reporter Sanford Jarrell concocted a charming tale about a floating speakeasy anchored in international waters just outside New York harbor—causing harbor police to embark on a frantic search for the phantom "sin ship"—that a reporter got fired for lying. Unfortunately for Jarrell, he perpetrated his hoax just as the news industry was developing a bad case of wanting to appear that it had ethics. (Though it also wanted plenty of sensational stories, creating—many would argue—an inevitable tension.) Since then, the noisy firing of rogue reporters has been a recurring feature in the world of journalism.

A Rogue in Red China

In 1972 Bob Patterson filed a series of groundbreaking reports for the San Francisco *Examiner* about his secret odyssey through Red China. These reports were made all the more remarkable when it was learned Patterson had never left Hong Kong.

Jimmy's World

In 1981 Janet Cooke won a Pulitzer Prize for her *Washington Post* articles about an eight-year-old heroin addict named Jimmy, but had to return the Pulitzer when her editors figured out that Jimmy didn't exist. Her argument that someone like Jimmy could exist, given the drug problem in Washington, D.C., didn't win her much sympathy, especially from the police who had been frantically searching for the boy. She later sold the story rights to her escapade for a cool $1.5 million.

Glass Works

Stephen Glass was a young writer on the fast track for success at the *New Republic*. During the late 1990s he always seemed to get the scoops. His most celebrated article, "Hack Heaven," told the story of a fifteen-year-old hacker who broke into the computer systems of Jukt Micronics and then extorted money (and a job, a Miata, a trip to Disney World, and a lifetime subscription to *Playboy*) from the software corporation. The article captured the topsy-turvy culture of the dot-com boom. Too bad Jukt Micronics only existed in Glass's imagination. The *New Republic* fired him when they found out, but he later cashed in his notoriety for a six-figure book deal.

Gray Lady Down

Reporter Jayson Blair claimed to be traveling the country, doing research and conducting interviews. In reality, he spent most of his time in a New York City Starbucks, sipping coffee and lifting details from other journalists' work. For this reason, his employers showed him the door in 2003. What made this shocking was that he was employed by the *New York Times,* the so-called Gray Lady of journalism and the most respected paper in the United States. This proved, to anyone who still doubted it, that rogues could pop up anywhere. Blair copied the strategy of Stephen Glass and softened the pain of his dismissal with a book deal.

Jayson Blair, 1. n.: A former reporter for the *New York Times*. **2. v.:** To fal-
sify or add phony details to a document, as in "I Jayson Blaired my resume."
(Usage seen on Gawker.com, May 14, 2003.)

Rogue War Reporters

When coalition troops rolled into Iraq in spring 2003, Swaziland state
radio sent journalist Phesheya Dube to Baghdad to cover the fighting. Day
after day, listeners heard live reports from the intrepid reporter—much to the
alarm of his colleagues at home, who frequently urged Dube to stay out of
harm's way. Dube, however, seemed totally unconcerned about his safety. The
reason why became apparent when someone spotted him strolling around
Mbabane, the Swaziland capital. Dube, in fact, had never gone to Baghdad.
As one member of the Swaziland parliament put it, he had been "broadcasting out of a broom closet" in Mbabane, passing wire reports off as his own
eyewitness accounts.

Dube represents a distinct subclass of rogue reporters—the rogue war reporter. These journalists creatively combine the glory of being on the front line
with the safety of remaining at home.

Some rogue war reporters travel to the war region, but avoid the hazards of
actual combat by filming reenactments of events. For instance, at the start
of the second Iraq War, Sky News reporter James Forlong broadcast footage
of a cruise missile firing from the HMS *Splendid*—neglecting to tell viewers
that the scene was staged for his benefit, and no missile was actually fired. Forlong resigned, whereas Dube was never reprimanded (and probably still works
at Radio Swaziland today).

Constructed Quotation, n.: A quotation attributed to an interviewee that was
in reality written by a reporter after the interview. Usually the interviewee
approves the phony quotation. It's a case of "you should have said this, so
why don't we pretend you did."

Keeper, n.: A story a journalist holds on to for publication at a more opportune
date. This strategy commonly involves sitting on a story about an embarrassing incident in a politician's past until the night before the election, when
it will have maximum impact.

Time Shifting, v.: Writing in the past tense about an event that hasn't yet happened. Usually done to make deadlines for short-lead publications. The danger is that the story might still predate the event. This happened in 2005 when the *Boston Globe* described in great detail the slaughter of baby seals by hunters off the coast of Newfoundland. However, the hunt hadn't yet taken place.

Predetermined Story Line, n.: The plot outline reporters often draft before an event. This allows the reporter to plug details into the predetermined story line once the event has happened, and quickly file a report. The story line's accuracy is of secondary importance.

REALITY RULE 10.2

Reporters sometimes forget that information is only as good as its source.

Rogue Sources

Sometimes what you read in the paper or see on the nightly news isn't true, but not because a reporter deliberately lied. Instead, a reporter relied on a questionable source and got taken in by a hoax—in other words, the journalist didn't do his homework. The history of journalism is full of spectacular goofs.

Monte Christo Pistols

In 1856 the London *Times* sparked a transatlantic row by publishing—as proof of the barbaric nature of American society—a letter describing a series of duels fought with Monte Christo pistols on a Georgia train, while passengers ignored the bloodshed. The *New York Times* angrily denied that such duels had ever occurred, and the London *Times* realized it had been duped when it learned that "Monte Christo pistols" was Southern slang for bottles of champagne.

The Hitler Diaries

In 1983 *Der Stern* thought it had scored a journalistic coup when it obtained the secret diaries of Adolf Hitler, supposedly hidden in East Germany since the end of World War II. The German magazine wanted so badly for the diaries to be real that it ignored obvious evidence to the contrary, such as Hitler's well-known dislike of keeping personal records. *Der Stern* only admitted the diaries weren't real after it became clear that they were written on paper manufactured well after the war's end, and that their contents had been lifted from an edition of *Hitler: Speeches and Proclamations.* All told, the debacle cost the magazine upward of $24 million.

Whatever Happened to Buckwheat?

In 1990 the news show 20/20 aired an interview with William Thomas, the actor who played Buckwheat in the Our Gang comedies of the 1930s and '40s. 20/20 claimed Thomas now lived in Tempe, Arizona, and worked as a grocery bagger. But the man 20/20 interviewed was an impostor named Bill English who had been claiming to be Buckwheat for thirty years. 20/20 sheepishly admitted its mistake the week after the segment aired. In the ensuing scandal, a producer was fired, and the son of the real William Thomas (who had worked as a film technician before dying in 1980 at the age of forty-nine) sued the network for negligence.

The Almost Death of a President

In 1992 CNN almost reported that the first President Bush had died, after it received a phone call from a man claiming to be the president's heart specialist on board Air Force One. Anchorman Don Harrison interrupted the regularly scheduled broadcast to deliver the news, but, just in the nick of time, someone at CNN realized it was a hoax, and the producer yelled "Stop! Stop!" Viewers could hear shouting, but didn't know what it was all about. The caller turned out to be mentally unstable.

The Diana Tapes

In 1996 the *Sun* claimed to have a videotape of Princess Diana frolicking in her underwear with cavalry officer James Hewitt. Hot stuff. But the tape was a phony shot by an amateur filmmaker in a London suburb using two Diana lookalikes and one fake Hewitt. The total cost of making the film was $1,300. The filmmaker reportedly sold the tape to the *Sun* for six figures.

The Marilyn-JFK Letters

In 1997 ABC prepared a $2 million three-part documentary about the relationship between JFK and Marilyn Monroe, alleging not only that the two had engaged in a longtime affair, but that JFK had intended to establish a trust fund for Monroe's mother, to buy the actress's silence. ABC's proof for these spectacular claims? JFK's love letters. But just in time to scuttle the series, ABC discovered the letters had been produced on a typewriter that wasn't manufactured until after Kennedy's death. Another problem was that the addresses on the letters contained zip codes, though zip codes only came into use in 1963—again, after JFK's death.

Rather-gate

In 2004 Dan Rather reported on 60 *Minutes* that CBS had obtained documents proving President Bush had disobeyed orders while serving in the National Guard and had then used his family's influence to cover up his poor service record. The documents allegedly came from the files of Colonel Killian, Bush's commanding officer in the Guard. Almost immediately, amateur sleuths pointed out on the Internet that the documents looked an awful lot like they had been created on a computer using Microsoft Word—a sure sign of forgery, since Microsoft Word didn't exist when Bush served in the Guard. CBS didn't pay much attention to these sleuths, but when the network realized its source for the documents, Bill Burkett, had lied about how he obtained them, it decided it could no longer vouch for their authenticity. Rather apologized for airing the story.

Fact Gap, n.: The disparity between what the public believes to be the facts and what actually are the facts. Example: a June 2003 poll revealed that half the public believed Iraqis to have been among the nineteen hijackers on September 11. In reality, no Iraqis were among the hijackers. Analysts attributed this "fact gap" to both misleading news reports and the Bush administration's efforts to link Iraq to terrorist organizations.

case file: Mr. Man on the Street

Reporters enjoy swooping down on random pedestrians and quizzing them about the latest headlines. It's easy to do and conveys a populist, democratic tone. But have you ever wondered who the man on the street really is? What if it were the same guy being asked for his opinion again and again?

In mid-2003 a few media critics noticed that something like this appeared to be happening. The same name kept popping up in "man on the street" interviews. Greg Packer, a highway maintenance worker from upstate New York, had been quoted by the *New York Times,* the *New York Daily News,* the *Los Angeles Times,* the *New York Post,* the *Philadelphia Inquirer,* the London *Times,* and other publications. He had also appeared on CNN, MSNBC, and Fox. But he was always described as nobody special, just a random person encountered on the street. How had he become the go-to guy when the media needed a "man on the street"?

It turned out that Packer was a man with a curious hobby. He camped out to be first in line at celebrity events. When media arrived to cover the event, he was front and center, ready to answer questions should a reporter want to talk to a fan. Often Packer waved at reporters to urge them over. Not realizing he was a serial front-of-the-line guy, the reporters happily interviewed him—again and again and again.

It helped that Packer was expert at delivering upbeat platitudes, the kind of stuff journalists could use to pad an article without rocking any boats. Take, for instance, his opinion on President Clinton: "He made his mistakes, like everybody else." Or on the U.S. invasion of Iraq: "We had to do whatever we had to do." Or on whether he preferred the Mets or the Yankees: "I'm for both teams...I'm a New York fan."

Packer was interviewed as an average Joe well over one hundred times before the media realized what was going on. When the story of his ubiquity broke, the *New York Daily News* dubbed him the "most quoted Everyman in the country." The Associated Press distributed a memo urging its reporters not to quote Packer anymore, but the news organization refused to say it would never again run his name, noting the possibility that he might one day actually do something newsworthy.

REALITY RULE 10.3

Truth is often stranger than fiction, but that doesn't mean every strange thing is true.

Satire Mistaken as News

In June 2002 the *Beijing Evening News* ran a story about unusual negotiations taking place between the U.S. Congress and the district government of Washington, D.C. Congress was threatening to leave Washington if the city didn't pay for the construction of a new Capitol building outfitted with a retractable dome. Was the story true? No. But was it a deliberate hoax? Also, no. A *Beijing Evening News* reporter had found the story on the website of the *Onion,* a satirical magazine, and neither he nor his editor had realized it was a joke.

As news sources proliferate (thanks to the Internet), mistaking satire for news is becoming increasingly common—and it doesn't only happen to Chinese reporters who aren't up on all the nuances of American culture.

In 2001 both cartoonist Garry Trudeau and the *Guardian* made reference to a study, conducted by the "Lovenstein Institute" of Scranton, Pennsylvania, that concluded George W. Bush had the lowest IQ of any American president of the past fifty years. Where had Trudeau and the *Guardian* learned about this study? In a press release forwarded to them via e-mail. That alone should have given them pause. The original source of the information was a humor website, linkydinky.com. The Lovenstein Institute and its IQ study were just a joke.

Trudeau and the *Guardian* were probably quick to believe in the authenticity of the Lovenstein Institute because its study confirmed what they were predisposed to believe. But that's another matter.

Satirical Prophecy, n.: A prediction or remark intended as a joke that later becomes true. For instance, joking that someday Arnold Schwarzenegger will be governor of California. (Wait! Oh my God! That's already true.)

> ## Reality Check: I-69 Name Change
> Did newspapers seriously report in November 2004 that Indiana congressman John Hostettler had introduced legislation to change the name of Interstate 69 to the more "moral sounding" Interstate 63?

The first newspaper to print this story as fact was the *Sierra Times,* and other papers (some as far afield as Belgium) soon followed suit. But these papers had been fooled by a satirical article on the *Hoosier Gazette,* an on-line humor site created by Josh Whicker. The *Hoosier Gazette* article quoted Hostettler as saying, "Every time I have been out in public with an 'I-69' button on my lapel, teenagers point and snicker at it. I have had many ask me if they can have my button. I believe it is time to change the name of the highway. It is the moral thing to do." After receiving a torrent of phone calls about the story, Hostettler's office issued a statement declaring the name-change idea absurd and assuring everyone that Congressman Hostettler was a "fervent supporter of I-69."

case file: The *Weekly World News* Effect

An article posted online on *Yahoo! News* in December 2003 reported that an unknown prankster had inserted outrageously incorrect translations into a Japanese-to-English phrase book. The Japanese phrase "Can you direct me to the restroom?" was translated into English as "May I caress your buttocks?" "I am very pleased to meet you" had become "My friend, your breath could knock over a water buffalo." Reportedly, thousands of Japanese tourists had been deceived and were being verbally assaulted, and in some cases, physically battered, after approaching people on the street and using these phrases.

Most people would have dismissed the article as a joke, if it hadn't appeared on *Yahoo! News,* which is usually a reliable source of information. And in fact the story was satire. So what was going on? The story's original source was the *Weekly World News,* a tabloid in which almost everything is a joke (comedy buffs would also have recognized the tale as the premise of a famous Monty Python skit). For some reason *Yahoo! News* had begun including *Weekly World News* stories in its "Entertainment News & Gossip" section without labeling them as satire. A fine-print credit to the *Weekly World News* was the only warning readers got. No news agencies repeated the article as truth, but the story of the bogus phrase book spread far and wide via e-mail.

Urban Legends Mistaken as News

In January 2002 Reuters news service reported that while using a toilet on a Scandinavian Airlines flight from Sweden to the United States, a woman had activated a high-pressure vacuum flush system that sucked her downward until her buttocks formed a perfect, airtight seal on the seat. Only after the plane had landed in America were ground technicians able to dislodge her. "She was stuck there for quite a long time," a spokesman was quoted as saying. The woman subsequently filed a complaint against the airline.

It was the kind of quirky story journalists love, and it soon appeared in numerous newspapers. But it wasn't true. Scandinavian Airlines checked its complaints and couldn't find any record of such an incident, but they did identify the tale as one of the fictional examples used when training flight crews to deal with emergencies. This was an example of that close cousin of satire mistaken as news—an urban legend mistaken as news.

Urban legends are sensational stories repeated by people who believe they're true. Reporters are no more resistant to their premises of deadly spiders hiding under toilet seats, bar-prowling kidney thieves, or $250 cookie recipes than anyone else. In fact, they may be less resistant because of their innate love of great stories. And so such tales are regularly offered up in the news as actual events, even though verifying details are always sketchy. (See chapter 1, "The Woman Who Gave Birth to a Frog.")

Reality Check: **Dangerous Jelly Mini Cups**
Did European Union bureaucrats really ban jelly mini cups,
as many news sources reported, because these bite-size candies
were deemed a threat to public safety?

We enter here into the realm of the euromyth, midway between satire and urban legend. According to popular rumor, overzealous EU bureaucrats have reclassified kilts as "womenswear," decreed that bananas sold within Europe not be "too excessively curved," mandated that joggers not go faster than six mph in city parks to avoid disturbing mating squirrels, and ordered that the word "pertannually" be removed from the EU constitution (citing it as meaningless) and replaced with the much clearer term "insubdurience." In reality, none of these things ever happened. They're all euromyths—ridiculous decisions attributed to EU bureaucrats.

Most euromyths are false, but occasionally a few turn out to be true, making all the others seem credible. For instance, in a 1979 directive EU bureaucrats really did reclassify carrots as a fruit, apparently because the Portuguese make carrot jam and anything used to make jam must be a fruit (at least for the purposes of paperwork). So did the EU ban jelly mini cups? Yes, and with some justification. Although these candies sound harmless, they have a nasty habit of lodging in children's throats. In fact, these candies had been outlawed in much of the world before the EU got around to banning them.

Penis-Melting-Zionist-Robot-Comb-Like, adj.: Having the quality of being insanely irrational, fantastically paranoid, and completely false, yet believed by many.

Penis-Melting Zionist Robot Combs

Sometimes very, very strange rumors get transmitted by the media. We're not talking about merely odd or disturbing rumors, such as urban legends or satires. No, we're talking about full-blown, howling-at-the-moon, pitchfork-waving, aluminum-tinfoil-hat-wearing insanity. When such madness rears its head, it is described as "penis-melting-Zionist-robot-comb-like."

The phrase derives from a mass panic that swept through Khartoum, the capital of Sudan, in September 2003. The panic was triggered by a rumor that a satanic foreigner was shaking hands with Sudanese men and thereby causing their penises to melt upward inside their bodies. One man claimed he was at the market when a stranger approached him, handed him a comb, and asked him to comb his hair. As the press later reported: "When he did so, within seconds...he felt a strange sensation and discovered that he had lost his penis."

Instead of debunking the rumor, the local media fanned the hysteria by offering hypotheses about who the satanic foreigner might be. The Sudanese journalist Ja'far Abbas, a columnist for the Saudi daily *Al-Watan,* made this observation:

> No doubt, this comb was a laser-controlled surgical robot that penetrates the skull [and passes] to the lower body and emasculates a man!! I wanted to tell that man who fell victim to the electronic comb: "You jackass, how can you put a comb from a man you don't know to your head, while even relatives avoid using the same comb?!" ... That man, who, as it is claimed, is from West Africa, is an imperialist Zionist agent that was sent to prevent our people from procreating and multiplying.

While it's hard to argue with the logic of Ja'far Abbas's reasoning (since it displays no logic), the almost certain probability is that the Sudanese rumor was not evidence of imperialist Zionist agents armed with emasculating laser-controlled robot combs. Instead, it was a manifestation of a Koro epidemic, which is the term for a shrinking-penis panic. Strangely enough, historical records contain numerous examples of such epidemics.

James Taranto, writing for the *Wall Street Journal,* is credited with introducing American readers to the story of the Sudanese panic and coining the phrase "penis-melting Zionist robot combs." As an adjective, it is to be used sparingly, reserved for only the weirdest of the weird stuff that crosses the newswires.

REALITY RULE 10.4

The world as it appears on the nightly news should not be confused with the world as it is in reality.

Media Contamination, n.: The skewed perception of reality that results from overwhelming media coverage of an event. First used by Judge Lance Ito during the O. J. Simpson trial.

case file: "I Can't Quite Place That Accent"

In early 2003, during the buildup to the second Iraq war, CBS News scored a journalistic coup: an exclusive interview with Saddam Hussein. When 60 *Minutes II* broadcast the interview, the show provided a voice-over translation of Hussein's responses, which is standard practice in the news industry. But viewers didn't know that although the translation was perfectly accurate, the voice-over's thick Arabic accent was not. The voice didn't belong to an Arabic speaker at all, but to Steve Winfield, an American actor who specializes in faking accents. CBS hired Winfield to read the translation in phony Arabic-ese. Apparently the network thought U.S. audiences would get confused if Hussein (as well as the person speaking his words) didn't sound foreign enough. Rumors that Dan Rather had for years been faking a Texas accent remain unconfirmed.

CNN Effect, n.: The phenomenon of government policymakers making decisions based on what they see on cable news stations such as CNN, rather than on what their own intelligence sources say. In an example of the unreal determining the real, any errors in the news broadcast quickly become the basis for real-world actions.

VCNC (Vast Cable News Conspiracy), n.: The theorized conspiracy among cable news networks to present the public with a fake version of reality.

Hey, I Didn't Write That: Phony Bylines

Just because a reporter's name appears as the author of an article doesn't mean the reporter actually wrote it. Editors routinely delete or add sections at will. Usually the final product resembles the writer's original story, but not always.

In July 2003 Deanne Wrenn submitted to Reuters a story about U.S. Army private Jessica Lynch's homecoming from Iraq. When the story appeared online, most of what Wrenn had written had disappeared, and the article's tone had shifted, from sympathy toward Private Lynch to criticism of how the private's experiences in Iraq had become a "media fiction." Only a few sentences in the final paragraph were Wrenn's original words. Over the next day even this small contribution vanished as editors continued to update and alter her story. Ultimately not a word of what she had written remained, and quotations from sources she had never interviewed had been added. Yet her name remained on the byline.

How common is this phenomenon? It's hard to say because most writers don't publicly complain when it happens to them. After all, they're getting a publication credit. Writers are typically more worried about the opposite phenomenon: when their names don't appear on stories they know they wrote every word of.

Plastic-Robot Vibe, n.: The feeling you get from newscasters (or other media personalities) who seem strangely artificial, as if built out of plastic and machinery rather than flesh and blood.

REALITY RULE 10.5

"News is what people want to keep hidden; everything else is publicity."*

Where News Really Comes From

The romantic image of where news comes from has journalists pounding the pavement and burning up the phone lines looking for important stories to report. The reality is that most of what you see or read in the news is fed to reporters by public relations firms.

Here's how it works. Corporations hire PR firms (or in-house media relations staff). These PR firms then try to get journalists to report favorably on what their clients are doing, or whatever ideas their clients want promoted, by sending out thousands of press releases and suggesting story ideas directly to reporters. (Plus, it never hurts to send a reporter a gift basket!) The reporter's job is to sift through this avalanche of information and decide what in it is entertaining enough to be newsworthy. By some accounts, over 70 percent of what we receive as news originates from PR firms.

---

*Bill Moyers, *NOW,* December 17, 2004.

A favorite tool of PR firms is the video news release (or VNR). VNRs are publicity videos designed to look like news segments, including fake reporters who deliver positive commentary about the corporations who have hired them. PR firms send these VNRs to TV stations that then reedit them to look like material the stations produced themselves. The VNR ends up seamlessly integrated into news broadcasts. Stations like this deal because it means free content (always important in these times of ever-shrinking budgets). Most viewers never know they're watching PR-created "news."

Fake Government News

Corporations have been supplying TV stations with video news releases for years, and media critics have never liked the arrangement. But when it came to light that the government was supplying stations with VNRs, the critics hit the roof. Because when corporations create fake news, it's covert advertising. But when the government does the same thing, it's covert propaganda, which is a lot creepier.

Government agencies began creating VNRs during the Clinton administration, and the practice has accelerated under Bush. If you've watched the evening news in the past few years, then you've probably seen a government-created news clip. But you wouldn't have known it, because the government is hardly ever identified as the source of the footage.

Hundreds of these clips have appeared in news broadcasts nationwide, but the one that caught the public's attention was a segment designed to promote a controversial new Medicare law. It featured a "reporter" who cheerily helped viewers "sort through the details" of the legislation, not once mentioning that it had been widely criticized as a giveaway to pharmaceutical corporations. The clip concluded with her saying, "In Washington, I'm Karen Ryan reporting."

What infuriated critics was that Karen Ryan wasn't reporting. She was reading from a script prepared by the Department of Health and Human Services—a fact never mentioned when the segment aired in news programs throughout the nation. As Ryan later put it, she was a "paid shill for the Bush administration." The Cleveland *Plain Dealer* put it even more bluntly: KAREN RYAN, YOU'RE A PHONY.

REALITY RULE 10.6

"Journalism is founded on the premise that reality can only be shown through other people's statements."*

Phony Media Objectivity

The news industry likes to maintain the appearance of objectivity. In an ideal world this would mean clearly identifying the source of all information presented to the public, noting all biases or affiliations, and challenging sources to verify their claims. In practice, "objectivity" consists of finding two people with opposing viewpoints, allowing them each to make a sound bite, and leaving the audience to figure it out from there. But if a news organization has its own spin on the issue, then it can use a variety of tricks to surreptitiously promote one point of view, or shade how the public perceives events, without actually lying. Entire books have been devoted to these tricks, but here are a few of the most well known:

The Misleading Statistic: A statistic is used to imply one conclusion, without acknowledging that the same data could be used to support other conclusions. For instance, ever hear the gloomy statistic that 50 percent of all marriages end in divorce? Journalists cite it a lot because it's an attention-getting number. But the truth is less clear-cut. The figure comes from an old study by the National Center for Health Statistics that found that, in one year, there were half as many divorces as there were marriages. The problem is that it's hard to extrapolate from what happened in one year to what will happen in all marriages. Moreover, the figure doesn't acknowledge variations within the population (such as, people who get married very young tend to divorce at a far higher rate than people who marry later in life). Aaron Levenstein famously remarked that statistics are like bikinis: What they reveal is suggestive, but what they conceal is vital.

---

*Chuck Klosterman, *Sex, Drugs, and Cocoa Puffs* (New York: Scribner, 2003).

The Phony Crime Wave: The media holds the public's attention during periods of slow news by reporting every crime that would normally go unmentioned. This creates the false (and scary) impression of a crime wave in progress. For instance, in 2002 a few dramatic child abduction cases made headlines, prompting the media to cover every new abduction. The public became so alarmed by this apparent crime wave that the White House convened a special Conference on Missing, Exploited and Runaway Children to address the issue. The irony was that the number of abductions had actually declined, from 263 in 2001 to 201 in 2002.

The Generalization from a Single Example: A reporter makes a sweeping statement (such as "more commuters are deciding to bike to work instead of drive"), but backs it up with only one or two examples (one of which might be his neighbor, whose decision to bike to work inspired the story). Single examples tend to stick in people's minds (especially with repetition) and therefore lead audiences to believe they represent a larger trend, even if the reality is just the opposite.

The Favored Source: Journalists aren't supposed to state their own point of view, but there's nothing to stop them from only interviewing people with whom they agree. Reporters often rely heavily on a few favorite sources who can be counted on to say the right things. In this way, the media can maintain the guise of objectivity while simultaneously creating the impression that there's really only one credible side to an issue.

Fringe Sources: While the favored-source trick can be used to create a false consensus, the fringe source can create false controversy. Reporters will go to great lengths to quote people on either side of an issue, even if this means reaching out to the lunatic fringe to find a source. And so we might get a statement by a leading scientist contrasted with a quotation from the head of the local Bigfoot Watchers Club, as if the two were equally credible. Or the media will ignore the mainstream altogether and find lunatic fringers on both sides—because screaming extremists always make better TV than middle-of-the-road sorts who debate more politely.

The Unflattering Close-up: Want to make someone look nervous or guilty? A close-up will emphasize every nervous tic or bead of sweat. Alternatively, a shot from below increases a person's stature, whereas a shot from above shrinks it. Lighting also makes a big difference. *Time* magazine got in trouble when it used O. J. Simpson's mug shot on its cover shortly after his arrest—and intentionally darkened his image, as if to make him appear untrustworthy. *Newsweek* used the same image but didn't darken it.

The Tight Crowd Shot: Five placard-bearing protestors gather outside city hall to demand the legalization of domestic ferrets. Not much of a protest, but if the camera zooms in close, those five protestors can be made to look like fifty. A small demonstration is thereby transformed into a massive outpouring of citizenry for the evening news. A notorious instance of this occurred in April 2003 when a crowd pulled down Saddam Hussein's statue in Baghdad's Paradise Square. The first televised scenes of the event, shot from a close angle, seemed to show a large crowd. News broadcasts presented the footage as evidence of Iraqis rejoicing at the dictator's downfall. But shots that surfaced later, taken from a wider angle, revealed the square to be almost empty. (At the time the statue came down, most Iraqis were hiding in their homes, unaware the fighting was over.)

Push Poll, n.: A poll in which questions are phrased in such a way as to push people toward certain conclusions. Instead of asking "Which candidate are you planning to vote for in the upcoming election?" the push poll would ask "Given the evidence that candidate *X* is a liar and a cheat, which candidate are you planning to vote for?"

ENTERTAINMENT 11

Once upon a time, forms of entertainment were few and simple: conversation, music, and dance. Nowadays our options have expanded considerably. With movies, radio, TV, and video games, there's always something to see or do. Many fear this barrage of entertainment is eroding the barrier between reality and fantasy. But for others the only concern is the mystery of how there can be five hundred channels on their TV, and nothing worth watching.

REALITY RULE 11.1

There's nothing real about reality TV.

Fake Reality TV

As long as there's been TV, there's been reality TV. And as long as there's been reality TV, producers have been faking the reality portion of it.

The basic premise of the reality genre is to place people in front of a camera and record their honest, unscripted reactions to events. Audiences like the spontaneity of reality shows, and TV studios love that they're cheap to make. It's a match made in heaven. But TV producers need content that will reliably entertain, and much reality is ugly and dull. Which is why producers have a habit of stepping in to goose things up a bit, either on the set or in the editing room. They can't help themselves—there's too much money involved to do otherwise.

1950s: Quiz Shows

Audiences in the 1950s were glued to their sets watching the drama of everyday people winning or losing thousands of dollars in the quiz shows that were one of the earliest forms of reality TV. But a series of scandals at the decade's end revealed that corporate sponsors were picking who won and who lost.

The most notorious quiz show fraud occurred on the program *Twenty-One*. For a while contestant Charles Van Doren—an instructor at Columbia University and son of the Pulitzer Prize-winning poet Mark Van Doren—seemed unbeatable. Week after week he won, racking up prize money of $129,000 and becoming one of the most famous people in America, revered as the epitome of elegant, cultured genius. But Herbert Stempel, a previous contestant on the show, became jealous of Van Doren's success and revealed that he had been instructed to let Van Doren win. Not only had Van Doren been given the answers by the producers of the show, he had also been coached to draw out the tension by pretending to struggle to come up with correct answers. The *Twenty-One* scandal ended the reign of the prime-time quiz shows, but it didn't end fake reality TV.

1980s: Daytime Talk Shows

In the 1980s daytime talk show hosts like Oprah Winfrey, Sally Jessy Raphaël, Phil Donahue, and Geraldo commanded huge audiences. Their appeal lay in the real people who would appear on their shows, brazenly confessing all manner of taboo vices and problems. Topics ranging from "caring for disabled lesbian lovers," to "makeovers for drag queens," to "I'm sixteen and I'm a nymphomaniac" earned the shows the label "Trash TV."

Skeptics suspected at least some of the guests were fakes or actors. And the skeptics were right. In 1988 it came to light that one couple, Tani Freiwald and Wes Bailey, had appeared on numerous talk shows by claiming to be different people suffering from different problems. On the *Oprah Winfrey Show* Freiwald posed as Bailey's sex-hating wife. On the *Sally Jessy Raphaël Show* she became a sex worker trying to cure Bailey's impotence, and on *Geraldo* she was transformed into a sex surrogate hired to help Bailey, who now claimed to be a thirty-five-year-old virgin.

The talk shows promised to reform and better screen their guests. But ten years later a rash of fake-guest scandals erupted in both America and England. Cases included a woman who shaved her head and pretended to have cancer in order to get on *Oprah,* and a wagonload of phony guests—recruited from an entertainment agency—who appeared on the BBC's *Vanessa Show.* The BBC canceled the *Vanessa Show,* and other programs promised to conduct internal investigations. But rumors continue to swirl—with the *Jerry Springer Show* in particular attracting many of them.

2000 and Beyond: Reality TV

The real-life-soap-operas and extreme-challenge-contests phase of the reality phenomenon kicked off in 1992 when MTV debuted *The Real World,* in which cameras recorded the tribulations of seven young strangers living in a New York City apartment. This was followed by the 2000 success of CBS's *Survivor,* about sixteen "castaways" who had to survive on a desert island while voting a fellow contestant off the island each week. (Europe had its own version of *Survivor* slightly earlier.)

Since 2000 reality programming has spread across the airwaves like a fungus, but claims of fakery have plagued virtually all the major shows. With *Survivor* it's accusations that votes were rigged, shots were staged, and cast members were hired through modeling agencies. (The show's producer insists the castaways are all normal people who independently submit applications.) On *American Idol* viewers have complained that their phoned-in votes don't seem to get counted. On *The Osbournes* the family's teenage children have claimed certain scenes were staged for dramatic effect. And the list goes on and on.

Even less sensationalized fare has been rocked by scandal. The PBS series *Antiques Roadshow* seemed about as homey and noncontroversial as a program could get. It featured professional antiques dealers appraising people's collectibles and family heirlooms. The fun part was when people discovered things they thought were junk were worth thousands of dollars. But in March 2000 the public learned that an appraisal in which a man brought in a rare sword he said had been lying around his attic had been staged. The man didn't think the sword was worth anything, so he had been using it to cut watermelons. The dealers then told him it was a rare Confederate sword valued at tens of thousands of dollars. Courtroom confessions later revealed that the entire appraisal, including the story about cutting watermelons, had been cooked up in advance by the dealers and the owner of the sword, who was a high school friend of one of the dealers. The sword, however, was real.

With audiences growing more cynical about the reality of reality TV, studios began to design shows that were openly dishonest. In this vein Fox debuted *Joe Millionaire,* on which women competed for the affections of a man they thought was a millionaire, only to learn at the end of the series that he was a "$19,000-a-year construction worker." But even here not all was as it seemed. Critics pointed out that Fox's faux millionaire was a swimsuit model as well as a construction worker and earned far more than $19,000 a year. There were even rumors that he really was a millionaire. If true, this definitely would have been a sign of the times—faking that you're faking it so that you can fake it.

Celebreality, n.: Reality TV programming that focuses on the normal, everyday lives of celebrities. Examples include *The Osbournes* and *The Anna Nicole Smith Show.*

First-Season Syndrome, n.: A theorized pattern on reality shows whereby only the first season is real (in the sense of being unscripted and spontaneous). In subsequent seasons players are aware of the show's format and possible strategies and therefore no longer display genuine reactions, but merely play to audience expectations.

Faux-lebrity, n.: A star of a reality TV show who is well known enough to be recognized, but will never attain the status or commercial appeal of a celebrity. Also known as a "surface celebrity."

Reality Check: Bizarre Reality TV Concepts

In the current glut of reality TV shows, producers are struggling to come up with ever stranger, more sensational premises that will stand out from the crowd and bring in new viewers. Below, see if you can separate the shows that are real (in the sense that studios have either seriously considered or have already produced them) from the ones that are jokes.

Sperm Race TV

Premise: The finalists of a group of men competing to father a child square off in a "sperm race." A fiber-optic camera films their sperm inseminating the woman's egg. The winner is the man whose sperm first inseminates the egg.

The program sounds like a hoax—and like an ethical minefield. But in 2004 Brighter Pictures, a subsidiary of Endemol in Britain, confirmed it had such a project in the planning stages. Faced with criticism, it defended the program by insisting the show would include "a tremendous amount of science." Brighter Pictures had earlier created a show called *There's Something About Miriam,* about men competing for the affection of a woman who turns out to be a transsexual.

Lapdance Island

Premise: Ten men are stranded on an island with forty professional lap dancers. The man who resists the temptations of the dancers longest wins.

Britain's Channel 4 ran ads in mid-2003 encouraging men to apply to be on this show, and soon received over twenty thousand applications. But in August the channel announced the program was a hoax designed to promote *The Pilot*

Show, a new Candid Camera–style comedy on which hoaxers fooled people into believing they were participating in absurd (but fake) reality programs. As the response Channel 4 got from *Lapdance Island* demonstrated, *The Pilot Show* will never have a problem finding people to fool (as long as their hoaxes involve being seduced by lap dancers).

Quarantine

Premise: Contestants are locked in a lab and exposed to contagious diseases. The person who remains in the lab longest wins £100,000.

In early 2004 the British *Daily Mirror* ran an ad seeking contestants for a reality show with this premise. The ad read: "Could you be a guinea pig in our virology lab? Not worried about looking and feeling your worst on live TV?… Don't mind the nation seeing you at your lowest ebb? If you want to become a star in a week (and rich, too) then we want to hear from you." Within a few days the paper had received over two hundred applications. Medical doctors were horrified and blasted the idea in the press. Thankfully it turned out to be an experiment "to discover just how far people will go in their pursuit of fame." As this hoax revealed, they'll go pretty far.

Seriously, Dude, I'm Gay

Premise: Heterosexual men compete to convince "a jury of their queers" that they're gay. Challenges include coming out to friends and going on blind dates with gay men. The contestant who can best pass for gay wins $50,000.

In May 2004 the Fox network announced this program would air in June. The show, as Fox's press release put it, would be a humorous take on "a heterosexual male's worst nightmare." The press release wasn't a joke. The network had already filmed an episode. But after facing a huge backlash, Fox canceled the series a few weeks later. *Seriously, Dude, I'm Gay* never aired.

Antebellum Island

Premise: Twelve strangers are stranded on an island that occupies an alternative reality in which the South won the Civil War. They compete to win $1 million (in Union money).

There have been several history-based reality shows. In 2002 the BBC aired *The Trench,* in which contestants struggled to survive in the simulated environment of a First World War trench. However, no reality program has yet resurrected the Confederacy. *Antebellum Island* was a spoof presented by the humor magazine *The Onion,* which joked that the show's motto would be "Secede, Suppress, Survive."

Dust to Dust

Premise: A corpse is televised as it rots. That's the show. No one wins a prize.

In late 2004 Channel 4 announced it was seeking a terminally ill patient willing to donate his or her corpse to such a show. In other words, the producers were looking for someone willing to die to get on TV. (It would be heartwarming to know you've got a production team waiting for your demise.) Channel 4 insisted the show would have great scientific and educational value.

Win the Green

Premise: Illegal immigrants living inside the United States brave challenges such as eating beetles or lying inside sealed coffins filled with rats in hopes of winning a year's worth of free legal services to help them obtain a green card.

Win the Green (titled *Gana la Verde* in Spanish) has aired on Spanish-language stations in Los Angeles since July 2004. Immigrants-rights advocates have blasted the show for exploiting the desperation of undocumented immigrants. Contestants seen on air are also potentially exposed to the danger of deportation. But the show's producers claim they have a long waiting list of people who want to be on the show, and have received no complaints from viewers.

Fake Bloopers

Shows that feature bloopers, outtakes, and amusing scenes caught on video have long been a TV staple. But although blooper shows claim to screen material for authenticity, audiences shouldn't believe every clip is real. Many of the spills and slipups aren't bloopers at all, but carefully choreographed fakes.

Demand for bloopers far exceeds the supply, and entrepreneurs have stepped in to fill the gap. Fox's *Stupid Behavior Caught on Tape* showed an aerobics instructor getting hopelessly tangled in a jump rope, but reporters who saw the original tape could hear an offstage director shouting directions. *Caught on Tape!* (similar name, different show) captured the world's worst employees: a pizza chef casually serving customers food he'd dropped on the floor, a hapless sandwich maker, and an unhygienic deliveryman. A closer look revealed that all three employees were the same man, who happened to be the video's producer. According to a report that aired on Bravo, *The Reality of Reality: How Real Is Real?*, as many as 75 percent of the bloopers collected by the clip-show business may be fake, which adds up to an awful lot of bogus blunders.

Yarase, n.: A Japanese term for the staged events common on reality shows. Reality shows are particularly popular on Japanese TV, and are notorious for going to extremes of weirdness and cruelty that most American and European shows don't dare. Japanese fans of these programs assume that the most shocking scenes are just "yarase," which gives the fans an excuse for not being too disturbed by what they see.

Fake Documentaries

Even documentaries are not always as real as they seem. British documentaries, in particular, have been prone to fakery in recent years.

Only after parts of *The Connection* had aired in the United States on CBS's *60 Minutes* in 1998 was the Carlton Television documentary about Colombian drug smugglers exposed as a near-total fake. The Colombians were actors, the heroin was sugar, and the central character—a mole hired to smuggle drugs on flights from Colombia to Britain—was a car-park attendant who had never smuggled anything. Then there was *Daddy's Girl,* a Channel 4 film about incestuous fathers and daughters that had to be scrapped when the featured father and daughter were revealed to be unrelated. Channel 4 was also censured for *Chickens,* in which viewers were never told that scenes showing young male prostitutes in Glasgow negotiating with clients were staged by members of the production team.

However, nature documentaries may be the most egregious offenders, simply because they seem above reproach. How could footage of mating polar bears be faked? But in a 2004 article, Sir David Attenborough revealed some of the tricks of the trade. Mating polar bears, for instance, would likely be filmed in a zoo, with footage spliced in to make it appear the bears were in the wild. Or a dramatic scene of a falcon catching its prey could be faked by filming three independent shots: one of the bird's prey, a second of the bird swooping downward, and a final shot of feathers flying into the air (tossed up by a member of the film crew). These shots would then be combined to form one scene.

The most infamous phony nature footage appeared in the 1958 Disney documentary *White Wilderness.* As part of its presentation of Arctic wildlife, the film showed lemmings jumping into a river to commit suicide, as legend has it they do. Except that lemmings don't really commit suicide: They sensibly avoid large bodies of water. So to get the shot the filmmakers had to round up some lemmings and herd them off a cliff. PETA would have been horrified. As a result of this faked scene, lemming suicide became an accepted fact in popular culture for decades afterward.

Just-Add-Water Celebrity, n.: An instant celebrity created by marketing hype. Typically lacking in the qualities—such as talent, charisma, wealth, or family name—whereby other celebrities earn their fame. Examples include the stars of *American Idol.*

REALITY RULE 11.2

In real life no one has magical powers and stories don't always have happy endings.

Reality Blurred

Movies depend on the suspension of disbelief, but when the lights go up you're supposed to return to real life. This proves more difficult for some fans than for others.

Diehard fans of *Star Trek, Star Wars,* and *The Lord of the Rings* are among the most notorious for acting as though the movie worlds they love are real. You find them arguing over the finer points of the elvish language, or dressed as Spock or Princess Leia at conventions. Sometimes they even make real life correspond to their fantasies. *Star Trek* fans organized a massive write-in campaign that got a space shuttle named after the fictional USS *Enterprise*. In a surreal twist, later *Star Trek* episodes showed a space shuttle mural in the captain's office, implying that the USS *Enterprise* was named for the space shuttle *Enterprise*. *Star Wars* fans in Great Britain and Australia topped this by listing "Jedi" as their religion on census forms. In both countries roughly as many Jedis as Jews were recorded.

It's easy to tease science fiction and fantasy fans for their role playing, but occasionally the blurring of movies and reality has more serious consequences. In 2001 a Japanese woman, Takako Konishi, was found frozen to death in the woods outside Fargo, North Dakota. Police who spoke to her a few days before her death believed she came to Fargo to search for a briefcase full of money that a character in the 1996 movie *Fargo* buries in a snowy ditch. The officers explained that the movie was fiction (and, ironically, the movie's action does not take place in Fargo), but she didn't seem to understand, and off she went. A filmmaker who later investigated the circumstances of her death came to believe that she wanted to commit suicide, not search for lost treasure. If so, why she chose to travel to Fargo to die is still not clear.

Video gamers can also lose the ability to distinguish between virtual and reality. In *Wired* magazine, Daniel Terdiman described one gamer who became so obsessed with the virtual challenge of picking up objects with a ball that, driving down Venice Boulevard (in real life), she found herself swerving to the side of the road to pick up objects such as mailboxes. Other players have lost their jobs and families due to gaming addictions. Addicts can become so absorbed in their virtual worlds that they won't leave the computer to go to work, to say hello to a spouse, or even to use the restroom—necessitating "piss pots" beside the computer. Should you find yourself reluctant to put down *this book* despite a burning need to go to the bathroom, there is a perfect solution. Read the book on the toilet. You have my permission.

CSI Effect, n.: The belief that all criminal cases are solved using the high-tech, forensic science seen on TV crime shows such as *CSI*. Lawyers have noticed that the lack of such high-tech evidence can seriously prejudice a jury against a prosecutor's case. A manifestation of the pervasive if-it's-not-like-what-we-see-on-TV-then-it-can't-be-real mentality.

case file: The Klingon Language

The *Star Trek* universe is fictional, as are the Klingons who inhabit it. The Klingon language, however, is real and thriving.

Klingon as a speakable language came into existence thanks to Marc Okrand of the University of California, Berkeley. He created it in 1979 at the request of Paramount Pictures executives who wanted the Klingons in the first *Star Trek* movie to sound realistic. Okrand expanded the language for the third movie in the series and adds to it to this day. But fans gave the language an independent life.

A group of hardcore fans banded together in 1992 to form the Klingon Language Institute, dedicated to the study and promotion of Klingon. Their efforts have been impressive. Two members, Andrew Strader and Nick Nicholas, translated Shakespeare's *Hamlet* into Klingon, inspired by General Chang's remark in *Star Trek VI: The Undiscovered Country* that "Shakespeare is best read in the original Klingon." Another member, Dr. d'Armond Speers, embarked on an experiment to raise his son as a bilingual speaker of English and Klingon. From the day his son was born, Speers spoke only Klingon to him, while his wife spoke English. But Speers had to abandon the experiment when his son stopped responding to Klingon. Evidently the kid realized that being fluent in Klingon would doom his chances of dating in high school. There was also the minor problem that Klingon had no words for everyday items such as "diaper" or "table."

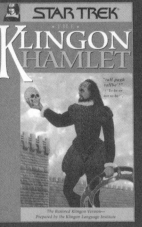

Photo courtesy of Pocket Books

The Klingon Hamlet

Klingon received official recognition in 2003 when the Oregon mental health authority added the right to have a Klingon interpreter to its list of patient privileges, noting that "there are some cases where we've had mental health patients where this was all they would speak." The decision was tongue in cheek (they've never really had a patient who speaks only Klingon), but should a Klingon wander off course, land on Earth, and find itself in an Oregon mental health facility, the officials there will be ready.

Snob Hit, n.: A boring movie or play that people pretend to like because they think they're supposed to like it.

Unread Bestseller, n.: A book that many buy, but few actually read.

REALITY RULE 11.3

"In Hollywood it's good to be yourself, but it's even better to be someone else."*

Real Person, n.: Someone who is not an actor.

Half-People, n.: People who become so accustomed to presenting an image or caricature of themselves in public that they're eventually reduced to caricature in private life as well (i.e., celebrities). Coined by Andy Warhol.

Ghostwriters and Ghost Reviewers

Literal-minded readers might assume an autobiography is written by its subject. After all, the definition of an autobiography is "an account of somebody's life written by that person." But the more famous the person is, the more probable it is that the menial task of writing was farmed out to a lowly ghostwriter (who will be lucky to get a thank-you on the acknowledgments page). That's understandable. Celebrities don't have time to write.

What's more surprising is when the "author" of an autobiography doesn't read his own book. After Ronald Reagan's ghostwritten autobiography came out in 1990, the former president said, "I hear it's a terrific book! One of these days I'm going to read it." A joke, probably. But basketball player Charles Barkley was far more serious in 1993 when he finally looked at his own autobiography after its publication and publicly complained he had been "misquoted" in it.

---

*Geoff Pevere, "Great Fakery Is the Coin of the Hollywood Realm," *Toronto Star,* December 13, 2002.

Reviewers are also notorious for not taking time to crack open a book. As the Scottish reverend Sidney Smith remarked, "I never read a book before reviewing it; it prejudices a man so."

Synthespian, n.: A virtual actor created through digital animation. Examples include Buzz Lightyear from *Toy Story* and Gollum from *The Lord of the Rings*. In 2003 *MTV Movie Awards* became the first show to reward the best "virtual performance."

Celebrity Worship Syndrome, n.: An obsessive fascination with the lives of the rich and famous. Psychologists speculate that people who exhibit this syndrome have difficulty forming real relationships with those around them and therefore form imaginary relationships with the people they see on screen.

Celebrity Imposters

Modern society is full of people claiming to be celebrities when they're not. At one end of this spectrum are the con artists. The R&B singer Elgin Lumpkin should have had a double measure of immunity from such identity thieves. First there was his stagename: Ginuwine. Then there was the title of his hit song: "Can You Tell It's Me." Neither did the trick, however, because in 2001 a con artist walked away with $25,000 by posing as the singer and convincing concert promoters to send him deposits on future performances. One of his victims finally cottoned to what was going on and warned him, "We know you're not the real Ginuwine." The faux Ginuwine is now serving time.

At the other end of the spectrum are the legal imposters: celebrity look-alikes who entertain at corporate functions, fundraisers, and parties. Fake Elvis Presleys are so popular they come in every shape, size, and form—fat, skinny, old, young, black, white, and airborne (as in the Flying Elvises featured in 1992's *Honeymoon in Vegas*). Buck Wolf, entertainment editor for ABCNEWS.com, has compiled a list of fake Elvii that includes Elvis Herselvis (the lesbian Elvis), Green E (the environmental Elvis who sings "In the Landfill"), El Vez (the Mexican Elvis who sings "In the Barrio"), Cop Elvis (a former New Zealand policeman fired for refusing to remove his blue suede shoes while on the job), and Extreme Elvis (a 350-pound stripteasing Elvis).

Oomposter, n.: One who pretends to have played an Oompa Loompa in 1971's *Willy Wonka and the Chocolate Factory.* In 2005 a Nevada man admitted that for over thirty years he had been lying to the media about having been one of the diminutive stars of Mel Stuart's classic.

Online Imposters

Between the criminals and the professional look-alikes lurks a whole range of celebrity wannabes driven by a variety of motives—parody, wish fulfillment, and ego-gratification among them.

Weblogs, in particular, have become a vehicle for celebrity wannabes, owing to the ease with which you can pretend to be anyone you want to be online. One of the more memorable fake celebrity blogs was the Bill Clinton journal that appeared in 2004 just as the former president launched a book tour to promote his autobiography. While Clinton's official memoirs may have been a bit dry, his (faux) weblog was far racier. The pseudo-Clinton divulged secrets such as his favorite sexual position (something he called "the Terminator") and his nickname for Hillary ("the dragon lady").

Another popular faux blog claimed to be authored by Nick Nolte. It had the weathered actor musing on topics such as blenders, billiard tables, the "blahs," and David Bowie's song "Cat People." (He wondered if Bowie was "talking about cat people in the sense of some sort of society of cat mutations or if he just means humans who happen to like cats?") Nolte's blog attracted quite a following—including the real Nick Nolte's lawyer, who sent its creators a cease-and-desist letter.

Many celebrities do maintain websites and weblogs, and will correspond with fans via e-mail. But if you meet an A-list star in a random chat room, be skeptical. In 2004 a girl from Chile met a guy online who said he was Daniel Radcliffe, the actor who plays Harry Potter. She only realized he was lying after she traveled to England (with her mother), knocked on Daniel Radcliffe's door, and was told the actor had no idea who she was.

Surgical Look-alikes

For some people, impersonating their favorite celebrity online isn't enough. They want to become that celebrity in the flesh. And with plastic surgery they can. In 2004 MTV debuted *I Want a Famous Face,* a program that followed young people as they surgically refashioned themselves to look like their Hollywood idols. Episodes included a woman who turned herself into Kate Winslet, twins who turned into Brad Pitt, and (in what was probably the most notorious episode) a transsexual who transformed himself (herself?) into Jennifer Lopez.

Celebrities Who Are Imposters

While many people impersonate celebrities, a popular conspiracy theory holds that certain celebrities are themselves imposters. This theory is most frequently applied to Paul McCartney, because of the 1969 rumor that Beatles albums contained clues confirming the musician's death. For instance, play the *White Album* song "Revolution 9" backward and you will supposedly hear the phrase "Turn me on, dead man"—as clear a clue as any. The real Paul McCartney, so the story goes, died in a car accident on November 9, 1966. Worried about the effect this would have on their future, the band replaced McCartney with a look-alike named William Campbell. Thus, the current McCartney is not the real McCartney. So far Sir Paul has refused to admit he's a fake.

More recently a Scandinavian woman named Lisa Johansen claimed to be the real Lisa Marie Presley. According to her, for her own safety she was whisked away to Scandinavia shortly after the death of Elvis, and a body double was put in her place. She was to come out of hiding when she came of age, but the fake Lisa Marie usurped her position. Johansen claims that facial analysis proves her to be the real deal, but the other Lisa Marie doesn't seem to be losing any sleep over the challenge.

George Spelvin, n.: A name used in movie credits and theater bills to disguise the fact that an actor is playing dual roles. The tradition of using this name dates back to 1906. In the 1970s a porn star had a career as Georgina Spelvin.

REALITY RULE 11.4

Technology can hide even the most glaring lack of talent.

Milli Vanilli 1. n.: A pop duo from the late 1980s. **2. v.:** To lip-synch a song. Example: "We were going to sing that for real, but instead we Milli Vanillied it." **3.** To have your work passed off as another's; to be plagiarized. Example: "I'm so mad that my roommate Milli Vanillied my term paper." **4. v.i.:** (obscure usage) To be given a Milli Vanilli album as a present. Example: "I was Milli Vanillied this Christmas."

Karaoke Culture, n.: A society in which imitation passes for reality and originality is nonexistent. Derives from a statement by Malcolm McLaren, the former manager of the Sex Pistols: "Today we live in a karaoke world. A world without any particular point of view...liberated by hindsight, unencumbered by the messy process of creativity, and free from any real responsibility beyond the actual performance."

Soundtrack Autism, n.: The inability to know what emotions you're supposed to be feeling unless cued by a soundtrack.

Lip-synching

Pop music is big business. Creating it requires teams of producers, sound engineers, and musicians—and an attractive face to sell it to the public. Whether the owner of that face can also sing is of secondary importance. Her voice can be improved or replaced entirely using technology. But for marketing reasons, the music industry likes to pretend otherwise. It pretends pop stars make their own music and can sing without a pant or a gasp while executing complex gymnastics routines during concerts. That this is simply not true has been proved by twenty years of lip-synching scandals.

Milli Vanilli's 1988 singles "Girl You Know It's True" and "Blame It On the Rain" raced up the charts thanks in large part to the good looks and great dance moves of the group's singers, Rob and Fab. But after falling out with Rob and Fab, the group's producer, Frank Farian, disclosed in 1990 that the duo had sung neither on their debut album nor in concerts, but relied on anonymous studio vocalists. Rob and Fab's sole contribution was as eye candy for the crowds. The public backlash was swift and unforgiving. The duo were stripped of their Grammy Award, and consumers filed a class action suit against the group and their record company. Rob and Fab were banished to the twilight world of celebrity has-beens, and Milli Vanilli became the poster child of lip-synching.

The Milli Vanilli debacle scared the industry, but it didn't slow the lip-synching phenomenon. Virtually all the major pop stars (Madonna, Britney Spears, Shania Twain) are rumored to lip-sync during concerts. In October 2004 Ashlee Simpson became the latest star to be caught in a lip-synching snafu. As she stood on a *Saturday Night Live* stage, her vocals began blaring through loudspeakers before she even had the microphone to her mouth. Her record company blamed this on a "computer glitch," but Simpson's manager-father blamed his daughter's acid reflux. His logic was that she would normally never lip-sync—of course not—but her throat was sore, so she had to. Tiny violins accompany this sob story.

Singers aren't the only ones called on to mime to prerecorded music. Entire bands—it's said virtually all the bands that appear on European music shows such as *Top of the Pops*—are reduced to stage furniture, mutely going through the motions of playing their instruments. From the point of view of concert promoters and the producers of live television shows, this insures against screwups—as long as the band doesn't rebel by stopping their act while the music continues.

Sometimes even the audience noise is faked. Television viewers have long been familiar with canned laughter, invented by engineer Charles Douglass in the 1950s. Laugh tracks' effectiveness (and thus their appeal to TV producers) lies in the fact that people tend to laugh when they hear other people laughing, and to cheer and clap when they hear others doing the same. Hearing silence makes people uncomfortable.

This psychological principle has not been lost on entertainment professionals outside the television industry. Crowd noises on many "live" concert recordings are dubbed in to make the events sound more exciting. And, taking the idea a step further, stadium owners can pipe in cheers and applause to loosen up audiences during sporting events. In 1997 the New York Nets management admitted to playing fake crowd noises over the speakers during home games at Continental Airlines Arena. However, they firmly denied placing blow-up dolls in empty seats.

Soon real people won't be required at concerts at all. Prerecorded band tracks can play in arenas to the cheers of fake crowds.

Sarcastic Clap, n.: A slow clap meant to convey derision, not appreciation.

Voice Tracking, v.: Using prerecorded DJ segments in radio broadcasts. Much of the DJ patter heard between songs on commercial stations is recorded days in advance, though it sounds live.

Reality Check: Metallica's Trademarked Chords

Did the rock group Metallica sue the band Unfaith for using the chord progression E to F, claiming Metallica had trademarked that sound?

It was the kind of litigious insanity that makes people howl with protest: world-famous Metallica suing an obscure Canadian group to stop it from using the chord progression E to F. According to a press release that appeared on the Internet in July 2003, Metallica wanted to prevent Unfaith from causing "confusion, deception and mistake in the minds of the public." The release elaborated: "We're not saying we own those two chords, individually—that would be ridiculous. We're just saying that in that specific order, people have grown to associate E, F with our music." Given that Metallica was at the forefront of efforts to stop the file-sharing network Napster, the story seemed believable to a lot of people. DJs railed against Metallica's action, and music fans everywhere denounced the band. But it was all a hoax concocted by Unfaith's lead singer, Erik Ashley. He had planted the story on his band's website, and backed it up with a fake MTV news page. None of Unfaith's songs even used an E to F chord progression.

Encore Bloat, n.: When bands conclude concert performances early, then return to the stage for an endless round of encores. Bands seem to think this is giving the audience something extra for their money, as if playing a full set is an act of generosity. Concertgoers paying through the nose to be there are not so easily fooled.

ADVERTISING 12

In ancient Greece all trade-related activities were confined to marketplaces set off by clear boundaries because of the belief that such dealings, though necessary, promoted antagonistic, dishonest relationships. Sellers had a natural motive to lie and cheat, to say anything to get people to buy their products: *It's new and improved! It's got more stain-fighting power! It's now longer lasting!* The Greeks didn't want that perfidy leaking into everyday life. Today we sporadically pay lip service to that ideal. For instance, we make a show of keeping advertisements separate from articles in newspapers. But, in reality, the boundaries of our marketplaces have disappeared. Advertising is everywhere. This is one of the major reasons we live in the age of b.s.

REALITY RULE 12.1

You may never even know you're being advertised to.

Fake Testimonials and Fake People

Advertisers accept that consumers might not believe them if they say the vacuum cleaner they're selling is the greatest thing in the world, but they always hope that if they can get Mr. Average from Arkansas to say it, everyone will think it must be true. Thus we're bombarded with a constant stream of third-person product testimonials. Most consumers are jaded enough to realize that testimonials accompanying dubious products such as penis-growth pills are fictitious ("I gained three inches in the first month," says John from Muskogee), but they're less likely to realize that major corporations also resort to fake testimonials.

The Microsoft Switch Campaign

Apple Computer's high-profile "switch" campaign was built around everyday computer users describing why they switched from Windows to a Mac. There's never been any suggestion that these testimonials were fake. Some of the people in the ads may even have been a little too real for Apple's liking. A teenage switcher named Ellen Feiss earned worldwide notoriety for appearing to be stoned in her ad. She later admitted she had been foggy-headed from allergy medicine, but insisted she never took anything illegal.

The success of Apple's campaign apparently got Microsoft jealous, because in 2002 it debuted its own switch ad online. Beside a picture of a woman the text read, "After eight years as a Macintosh owner, I switched to a PC with Windows XP and Office XP. Why? It's about more and better. " Internet sleuths quickly deduced that the woman pictured was unlikely to have written the testimonial, because the photo came from a commercial library of stock images and had appeared

The questionable confession of a Mac to PC convert

in other ads. Ted Bridis, an Associated Press reporter, then discovered that the testimonial's author was Valerie Mallinson, a Microsoft PR rep. When challenged, Mallinson insisted the ad wasn't deceptive because she really had "made the switch," but when the only switcher a company can drum up is its own PR rep, the endorsement isn't quite as persuasive. Microsoft quietly retracted the ad.

Advertainment, n.: An advertisement camouflaged as entertainment. BMW has paid well-known directors to create short films featuring its cars, and allows these films to be viewed online for free. But the broader trend is toward inserting product plugs directly into existing forms of entertainment such as movies, music, TV shows, and books. In 2005 McDonald's offered to pay rap artists who used the words "Big Mac" in their lyrics up to five dollars every time the track played on the radio. (But they weren't willing to pay me anything to change the title of this book to *Hippo Eats Big Mac*.)

David Manning

In an egregious example of fake testimonials, *Newsweek* revealed in 2001 that Sony Pictures had included quotations from a fictitious reviewer, David Manning, in print ads for many of its movies. Predictably, David Manning loved all the stinkers other reviewers panned. He even praised the Rob Schneider comedy *The Animal* as "another winner." (I saw *The Animal.* I can think of many words to describe it. "Winner" would not be one of them.)

Sony pulled the ads, but defended the invented reviews as a form of free speech. When filmgoers filed a class action suit, the judge ridiculed the free speech defense, and the company had to pay a $1.5 million settlement as well as $325,000 in fines to the state of Connecticut—making David Manning one of the most highly paid or, at least, costly movie reviewers in history.

But not costly enough, because Sony subsequently got caught using fake testimonials in TV ads for *The Patriot*. The ordinary moviegoers interviewed as they left a theater were actually Sony employees. Which makes you wonder: Does *anyone* see Sony movies who hasn't been paid to do so?

Advertorial, n.: Editorial content in newspapers and magazines that contains disguised advertising. An article in a food magazine might list great places

to eat without revealing that it's only including restaurants that have advertised in the magazine.

Fake User Posts

Traditional fake testimonials appear within an ad, so consumers have some
warning they might be bogus. A far more devious tactic is to post fake testimonials on Internet message boards or in newsgroups.

Say, for instance, that a person decided to do some research before choosing
what brand of digital camera to buy. Not trusting the information available from
advertisers, she might browse through what people who had used the products
had to say on message boards. But assuming the comments she finds are real and
honest would be a bad idea, because advertisers now spend a lot of time posting fake testimonials on message boards and in chat rooms. The FTC calls this
practice "disguised advertising." Even negative comments can't be trusted, because they may be a marketer's effort to discredit a rival company's product.
Hollywood studios routinely spam movie message boards with fake audience reviews of their latest releases, just as authors use fake names to post glowing
Amazon.com reviews of their own work. (See chapter 6: Fake User Posts.)

Astroturf, n.: 1. A brand of artificial grass (spelled AstroTurf) registered as
a trademark of Textile Management Associates. **2.** Any form of communication deceptively designed to appear as though it is part of a genuine
grassroots campaign. This usage is believed to have been coined by former
senator Lloyd Bentsen (D-Texas).

Astroturf Campaigns

Advertisers and PR firms don't limit themselves to Internet chat rooms.
Wherever the public has a chance to voice its opinion, marketing flacks will insert their own phony endorsements. A target of choice is the letters to the editor section in newspapers, where the average person is supposed to be able
to get his or her two cents heard. Instead, PR firms flood newspapers with fake
letters. Their aim is to simulate the appearance of genuine grassroots movements (thus the name astroturf campaigning), as if thousands of people had
spontaneously decided to write in about whatever the issue might be.

Although newspapers screen for astroturf, an enormous amount of it slips through. For instance, in 2003 Democrats noticed similar letters in support of President Bush's economic policies appearing in papers such as the *Boston Globe,* the *Cincinnati Post,* and the Fort Worth *Star-Telegram.* The letters all started with the line: "When it comes to the economy, President Bush is demonstrating genuine leadership." The letter was traced back to a Republican website, gopteamleader.com, that had posted it and was encouraging readers to print it out and send it to local papers. Thus, an instant grassroots movement was created.

Astroturf is used by those of all political persuasions. Even animal-rights activists were accused of using astroturf-style techniques to simulate support for a proposed amendment to Florida's constitution that would have granted rights to pregnant pigs. In fact, every major corporation, political party, and activist group engages in the practice. They believe that if their rivals are doing it, they can't afford not to. Meanwhile, genuine public discourse becomes a memory from the distant past.

case file: Microsoft Raises the Dead

In 1997 the Justice Department sued Microsoft for violating antitrust laws. As the case dragged on, the stakes became higher and higher, with the court eventually threatening to divide the software giant into smaller entities. But the software maker had one consolation: A vast citizens' movement was rallying to its defense, demanding in letters to states attorneys' general offices that the government get off the company's back. These outraged citizens even organized themselves into pro-Microsoft groups, with names such as Americans for Technology Leadership (ATL), Citizens Against Government Waste, and the Freedom to Innovate Network.

This groundswell of support made Utah's attorney general Mark Shurtleff suspicious, so he took a closer look at the pro-Microsoft letters he had received. He noticed they were peppered with similar phrases—such as *strong competition and innovation have been the twin hallmarks of the technology industry* and *the technology sector must remain free from excess regulation.* Also, some of the letters had arrived from nonexistent towns such as Tucson,

Utah, and, strangest of all, two of them included handwritten notes in the margin stating that the correspondent was dead.

To Shurtleff this meant one of two things: Either a zombie army was rising up from the grave to defend the right of Microsoft to crush its competitors, or the grassroots campaign was phony. He guessed it was the latter, and he was right. The pro-Microsoft campaign turned out to be one of the most elaborate astroturf schemes on record.

Microsoft had surreptitiously funded the citizens' organizations to serve as front groups. Paid PR grunts at these organizations then conducted polls to determine the level of public support for Microsoft. Respondents who voiced support for the software maker were sent letters, many of them individually composed by PR grunts to ensure a personal touch, that they were instructed to sign and forward on to their state attorney general. A handstamped, pre-addressed envelope was provided.

Unfortunately for Microsoft, two of the recipients on its mailing list were dead. The family members of the deceased diligently carried out Microsoft's instructions and sent the enclosed letter to the attorney general, but added a note explaining that the person whose name appeared on the signature line had passed away. This honesty inadvertently exposed the artificial nature of the entire campaign.

Faced with widespread criticism, an ATL spokesman denied anything untoward had been done, stating that the techniques used to orchestrate a campaign on Microsoft's behalf were "fairly common practice"—which means, I suppose, that the dead must be a more active lobbying group than previously realized.

Leaner, n.: A marketer hired to hang out undercover in bars and buy drinks for cool-looking people. The drinks are covert product samples. The idea is to influence or "lean on" trendsetters, so that they'll adopt the product and influence their friends to use it.

Roach Baiting, v.: Hiring undercover marketers to hang out in public and visibly use a product. Similar to the use of leaners, but rather than influencing trendsetters the marketer is herself the trendsetter influencing roaches (consumers) to follow her lead.

Operation Fake Tourist

Anything you come across in a paper or on the Internet may have been planted by an advertiser. Okay, you may think, I just won't believe everything I read. But the b.s. doesn't end there, because anyone you talk to in a public place may be an advertiser in disguise.

In a new promotional gimmick called covert sampling, marketing firms pay attractive young women to go to bars or nightclubs and pretend to be celebrating a birthday or cheering up a friend who just got dumped. This is their excuse to buy everyone in the place a drink—a disguised product sample. In other words, that woman who's flirting with you, dancing with you, and who just bought you a drink is only trying to get you to become a cranberry vodka consumer.

Sony Ericsson Mobile Communications took this idea to a new level in 2002 when its marketing firm hired actors to prowl the streets of Manhattan and Seattle posing as tourists. Their mission was to ask random pedestrians to take their picture using their new T68i digital camera/phone. Anyone who agreed would be given a rundown of the camera's snazzy features, without the actor ever breaking out of the chatty sightseer character. The campaign was dubbed Operation Fake Tourist. Female models were also hired to hang around in bars and strike up conversations in which they interwove references to their amazing new phone.

It's hard to imagine how marketers could extend their reach into everyday life any further, unless they perfect an invasion-of-the-body-snatchers–style virus that transforms normal people into corporate shills. If your elderly aunt starts babbling hysterically about the features of her new mobile phone, then watch out. The infection may have begun.

Magalog, n.: A shopping catalog camouflaged to look like a magazine.

Faux-rilla Marketing, n.: Guerrilla marketing (i.e., the use of unconventional techniques to publicize a product) that relies on fake elements. Two examples: in 2001 the Gap clothing chain spray-painted fake graffiti on its store windows to lend itself some counterculture cool. And in 2003 Dr

Pepper/7-Up sponsored a faux grassroots network of bloggers to hype its milk drink, Raging Cow. This latter effort only inspired real bloggers to boycott the drink.

Subviral Marketing

Advertisers love the Internet. Why? Because e-mailers love to forward funny ads to their friends, and they do it free of charge. This phenomenon is called viral marketing because the content spreads like a virus, and it's given a new lease on life to many ads that were too racy, raunchy, or just plain stupid to make it in mainstream markets.

However, some of the most popular ads on the Internet aren't created by advertisers. They're ad parodies created by random pranksters. Or are they? Conspiracy theorists suspect otherwise. They're convinced the parodies actually are the work of the companies they supposedly spoof. The faux ads spread everywhere and generate all kinds of free publicity, but by claiming they had no role in their creation, companies can distance themselves from any criticism. They get to have their cake and eat it too. It's hard to prove that companies do this, but (assuming they do) the concept is called subviral marketing. A few of the more notorious parodies suspected of being subviral ads include:

The PUMA Oral Sex Ad

The Ad: A glossy image shows a young woman, visible from the shoulders down, kneeling in front of a man, visible from the thighs down. The viewer can't see what's going on, but it's easy to guess because

some kind of milky liquid has landed on the woman's thigh. The woman and the man wear PUMA sneakers; the woman's PUMA handbag lies in the foreground; and a PUMA logo is stamped in the lower-right corner of the image.

Whodunit: The ad appeared on European websites in February 2003, and on American sites a month later. In fact, it was all over the Internet—as was the discussion about where it came from. Rumor held it had run in the Brazilian version of *Maxim*. But PUMA soon denied this, announcing it was in no way responsible for the image, and threatening legal action against anyone who reproduced it. This led to further Internet speculation that PUMA had created the ad. First, why would anyone bother to parody PUMA except PUMA itself? PUMA's rival Pony had recently generated enormous buzz by hiring porn star Jenna Jameson to appear in its ads. It seemed too coincidental that a sexy parody was now helping PUMA steal Pony's thunder. Second, the empty threat of legal action (there was no legal basis for suing) guaranteed the image far more attention than it otherwise would have received, and therefore seemed the perfect move for a company if it wanted to stoke the controversy. Finally, although the image was graphic, it was no worse than many real ads, such as a Gucci ad in the February 2003 issue of *Vogue* that showed a model pulling down her underwear to display pubic hair shaved into the letter G.

Other theories were that PUMA's rival Adidas created the image; that it was a spec ad (speculative ad—agencies create these to show potential clients the work they're capable of); that it was an in-house joke produced by someone at PUMA but never intended for public viewing; or that it was the work of an unknown Photoshop-skilled prankster. No one has stepped forward to take credit for the racy PUMA ad, so choose whatever theory you like.

The MasterCard "Perfect Date" Priceless Parody

The Ad: A video clip shows a young man saying goodnight to his date in front of her family's house. A voice-over says, "A night out on the town, $75." Then the guy starts to plead for oral sex. The voice-over interjects: "Getting the nerve to ask such a question, $12 bottle of wine." After some back and forth (she resists, he begs) the porch light suddenly comes on, and the girl's sister opens the door to say, "Dad says to go ahead and give him a blowjob, or I can do it, or if need be he'll come down and do it himself, but for God's sake tell him to take his hand off the intercom." The voice-over returns: "Having a girlfriend whose father has a sense of humor, priceless."

Whodunit: The MasterCard priceless ads are among the most parodied in the world, which isn't surprising given that they air in ninety countries and are familiar to millions of people. MasterCard denies having created this parody. However, the *Guardian* claims sources inside the industry report the parody "was produced in cahoots with MasterCard's U.S. agency," thereby making it "the highest-profile subviral yet." It's up to you to decide whom to believe: MasterCard, or the *Guardian's* unnamed sources.

The Volkswagen Suicide Bomber Ad

The Ad: A man wearing a Palestinian-style scarf gets into a Volkswagen Polo. He drives off and stops outside a sidewalk café. He takes out a switch attached to a wire and presses it. A bomb goes off inside the car, but the car contains the explosion without suffering any damage. The tagline "Polo. Small but tough" appears on screen.

Whodunit: This ad attracted enormous controversy in early 2005, but it turned out Volkswagen was telling the truth when it denied any involvement. The piece was a spec ad made by professional filmmakers LAD (Lee and Dan). Reportedly Lee and Dan spent £40,000 to make the ad, since they shot it on 35mm film, but they probably didn't get Volkswagen's business. Rumor holds the Royal Society for the Prevention of Accidents also complained that the suicide bomber wasn't wearing a seat belt.

Subliminal Advertising

Conspiracy theorists tell us advertisers have been busy over the past half century hiding subliminal messages that send hypnotic commands straight to our subconscious brain. We have no power to resist. We see them and crave soda, popcorn, new cars, or cigarettes.

James Vicary Sells Popcorn

Subliminal advertising entered popular culture in 1957 when James Vicary announced he had rigged a camera at a movie theater in Fort Lee, New Jersey, to flash split-second messages such as "Hungry? Eat Popcorn" or "Drink Coca-Cola" during movies—causing concession sales to rise dramatically.

The advertising industry instantly latched onto the idea. Radio stations began broadcasting subaudible advertisements. A few even transmitted subaudible public service announcements, secretly warning listeners to stay off icy roads. Vicary made a fortune by offering the consulting services of his Subliminal Projection Company.

The public was terrified by the whole idea, which sounded like mind control. However, tests repeatedly failed to find that subliminal ads had any measurable effect on audience behavior. So how had Vicary gotten his results? The answer came in 1962 when he admitted in an interview with *Advertising Age* that his Fort Lee experiments had never happened. He had made it all up.

Subliminal Seduction

In 1973 Wilson Bryan Key's book *Subliminal Seduction* reinvigorated the debate about subliminal advertising. Key's titillating claim was that advertisers embedded lurid sexual imagery in seemingly innocent ads. For instance, in a Sprite ad he could see the hidden depiction of a woman having sex with a polar bear. In a later book he described an orgy he had spied in an ad for Howard Johnson's clam plate. These graphic images apparently triggered consumers' carnal impulses, enticing them to buy those products.

Products notorious for their supposed subliminal messages included a pack of Camel cigarettes that conceals a man with an erect penis in the front leg of the camel; and Pepsi cans that, stacked correctly, spell the word SEX. Pepsi withdrew these cans from the market in 1990 after a few people protested.

A few mischievous artists probably do hide sexual imagery in ads. And some people probably see way more in advertising imagery than is really there. But there's no reason such images would reduce us to helpless pawns in the hands of advertisers. Now, excuse me, I've got a sudden craving for a Sprite.

Reality Check: **The Little Mermaid Penis**
Can a penis be seen in the cover art for Disney's *The Little Mermaid*?

The idea of erotica hidden in Disney movies seems a bit far-fetched, but in this case it's true. One of the castle towers in *The Little Mermaid* video cover art is obviously phallus-shaped. Reports differ about whether the artist intended to place the penis there. The hidden body part caused such an uproar once Christian groups cottoned on to it that Disney removed it from the later laser disc release of the movie.

Other infamous examples of supposed Disney erotica include: an erection that the minister at Ariel's wedding in *The Little Mermaid* seems to sport (Disney explains the bulge away as his knee); the word SEX that forms in a cloud of dust halfway through *The Lion King* when Simba lies down on a cliff (Disney admits something is there, but says the letters spell SFX, a reference to the special effects team that worked on the movie); the phrase "All good teenagers take off your clothes" that the title character in *Aladdin* is said to whisper while standing on a palace balcony with Princess Jasmine (Disney claims he's saying "Scat, good tiger, take off and go"); and an image of a nude woman that appeared in a single frame of *The Rescuers*. The reality of *The Rescuers* nudity was confirmed when Disney recalled 3.4 million copies of the video in 1999 after realizing that a prankster had indeed inserted the offending frame.

REALITY RULE 12.2

Advertisers are guilty of lying until proved innocent.

Spinnish, n.: The language of spin, spoken by people in public relations.

Zen Spin, n.: The public relations strategy of not spinning a story in order to appear more honest. A nonspin form of spin.

Twisted Truth

You receive a piece of mail that declares YOU'VE WON $10,000,000! You tear open the envelope, only to find the fine print inside: "This is what we would be saying to you if you were our grand prize winner." Advertisers are full of bait-and-switch tricks like this. Technically they're not lying (so they can't be sued), but they're not being honest either. They're guilty of twisting the truth. Other underhanded schemes marketers use to get people to look at junk mail include phony official documents, phony personalized letters (often accompanied by phony handwritten notes on Post-its), and phony promotional checks.

case file: Man 1, Bank 0

In May 1995 Patrick Combs, a heavily-in-debt motivational speaker, was mailed a promotional check made out for $95,093.35. It looked real—until he saw the word "non-negotiable" stamped on it. On a whim, Combs decided to deposit the check at his bank's ATM machine and see what happened. To his surprise, the money was credited to his account.

Every day Combs checked his balance, expecting the $95,000 to have disappeared when the bank realized its mistake. But the days stretched into weeks, and Combs started to get excited. A teller had told him that according to a law designed to protect depositors, checks can't be returned after ten business days. Far more than ten days had passed, so although he could hardly believe it, the money seemed to be his.

A final test remained. Would the bank allow him to withdraw the money? Heart pounding, Combs went in and asked for a $95,000 cashier's check. The teller happily printed one out and Combs stashed it in a safe-deposit box.

Not long after this, the bank realized its mistake and made a series of threatening calls, warning Combs that he had committed fraud and demanding he give back the money. The bank also informed him that the ten-day rule was bogus. But by this time Combs had done a little research and knew he hadn't committed fraud because he had never endorsed the check. He had also discovered that banks were supposed to inform depositors within two days of learning that a check was no good. He told this to his bank, and the threatening calls stopped.

Combs's David-and-Goliath tale made headlines throughout the world. TV shows featured him, and Hollywood producers talked about turning his adventure into a movie. But how did it end? Did he get to keep the money? Unfortunately, no. Combs volunteered to return the check after negotiations made clear that the bank would take him to court otherwise. But he turned his experience into a one-man show that has probably earned him far more than $95,000 in the years he's been performing it. So he did find a way to turn a fake check into real money after all.

Puffery, n.: A legal term for exaggerated advertising claims that the average consumer would never take literally. Vague statements such as "They're great!" or "You'll love it!" are considered puffery, as opposed to specific, factually misleading statements, such as "It regrows hair!," which are considered false advertising. As cynics put it, puffery is a lie that doesn't work.

Retail Scams

The retail world is full of twisted truths. Items are labeled "made in the USA" even if the only part made in the United States was a tag sewn on in Los Angeles or a bumper screwed on in North Carolina. Merchandise is marked at sale prices, even if it was never sold at regular price. (By law, items must be offered at regular price 50 percent of the time before a retailer can advertise them as reduced to sale price, but this regulation is widely ignored.) And then there's the ubiquitous practice of "99-centing," whereby retailers sell a product at $19.99 rather than $20, because they think consumers will believe it's cheaper.

Consumer Reports's editors have cataloged an enormous number of misleading claims made by retailers over the years. A few of the all-time classics are below:

Consumers might have thought a "microwave spoon" was a spoon that could be heated in the microwave. Not so. If you read the fine print you discovered it was "not intended for use in a microwave." In other words, it was a spoon with which you could stir food that had been removed from a microwave—as you could with any other spoon.

A label promised a VHS Storage Case "automatically becomes portable when carried."

Those in need of a loan would have found it hard to pass up this offer from the Cleveland Finance Loan Company: "Pay nothing til first payment."

A health club advertised that, to fit the busy lives of its patrons, it was "open 24 hours, 5:30 AM to 9:00 PM."

The label on a pair of sunglasses assured buyers the lenses would "block over 100% of UV rays."

Dunkin' Donuts had a great deal for its customers: "Free 3 muffins when you buy 3 at the regular 1/2 dozen price."

Finally, a car dealership boasted of its half-price sale: "The price you see is half the price you pay." In other words, everything on the lot went for double the sticker price.

Photoflattery, n.: The tendency for objects in advertisements to look far better than they do in real life.

Hype Cycle, n.: The cycle—from initial interest, to unrealistic euphoria, to the inevitable crash of disillusionment (and sometimes a more realistic acceptance)—that overhyped products follow. Coined by the Gartner Group research firm.

case file: The Cesky Sen Hypermarket

Consumers in Prague could hardly avoid hearing about the new hypermarket, Cesky Sen, or "Czech Dream," opening in the Letnany Fairgrounds. There were flyers everywhere, as well as ads on billboards, at bus stops, in newspapers, and on TV. The store promised ultralow prices, such as TVs for nineteen dollars and mineral water for pennies, and a special surprise for anyone who came to the grand opening on May 31, 2003.

As hundreds of eager consumers got out of their cars that day they could see bright colors in the distance. Shopping bags in hand, they ran across the fairgrounds—only to find nothing but a 26-by-260-foot Cesky Sen banner fluttering in the wind. This was the special surprise.

In fact, there was no hypermarket, nor plans to build one. Student filmmakers Vit Klusak and Filip Remunda had set out to record what happened when consumers' expectations collided with reality. With the help of a grant from the Czech Ministry of Culture they had hired an ad agency to launch a massive marketing blitz to promote a nonexistent product.

What happened? Not much. As the angry, confused crowd grew in front of the Cesky Sen banner, Klusak and Remunda got on a stage to explain their project. Some people laughed; others booed and shouted curses at the filmmakers; and a few kids threw rocks at the Cesky Sen sign. But the filmmakers were prepared for this and started playing music through speakers to calm the crowd. Eventually most people shrugged and went home.

Klusak and Remunda's point was that advertisers play with our expectations all the time, raising them with big promises only to let us down by delivering nothing. What Klusak and Remunda did was no different, except they put themselves on a stage where people could throw rocks at them.

The pair said they would return the money they'd received from the Ministry of Culture if the movie they planned to make about the Cesky Sen experiment turned a profit. I've heard the film has since come out, but I've never seen it. Hopefully it, too, isn't a hoax.

REALITY RULE 12.3

All the world's an ad, and all the men and women merely marketers.*

Subvertisement, n.: An un-commercial. An advertisement created to subvert consumerism rather than promote it.

Ambush Marketing, v.: Purposefully undermining a marketing campaign. In 1998 the Coca-Cola Bottling Co. sponsored a Coke in Education Day in Columbia County, Georgia. The corporation offered $500 to the school that staged the most creative Coke promotion. Officials at Greenbrier High gathered students outside to spell "Coke" for a photograph, with executives from Coca-Cola Bottling watching. Just as the picture was taken, one of the students, Mike Cameron, took off his shirt to reveal a Pepsi T-shirt. The stunt ruined the picture and got Mike suspended, but it made him a

---

*Adapted from Buck Wolf, *The Wolf Files,* ABC News, who adapted it from William Shakespeare.

legend among culture jammers who love to throw wrenches in the spokes of corporate marketing efforts.

Amateur Publicity Stunts

With everybody selling something nowadays, the problem is getting heard above the clamor. If you're an amateur without much of a budget, then you've got to be creative. And no creative device has proved friendlier to the amateur, in terms of attracting attention on the cheap, than the hoax. Dream up an outrageous lie, toss it out there, and soon the public will be crowded outside your door. As can be seen from the examples below, the hoax can be adapted to solve almost any publicity problem.

The Case of the Pickled Dragon

Problem: Allistair Mitchell had self-published his book, but he needed to get it into bookstores. How could he attract the attention of a distributor?

Solution: Unleash a pickled dragon on the world.

In January 2004 an Oxfordshire man contacted the media, claiming he had found a tiny dragon—complete with wings, claws, and an umbilical cord—preserved in a jar of formaldehyde in his garage. The media had a field day. How had it gotten there? Was it a real creature? A local antiquarian took a look and pronounced it a fake. That was obvious since *dragons don't exist.* But the antiquarian theorized that it was evidence of a hundred-year-old attempted hoax. According to him, in the 1890s German scientists had given the dragon to the British Natural History Museum, hoping to fool their British rivals. But the British didn't fall for the prank and relegated the dragon to a warehouse, where it gathered dust until a porter took a fancy to it and brought it home. Decades later the porter's grandson found it while cleaning the garage.

The media ate this story up, but not a word was true. The dragon had been created by Crawley Creatures, modern-day model makers, at the behest of Allistair Mitchell, who played the part of the local antiquarian. One of his friends "found" the dragon. The unveiling of the elaborate hoax within a hoax generated enough publicity to persuade Waterstone Bookstore to offer Mitchell a distribution deal for his book. So who says hoaxing doesn't pay?

8march2003.com

Problem: How could Wakeman Publishing generate Internet buzz to promote Jêan Nemeyeth's novel, *The Shift of the Ages*?

Solution: Promise to reveal an astounding discovery to the world on March 8, 2003.

When the site 8march2003.com appeared online in October 2002, its anonymous webmaster claimed he had a secret to tell, but only on March 8, 2003. The secret involved an "astounding discovery" he made after finding an undeveloped roll of film while hiking in the mountains. The Internet, home to every conspiracy theory in the world, can't resist a secret, so all kinds of websites were soon speculating about what might be revealed. Was it something to do with extraterrestrials, or government secrets? Excitement increased when odd pictures were added to the site. Then March 8 arrived and the secret—that the site was a publicity stunt to promote Nemeyeth's book—was revealed. Anyone expecting something more exciting was disappointed. But Nemeyeth considered it a success. The characters depicted on the site tied in with characters from his book.

Emulator, n.: A consumer who buys products, such as sneakers, that allow him to fantasize about being someone else, such as Michael Jordan. Example: "I want to be like Mike."

Pseudo-event, n.: An event staged purely for the purpose of generating publicity, as opposed to a real event that doesn't need press coverage to validate it. Examples include press conferences, celebrity interviews, and award ceremonies. Coined by Daniel Boorstin in his 1961 work *The Image: A Guide to Pseudo-Events in America.*

> ### Reality Check: **Odd-vertising**
> Advertisers are going to increasingly bizarre lengths in their
> never-ending quest to get their ads in front of our eyeballs.
> But how bizarre? See if you can guess which of the following
> extreme advertising techniques are real, and which are fake.

Birdtyping

Did an Australian ad agency train flocks of geese to fly in formation and sky-write, or "birdtype," letters and corporate logos?

Australian writer Stephen Banham described skywriting geese in *Fancy,* a book that mixes factual and fictional stories about typography—with birdtyping being one of the fictional ideas. The story takes the form of a faux interview with Roman Kingsley, a geese trainer starting his flock with the obvious choice: *V* for Volvo. Curved letters, he notes, take the birds a bit longer to learn.

Bloodvertising

Did a company promoting a highly violent video game decorate bus shelters with blood-seeping advertisements, in which fake blood oozed out of cartridges, seeped down the inside of a clear plastic sheet, and dripped onto the street, with cleaners hired by the company periodically washing off the pavement?

Some companies know that blood and guts is where the money is. So when Acclaim Entertainment debuted its ultragory video game *Gladiator: Sword of Vengeance,* it highlighted the carnage factor with a "bloodvertising" campaign that ran for a week at selected UK bus stops. What this means, of course, is that advertisements involving other bodily fluids are sure to follow. Prepare for the worst.

Sno Ads

Have advertisements been painted onto fresh snow on ski slopes or on the sides of mountains?

Some people see pristine beauty; others see a canvas waiting for an ad to be plastered on it. Marketing executives naturally fall into the latter category. So it shouldn't have surprised anyone when SoCal Promotions announced in mid-2004 that it had developed a technique to paint "highly visible, unique, color advertisements" onto snow. Skiers, the company promised, could not avoid seeing the ads.

It also promised the ads would be 100 percent environmentally friendly. Nature lovers were still horrified, as was everyone who felt they should be able to spend a day outdoors without seeing a corporate logo on every mountain.

Freewheelz

Do advertisers provide free cars, in return for which recipients must allow large ads to be placed on the vehicle, listen to constantly streaming radio advertisements while inside it, and drive at least three hundred miles a week?

This idea began as a hoax, but entrepreneurs have since developed it for real (minus the streaming radio). In 2000 Ted Fishman wrote an April Fool's Day article for *Esquire* describing a company, Freewheelz, premised on the free-car-as-mobile-billboard idea. Little did he know that companies were already trying to make the business model work. Of course, this was during the dot-com bubble, when people could raise money for any harebrained scheme. Most of the free-car companies have now faded from the scene, but a few linger on. The catch is that sponsors are looking for high-visibility, always-on-the-road drivers. So you might be able to persuade a company to pay for your car if you're a taxi driver, but if you park in a garage all day, forget it.

Fetal Product Advertising

Are there prenatal education devices that project rhythmic sounds and brand names into the womb, familiarizing the fetus with corporate identities in the hope that it will grow up to be a loyal customer?

Prenatal education is all the rage among parents who want to give their babies every advantage, but it's hard to imagine parents who would approve of in utero commercials, and no marketers have yet tried to sell them on it. Though if they thought they could, I'm sure there'd be no stopping them. Maybe I shouldn't be giving them the idea.

Panhandler Advertising

Have advertisers given free laminated signs, displaying humorous messages such as, "At least I'm not spamming your e-mail," as well as the logo of a corporate sponsor, to panhandlers?

Denver-based Sumaato Advertising looked at all those panhandlers standing around holding will-work-for-food signs and thought, *That's a lot of advertising space going to waste.* So in May 2002 its employees drove around the city handing out new signs to homeless people. No money was exchanged. The panhandlers simply got more attractive signs in return for giving the ad agency free publicity. Critics blasted Sumaato for trivializing the homeless problem. The agency claimed it only meant to raise awareness of the issue. Nevertheless, sponsors haven't been eager to sign up the homeless as mobile billboards.

Urinal Advertising

Have advertisements been placed inside urinals in public restrooms?

When you can't go to the bathroom without seeing a commercial, then you know our culture has reached a tipping point. And, yes, that point has arrived. Richard Deutsch is the inventor of the Wizmark, the world's first "interactive urinal communicator." It sits inside the urinal, where it displays an ad and, when it senses motion, flashes lights and blares a taped message. Urinal users are unable to ignore it. Imagine a restroom full of these things blasting away at full volume, and you get a sense of the special hell Deutsch has brought into existence. So far Deutsch has signed up clients such as Country Music Television and Molson Breweries. And watch out, ladies. A version for women's restrooms is in the works.

Bro-ing, v.: Appropriating elements of African American culture in order to make a product seem cool. A play on "pro-ing," which is using endorsements by professional athletes to increase a product's appeal. Coined by Nike.

Body Ads

Those listening to the April 1, 1994, edition of National Public Radio's *All Things Considered* heard that companies such as Pepsi had begun to sponsor corporate logo tattoos. In return for permanently branding themselves, teenagers received a lifetime 10 percent discount on that company's products. Teenagers were said to be responding enthusiastically.

The news was an April Fool's Day spoof on our consumer-oriented society, in which all clothing seems to bear a corporate logo. NPR apparently thought people walking around with ad tattoos was too absurd to happen. NPR should have known better. Ten years later body ads were all the rage.

Body ads owed their transformation from hoax into reality to eBay. In August 2002 a woman offered to allow advertisers to tattoo their logo onto her husband's penis. Then, in August 2004, Jeremy Martin offered the back of his own bald head. These pioneering attempts at body advertising went nowhere, since eBay removed the auctions.

But the idea had been planted. In 2003 Justin Kapust, a student at Johnson & Wales University in Rhode Island, launched a company called Headvertise, which paid college students seventy dollars a week to wear temporary tattoos on their foreheads. He signed up clients such as Roommates.com and ClubZelis.com, but most of the students had other jobs, and their employers didn't like them showing up with huge ads on their foreheads. Soon after, the ad firm Night Agency debuted "ass-vertising." This involved "putting a logo, a web address, or a brief message on the seat of a pair of bikini style panties. The panties are then worn by beautiful girls, and revealed when appropriate in a 'mooning' fashion."

However, body ads didn't become mainstream until January 2005, when twenty-year-old Andrew Fischer of Omaha, Nebraska, auctioned on eBay one

Andrew Fischer, the human billboard, in Times Square

Photos courtesy of Chachi Kruel

The Forehead Ad Blocker™

month's advertising space on his forehead. It's not clear why Fischer's offer attracted so much more attention than earlier body ad schemes—maybe he had a bigger forehead—but whatever the case, the winning bidder gave him $37,375 to advertise its snoring remedy and whisked him away on a monthlong publicity tour that included appearances on *Good Morning America* and *Inside Edition.*

Inspired by Fischer's success, would-be body advertisers tendered space on every available body part: forehead, cleavage, buttocks—even, in one case, a pregnant belly. One extreme capitalist was willing to let advertisers tattoo their logo inside his body, on his colon. (Imagine the creative possibilities that would allow: "Coca Colon," or "Colon you hear me now?")

With this glut of body ads, it seemed escaping advertising would become impossible. Wherever you went—to work, to school, to the gym—some corporate sellout would be broadcasting a message at you from his forehead. Thankfully, inventor Chachi Kruel came up with the Forehead Ad Blocker™, which he offered for sale on (where else?) eBay. Thanks to Chachi we need no longer live in fear of the forehead-ad menace. This may indeed be proof that we can invent our way out of any problem.

BUSINESS 13

P. T. Barnum, the nineteenth-century master of the hoax, writes in his book *The Humbugs of the World*, "It would be a wonderful thing for mankind if some philosophic Yankee would contrive some kind of 'ometer' that would measure the infusion of humbug in anything. A 'Humbugometer' he might call it." This machine, Barnum mused, would sniff out all kinds of humbugs—such as watered-down milk or snake-oil medicine—fobbed off by businessmen on the public. Updated for modern times, a more appropriate term for the Humbugometer would be the Bullshitometer. It could definitely be put to immediate and practical use. Bullshit, after all, is the lifeblood of modern business.

REALITY RULE 13.1

Money is real only if everyone agrees to pretend it's real.

Unreal Money

Since the invention of money, people have been suspicious of it—paper money, in particular. The reason for this is that money doesn't have inherent value; it's just paper (or metal) unless people are willing to accept that it represents something more. Its value is a fake reality on which our society is based—an illusion with which everyone plays along because it's more convenient to carry around paper than to cart around things of real value, such as cows or sheep.

But while paper money is more convenient than bartered goods, it's also a lot easier to fake. And lots of people do fake it. Federal authorities estimate that over $40 million worth of counterfeit money is spent every year, and that amount is growing rapidly because of the ease with which color copiers and printers can be used for counterfeiting. If you find yourself stuck with funny money, you're supposed to report it to the police. But don't expect a refund. The only way to recover your loss is to trick someone else into taking the stuff. But that, of course, would be illegal.

Fake Money as Art

While paper money's functional worth is an illusion, its aesthetic value is genuine. It could even be considered art worthy of hanging on a wall, if we weren't eager to trade it for other things (such as art to hang on our walls).

For a number of artists this tension between money's aesthetic and economic functions has been a source of inspiration. Stephen Barnwell has created currency for the fictional land of Nadiria, as well as a history that explains how this lost colony of Antarctica was founded in 1866 and survived for thirty-three years until it mysteriously vanished. Nadiria's history can be read, and samples of its Dream-Dollars bought, at dream-dollars.com.

J. S. G. Boggs's fascination with money has led him much closer to the edge of the law. His drawings of dollars, euros, or whatever the currency is where he happens to be, are realistic enough to be mistaken for actual money, except that one side is blank (save for his signature and thumbprint). He spends his art-work in stores or restaurants by finding people willing to accept it at the face value it depicts, in exchange for goods or services. It's smart to take Boggs's offer, because collectors track down these "Boggs bills" and buy them for well upward of ten times their face value.

His art hasn't made Boggs many friends with treasury departments around the world. He's been charged with counterfeiting in Britain and Australia (in both cases juries found him not guilty), and the American Secret Service raided his studio in 1992 and confiscated thousands of his works. The Secret Service refuses to return these works, although it has never charged Boggs with a crime.

Ironically, as Boggs has become better known, counterfeit Boggs bills have started popping up. These are fakes of fakes. Boggs, however, told the collector who reported buying one of his spent bills for $2,000, only to learn it was the work of a copycat, not to worry too much about it. He figured the fake was a good one, so she got her money's worth.

Brief Safe, n.: Perhaps the grossest way ever devised to hide money—a money pouch disguised as a pair of soiled under-wear, complete with fake skid marks. Sold by Shomer-Tec, a law enforcement and military equipment firm. The ad copy for this product states, "Leave the 'Brief Safe' in plain view in your laundry basket or washing machine at home, or in your suitcase in a hotel room—even the most hard-ened burglar or most curious snoop will 'skid' to a screeching halt as soon as they see them." The ad notes that the briefs are available in only one color: white (with a bit of brown).

The Brief Safe

Strange Fakes That Pass for Real

Most counterfeiters go to great lengths to make their fake currency look convincing—at least under casual scrutiny. But some counterfeiters don't bother.

The $200 George W. Bush bill is a favorite among slacker counterfeiters. The front shows a likeness of George W. Bush and a treasury seal marked "The right to bear arms." The back shows an oil well and the White House lawn decorated with signs such as "U.S. deserves a tax cut," "No more scandals," and "We like broccoli." On January 28, 2001, a man served at a Danville, Kentucky, Dairy Queen drive-through window paid for his $2.12 purchase with one of these bills. The cashier happily accepted it and gave $197.88 in change—at which point the customer quickly drove off. The cashier later explained in her defense that she had believed the $200 bill to be legitimate because it was green, just like real money.

A $200 George W. Bush bill popped up two years later when a man used it to pay for $150 in groceries at a Food Lion in Roanoke Rapids, North Carolina. Once again the cashier accepted the bill and gave change. And in 2004 a cashier at a Fashion Bug clothing store in Pennsylvania gave $99 in change for another $200 W bill. It's a slow-moving Bush-bill crime spree.

European cashiers have proved no better than Americans at spotting obvious fakes, especially during the confusion that surrounded the switch to euros as Europe's official currency. In January 2002 a bartender in southern France mistook a customer's preferred Monopoly money for the new currency. Soon afterward German authorities discovered shoppers were

Nonnegotiable currency

using fake 300- and 1,000-euro notes adorned with pictures of buxom naked women. The European central bank had given the firm Planet-Present permission to distribute the bills as a publicity stunt, never realizing people might think the sexy money was real. I guess Europeans really are less prudish than Americans.

Stupid Counterfeiters

For every cashier who accepts obviously fake money, there's a counterfeiter who pushes her luck too far. Take Alice Regina Pike, who, in an apparent bid for the title Stupidest Criminal Ever, asked a Wal-Mart cashier to cash a $1 million bill. When the cashier refused, Pike tried to use the bill to buy $1,675 worth of merchandise. Still no luck. Finally the cops were called and took Pike away. (She should have tried with a $200 George Bush bill.)

Then there were the genius counterfeiters who successfully used their product to buy $300 worth of merchandise at Wal-Mart, then came back to the store a few days later to return the merchandise for real money. The cashier recognized the merchandise and handed back the bogus bills. The thieves walked out of the store, did a U-turn, and returned to complain that the money was counterfeit. The store manager told them if they had a problem with that, they could go to the police. They were never seen again.

Paste-up Scam, n.: A street con in which a stranger is approached and asked to make change for a twenty-dollar bill. Glancing quickly at the bill, the mark obliges. But the twenty is really a two-dollar bill with a twenty's corners pasted on. At a glance the two-dollar bill looks like a twenty.

Real Money Rejected

The Federal Reserve states that paper money's effectiveness derives from "the confidence people have that they will be able to exchange such money for real goods and services whenever they choose to do so." This confidence breaks down if legitimate money is rejected as counterfeit. That doesn't happen often, but when it does, the most frequent culprit is counterfeit-detection pens. These widely used pens contain a solution that reacts with starch to produce a black line. The expensive fiber used to make real currency doesn't contain starch, whereas the cheap paper commonly used to make counterfeit money does. So a black line should only appear on the fake stuff, unless starch got on real money, which can happen for any number of reasons—for instance, a prankster starching bills just to mess with subsequent holders.

A more unusual case of real money rejected as fake occurred in 2005, when Mike Bolesta tried to pay at Best Buy with fifty-seven two-dollar bills, which he happened to collect. Unfortunately, the clerk didn't realize two-dollar bills are legitimate—and neither did the police, who took Bolesta in to the station. Perhaps stores should hang signs for the benefit of their cashiers: two-hundred dollar bills fake, two-dollar bills real!

Fuzzy Math, n.: Economic calculations that don't make sense. First used by George W. Bush in 2000 to characterize Al Gore's proposed economic policies. More often used since 2000, to describe Bush's economic policies.

Strange Economic Indices

Economists create models that supposedly show how different events affect people's decisions to spend or save money. If an item becomes scarce, for instance, people will spend more to acquire it. That's the model of supply and demand. Economists also devise indices that measure what's happening in the economy overall. The Consumer Price Index (CPI), one of the best known of these indicators, tracks the prices of common household goods in order to reveal inflationary trends. Many other indices exist. Some of them have rather fanciful relationships to reality.

Cocktail Party Chatter Index (CPCI)

This index correlates the amount of cocktail-party chatter about a stock or commodity to its future value. A lot of talk about a stock is a bearish indicator that means its value will go down. (Once everybody knows about a stock, it's been overbought, and can only head south.)

Miniskirt Index

Increased miniskirt sales are said to indicate the economy is doing, or will do, well. The purchase of the miniskirt indicates optimism and vanity, emotions expressed more strongly in good times, but also has an economic effect of its own. First, it helps the clothing industry; second, miniskirts are usually worn when going out to show off, and more people going out benefits the food, beauty, and entertainment industries; third, miniskirts stimulate men, leading them to increase their economic activity as they strive to impress miniskirt wearers.

Lipstick Index

A rise in lipstick purchases is said to indicate a recessionary economic pattern, because when money is tight, women buy more small comfort items, such as lipstick, rather than large items such as clothes (miniskirts?). Supposedly after 9/11 lipstick sales rose sharply.

Golf Ball Index

More golf balls left unclaimed around golf courses is a sure sign times are good. In lean times people will hunt down balls, but when they're feeling rich they just buy more.

Aspirin-Count Index

Higher aspirin purchases signal a decline in stock prices. As market conditions worsen, people require more pain relief to function. (This indicator probably closely mirrors the alcohol index.)

Voodoo Economics, n.: Any economic theory based in fantasy, not reality. Coined by George H. W. Bush to describe the supply-side economic theory of his Republican rival, Ronald Reagan, who argued that the best way to stimulate the economy was to cut taxes for the wealthy, since this would encourage them to invest and create jobs. Oddly enough, once Bush was chosen as Reagan's vice president, he became a firm believer in the voodoo economics he had once derided.

REALITY RULE 13.2

The most important survival skill in any office is the art of b.s.

Shirk Ethic, n.: The opposite of work ethic. The belief that you should never put in a hard day of work if you can fake it instead. Strategies include leaving your office light on and a jacket on the back of your chair to make colleagues think you're still there; forwarding your office phone to your mobile phone, so you can pretend to be at work when you're at the golf course; and scheduling e-mails to deliver at night so it'll look to your boss like you're working late.*

Novelty Degree, n.: A phony degree received from a diploma mill.

Résumé Padding

Whether it's termed "putting your best foot forward" or "jazzing up your qualifications," everyone lies on résumés. In a 2002 survey commissioned by Office Angels, a UK temp agency, 80 percent of respondents admitted they were willing to do so. The other 20 percent were, presumably, lying. People typically stretch the truth about the dates of their previous employment (to cover embarrassing gaps), job titles, duties, and salaries. But the most serious lies concern education.

In today's workplace having an advanced degree can translate into higher pay, and having attended a highly ranked university such as Stanford or Harvard can be an important status symbol. So people have a lot of incentive to invent degrees, and not much stopping them from doing so. Lying about a degree is illegal in only a handful of states, and even then it's a misdemeanor, warranting a small fine but no jail time.

However, during the 1980s the FBI busted approximately twelve thousand people, working in a variety of professions, in Operation Dipscam (short for diploma scam). More recently a string of high-profile executives have been caught with phony diplomas, including the CFO of VERITAS Software (fake degree from Stanford Business School) and the CEO of Bausch & Lomb (unearned MBA from New York University). Ironically, lying about education seems most popular in the field of education itself, since teachers' salaries are often tied directly to their academic credentials.

If a teacher doesn't want to invent her fake degree from whole cloth, a vast market of diploma mills are ready and willing to help. These are fly-by-night "colleges" and "universities" that grant degrees to anyone for the right price. For instance, in 2004 eleven teachers in Georgia were found to have advanced degrees from Saint Regis, a fine Liberian educational institution that demands

---

*Jane Spencer, "Shirk Ethic: How to Fake a Hard Day at the Office," *Wall Street Journal,* May 15, 2003.

very little (nothing but payment, actually) from its students. Or there's Romanian-based Glencullen University, which has no campus and no faculty. Personally, I like to claim an MBA from General Delivery University's Ponzi School of Business. In a pinch, I'll add an advanced degree from GDU's School of Hard Knocks. GDU is a fictitious online university (bandersnatch.com/gduedu.htm) founded (as a joke) by Hugh Holub, but potential employers don't need to know that. GDU boasts it's "America's Only Genuine Diploma Mill."

Quantum Bogodynamics, n.: A theory of physics postulating that the universe contains objects of a bogus nature that infect surrounding areas with their bogusness. For instance, bosses often emit a high degree of bogusness, which explains why computers freeze, programs fail, and presentations go awry at an unusually high frequency when they're around.

Fake Sickies and Fake-ations

The British call it "faking a sickie"; Americans call it "taking a mental health day." One of the most common forms of office deception, it's calling in sick when you're actually quite healthy, in order to take a stealth vacation day. In both Britain and America, one-third of polled workers admit to having taken fake sick days, though I suspect the real number is much higher. According to surveys, British doctors suspect over 40 percent of requests they receive for sick notes are bogus.

Some of the more unusual fake sick day excuses encountered over the years by CareerBuilder, an online employment agency, include: "I tripped over my dog and was knocked unconscious," "I was sprayed by a venomous snake," and "A hitman was looking for me." (If a hitman were looking for me, I wouldn't stay at home like a sitting duck.)

The opposite phenomenon—faking a vacation to stay home sick—would be pretty pointless, but far more often than one might think people pretend to go to fancy resorts and stay at home instead. In Italy, where going on expensive vacations gives important bragging rights at the office, a 2003 poll conducted by the psychologists' association Help Me found that almost 7 percent of respondents planned to lie about where they went. They anticipated going as far as telling their neighbors they were leaving. Then they would buy a sunlamp, sit at home soaking up the rays, and resurface a week later with a great tan. Back at the office they would regale coworkers with tales of the Riviera resort where they stayed. Everyone does what they have to do to keep up with the Joneses.

Mutter Machine, n.: A device that emits background noise of conversation and laughter. Employees trapped in hermetically sealed office buildings and starved of human contact can thus be tricked into feeling they work in a lively, upbeat environment instead of the dreary solitude that is their reality. First reported installation—at the British Broadcasting Corporation's finance offices in west London.

Flex Space, n.: Temporary office space rented by a small business so that visiting clients think the company is bigger and more successful than it is. This is especially important if the company's real office is in a garage. Accommodations include tasteful wall art, a water cooler, and a receptionist. Entrepreneurs are expected to tell visitors that the offices aren't the business's permanent home, but many don't, and the receptionist won't rat them out.

Reality Check: **Outsourcing**

During the 1970s workers in manufacturing industries discovered their jobs had been relocated to factories abroad. More recently, white-collar workers have been shocked to find their own jobs outsourced. Is there any end to this trend? Try to guess if the following forms of the outsourcing phenomenon are real or fake.

Outsource Your Own Job

Is the new trend among Silicon Valley programmers to outsource their own jobs to India—paying the Indian programmer less than what they're receiving and pocketing the difference?

In July 2004 the *Times of India* asserted this was the hot trend among programmers, based on an anonymous source's statement: "About a year ago I hired a developer in India to do my job. I pay him $12,000 out of the $67,000 I get. He's happy to have the work. I'm happy that I have to work only 90 minutes a day just supervising the code. My employer thinks I'm telecommuting. Now I'm considering getting a second job and doing the same thing." It sounds like a great con, but because this story was based on a single unnamed source, it's doubtful there's much truth to it.

Outsource Drive-thru Windows

Has McDonald's been cutting costs by outsourcing the job of taking orders at their drive-thru windows to a company in North Dakota, where the minimum wage is only $5.15?

The microphones at drive-thru windows are usually so crackly it sounds as though the person talking to you is hundreds of miles away, but that you may actually be communicating via a long-distance connection seems bizarre. However, it is a possibility. McDonald's *has* been experimenting with outsourcing the drive-thru window ordering process such that, at a drive-thru in Oregon, you could be giving your order to someone in North Dakota (who then transmits your order back to the restaurant in Oregon). McDonald's denies this is an attempt to relocate jobs to states with lower minimum wages, and claims it's just about efficiency—as employees who have to take orders over the drive-thru microphone and deliver food at the same time make a lot of mistakes.

McJob, n.: A dead-end (hopefully temporary) job, typically in the service sector of the economy. Lacks the features real jobs used to provide, such as benefits or the potential for personal fulfillment.

Outsource Video Game Playing

Are players of online multiuser games such as Final Fantasy outsourcing the tedious parts of games to workers in poor countries?

Gamers are notorious for finding ways to hack the system, whether it's cheating with secret codes or, yes, paying people to play the boring parts for them. As reported in *Wired* magazine, in countries such as Russia and China workers are paid to play online games for one purpose—to earn in-game goods and currency that can then be sold to outfits such as Internet Gaming Entertainment (IGE), which resells them to Westerners. Gamers willing to pay to advance more quickly in multiuser games have created a thriving market for virtual goods. In 2004 writer Julian Dibbell earned $3,917 in one month by trading virtual goods, such as armor and gold pieces, used in the game Ultima Online—proving it's possible to earn a living entirely from imaginary products.

REALITY RULE 13.3

There's nothing like the promise of future wealth
to separate a person from his sanity.

Postcrash Realism, n.: A mood of caution and sobriety found among investors after a crash. Usually a fleeting condition.

Dead Cat Bounce, n.: A stock's temporary jump in value after a significant decline. Often incorrectly interpreted by investors to mean the downward spiral is over.

A Brief History of Bubbles, from Tulips to Dot-Coms

Give people the idea there's a quick and easy way to make a lot of money, and their grip on reality rapidly comes undone. Speculative bubbles throughout history have demonstrated that the greater the number of people throwing money at a dumb investment, the more eager everyone else is to do the same.

Tulip Mania

The first (and arguably most famous) bubble of the modern era was the seventeenth-century tulip craze in Holland. In 1636 word spread that wealthy people were willing to pay fantastically large sums of money for tulips, especially rare mosaic varieties that displayed brilliant flames of color. Prices were soon bid up, with a large portion of the population joining in the speculative fervor. People traded their life savings for bulbs, believing they could resell them at windfall profits. At the height of the mania a single rare bulb could fetch as much as a mansion. Charles Mackay, author of *Extraordinary Popular Delusions and the Madness of Crowds,* records that one unfortunate sailor arrived in Holland during the excitement and ate a tulip bulb he found on a merchant's counter because he mistook it for an onion; for this heinous crime he spent months in jail. But the mania was short-lived. By 1637 panic selling commenced, as people realized they were never going to make a return on their investments. The price of bulbs crashed, and many people were ruined.

The Mississippi and South Sea Schemes

Eighty years after the tulip mania, the belief that there was huge money to be made from trade with the Americas triggered speculative bubbles in France and England. There actually was huge money to be made, but nowhere near as fast or as effortlessly as speculators hoped.

The Scottish financier John Law led the mania in France. As head of the Mississippi Company, he talked up the seemingly limitless profits his venture stood to make from its monopoly on trade with the Mississippi region. The company's stock began to rise, and early investors made spectacular profits, leading to even greater excitement. The value of the company swelled dramatically until the summer of 1720, then collapsed. Share prices declined by 97 percent, the company went bankrupt, and the economy of France was placed in jeopardy. Law had to flee the country, and died penniless in 1729.

In England a similar debacle unfolded as investors bid up shares of the South Sea Company, which boasted monopoly rights on trade with the South Seas. Schemers took advantage of the nation's speculative mood by offering all kinds of harebrained investment opportunities, almost all of which found eager subscribers. These small-scale schemes were dubbed "bubbles," eventually giving name to the larger phenomenon. One bubble proposed to revolutionize the art of war by designing square cannon balls. Another invited the public to invest—with returns of over 100 percent every year—in "a company for carrying on an undertaking of great advantage, but nobody to know what it is." Within a day people had snatched up almost one thousand shares—whereupon the scheme's inventor took the money and ran, never to be seen again.

The South Sea house of cards came tumbling down in late 1720, when the company's value crashed. Complete financial disaster was averted thanks to actions of the British government, but huge numbers of people lost everything. Surprisingly, the South Sea Company survived the crisis and endured, in a reorganized form, until the 1850s.

Transportation Bubbles

In the coming years, popular excitement about new forms of transportation spawned a series of bubbles—in canal stocks during the 1830s, railroad stocks during the 1870s, and automobile and airline stocks during the Roaring Twenties. Demand for airline stocks became so great after Charles Lindbergh's 1927 transatlantic flight that any stock with the word "airline" in its name posted massive gains—including, notoriously, Seaboard Air Lines, a railway company. The bubbles of the 1920s ended with the Great Depression of the 1930s.

From Tronics to Dot-Coms

By the early 1960s bitter memories of the Great Depression were fading, and investors were looking for the next big thing. They found it in electronics. Any company with a variation of the suffix "tronics" in its name became a stock-market darling, propelling firms such as Circuitronics and Videotronics to dizzying heights and earning the bubble the nickname the tronics boom. The boom crashed in 1962.

But investors' passion for technology hadn't abated. It surged again in the 1980s with the biotech bubble, and reached a crescendo during the dot-com mania of the 1990s. In theory dot-com investors were excited about the communications revolution the Internet was facilitating. But in practice this excitement translated into a blind rush to buy the stock of any company with *.com* in its name. Purdue University professor Panambur Raghavendra Rau calculated that during the height of the mania, a company could add 28 percent to the value of its stock *in a single day* simply by adding .com to its name, even if the company had nothing to do with the Internet. He cited the example of Go-Rachels.com, which profited from its .com suffix despite being a potato-chip maker lacking any connection to the Internet. The business didn't even have a website.

But any association with the Internet was enough for dot-com-enamored speculators. Companies that were little more than Web portals were given valuations of billions of dollars; it didn't matter if they were making no money and couldn't explain how they planned to make money. Legend tells of a company that lured investors with a vague mission statement promising to "develop cool stuff," thereby offering the 1990s equivalent of "an undertaking of great advantage, but nobody to know what it is."

The dot-com bubble deflated slowly but relentlessly throughout 2000, leaving hundreds of thousands of portfolios in tatters. In the temporary backlash that followed, any association with the Internet became anathema. Rau estimated that during this period, companies could add an average of 29 percent to their value by dropping *.com* from their names.

Investors seem to have lost money but not enthusiasm. In 2003 a few traders thought they had found the next big thing in nanotechnology. Nanometrics (ticker symbol: NANO) happily benefited from the subsequent surge, though the company—a twenty-five-year-old maker of tools for the semiconductor industry—had nothing to do with nanotechnology. Then all eyes were on the gravity-defying real estate market. And, of course, there's always hopeful talk of a dot-com comeback!

Pump and Dump, v.: Hyping a stock to create buying interest and pump up the price, then dumping shares at a profit. A popular stock market con.

Poop and Scoop, v.: Swooping in to buy up shares after spreading negative rumors that cause a stock's price to depreciate; then selling at a profit once the rumors are discovered to be false, and the price of the shares has recovered. The opposite of the pump and dump scam.

Stockmarket Hoaxes

The stockmarket is full of sharks waiting to take the money of the gullible and inexperienced. And though the technology these sharks employ has changed over the years, their basic scam remains the same: using misinformation to manipulate stock prices.

The Civil War Gold Hoax

On May 18, 1864, two New York newspapers reported that President Lincoln planned to increase the size of the Union Army by four hundred thousand men, indicating the Civil War was likely to drag on for a while. Share prices on the New York exchange immediately dropped, but the price of gold rose, as gold was considered a safe, inflation-proof investment. However, traders soon discovered the news was bogus. A down-on-his-luck editor heavily invested in gold had paid street urchins to deliver phony dispatches from the Associated

Press telegraph office to the major newspapers, and two papers had printed the claim without fact checking. The editor was shipped off to prison at Fort Lafayette. Ironically, two months later, Lincoln announced he was increasing the size of the Union Army by five hundred thousand men.

Bre-X

In 1995 a tiny Canadian exploration company called Bre-X announced the discovery—confirmed by its geologist, Michael de Guzman—of a vast gold field, possibly the largest in the world, located in Indonesia. Shares of Bre-X rapidly rose from $2 to $286 on the Toronto Stock Exchange, until the company was valued at over 6 billion Canadian dollars. Two years later de Guzman jumped (or was pushed) from a helicopter and died in the Indonesian jungle. Days later, a rival firm announced that its own investigation had found no gold at the purported gold field site. The samples had been faked. At the end of one of the largest stock frauds Canada had ever seen, Bre-X shares were worthless. There are still rumors that de Guzman faked his death, since the corpse found in the jungle had been mostly eaten by animals, leaving little to identify.

The Emulex Hoax

On August 25, 2000, in a con that closely matched the 1864 Civil War gold hoax, an employee at Internet Wire, a wire service agency, distributed a false news release announcing an accounting scandal at a company called Emulex. The company's share price (which the employee had previously shorted, i.e., placed a bet that it was going to go down) plummeted, and the employee pocketed $250,000. A week later the FBI caught up with him. When authorities asked Internet Wire why it didn't have better safeguards against fake press releases, the agency responded that it did have strong security measures, but had been the victim of a sophisticated con artist. However, further investigation revealed that the rogue employee, a twenty-three-year-old college student, had simply handed the bogus news report to the night staffers, who immediately put it out on the wire. So much for sophisticated.

Reality Distortion Field, n.: A charismatic aura that allows some business-people to warp how those in their presence perceive reality. Such power can be both motivational and delusional. Coined by Bud Tribble at Apple Computer to describe his boss, Steve Jobs, and still used most frequently in reference to Jobs.

Time-Traveling Traders

The ultimate fantasy of every investor is to know in advance whether a stock will go up or down. One way to attain such knowledge would be insider trading, which is illegal. But another way would be time travel, which is not illegal (just against the laws of physics). Small wonder, then, that making a fortune via time travel is a recurring theme in popular culture.

The Time Travel Mutual Fund (on the web at timetravelfund.com) offers a novel way to tap into the benefits of time travel. The company will allow an initial ten-dollar investment with them to grow in value over the next five hundred years (or however long it takes to perfect time travel), at which point, thanks to the miracle of compound interest, it will have turned into millions. Then the fund will use this money to arrange for someone to travel back to the moment before the investor's death and suck him into the future, where advanced medicines will allow him to live forever (plus, he'll be rich). It's immortality and wealth for just ten dollars. What a bargain.

But one question that troubles would-be temponauts is why there aren't future time travelers among us now. Why hasn't anyone journeyed back to our era and cleaned up on Wall Street? In March 2003 a wire service story appeared to suggest someone had.

The article described the curious case of Andrew Carlssin, who had apparently begun his investment career quite recently with a mere $800. But in two weeks, through a series of spectacular trades, he had transformed this $800 into $350 million, which immediately caught the attention of the SEC. The SEC charged him with insider trading. How else could he have made such a perfect series of trades? But during interrogation Carlssin pleaded innocence, attributing his prescient knowledge of stock prices to his claim that he was a time traveler from the year 2256. Given his amazing track record, his explanation seemed oddly credible.

The story of the time-traveling stock trader spread far and wide, appearing in such august publications as the London *Times*. The SEC received so many inquiries about the case it eventually posted a statement on its website denying it had ever brought enforcement action against such a person. It turned out the tale had originally appeared in that fake-news culprit, the *Weekly World News. Yahoo! News* had picked it up, thereby lending it added credibility. (See chapter 10, the *Weekly World News* Effect.)

REALITY RULE 13.4

> **A good accountant knows that two plus two equals four. A great accountant knows that two plus two equals whatever you want it to equal.**

Quarterly Earnings Report, n.: An official document in which companies lie to their shareholders four times a year.

Transparency, n.: A public relations strategy of revealing just enough ugly truths about a company to look credible. Corporate America's buzzword in the wake of the numerous business scandals of the late 1990s.

Built on Bullshit: Business Megascams

If you were to hand a cashier a one-dollar bill and tell him it was a twenty, he'd laugh at you. But when a con artist in the business world tells people a one-dollar bill is a one-billion-dollar bill, time after time he gets away with it. When it comes down to it, the massive accounting frauds of recent years (Enron, WorldCom, Adelphia, et al.) aren't much more complicated than this. Because by claiming to have a billion dollars they didn't have, the companies attracted huge amounts of money from banks and investors—which is how the companies really made their cash. Such scams have been around long before Enron, et al.

The Swedish Match King

At the start of the twentieth century, Swedish businessman Ivan Kreuger controlled 40 percent of world match production and a massive financial empire. It's hard to overestimate his power. He had assets worth (in modern money) around $100 billion, and by the 1920s his conglomerate's stocks and bonds were the most widely held in the world. But the market crash of 1929 put a serious dent in his finances and sent his business into a tailspin. After he committed suicide (or faked it, according to persistent rumors) in 1932, auditors realized his empire had been nothing but a gigantic pyramid scheme. He had orchestrated a bewildering array of subsidiary companies, four hundred in total, that artificially propped one another up by extending one another credit. The long-concealed reality was that his debt exceeded that of Sweden.

The Great Salad Oil Swindle

At the peak of his operation in the early 1960s, Anthony "Tino" De Angelis, head of the Allied Crude Vegetable Oil Refining Corporation, claimed to have almost two billion pounds of vegetable oil sitting in his New Jersey storage tanks. Never mind that his tanks could hold, at most, sixty million pounds, or that two billion pounds was more than the entire annual world production. Having all this oil, he was able to borrow billions of dollars (inflation adjusted).

The prestigious American Express Field Warehousing Corporation was supposed to verify that De Angelis had all the oil he claimed, and occasionally sent someone to look at his tanks. Everything seemed to be in order, so the money kept flowing. But with this money De Angelis was buying futures in oil, betting its price would go up. Instead the price went down, and De Angelis found himself unable to repay his loans. When his creditors came to take possession of his collateral, they discovered there was hardly any oil. The tanks were connected by underground pipes. When an inspector came, he would see a full tank. But as he moved along the line, that tank would quickly be emptied and the oil piped to the next tank the inspector wanted to see. In 1965 De Angelis was sentenced to twenty years in prison (of which he served seven). It's estimated that almost $4 billion disappeared into his empty oil tanks.

Enron

In 1985 Kenneth Lay became CEO of a company named InterNorth, renamed it Enron, and launched it on a path toward global domination of the power industry. Over the next fifteen years the company grew at a staggering rate and investors fell in love with it, despite rumors about its unsavory business practices. For instance, it was widely alleged that by convincing power plants to shut down for unneeded repairs, Enron engineered a phony energy crisis that slammed Californians with record-high energy prices in 2000. Nevertheless, by 2001 Enron was America's seventh-largest corporation—on paper. But a mounting pile of debt and losses lurked behind the company's profitable veneer.

Part of Enron's success strategy was pure showmanship. For example, employees later confessed they were occasionally required to man a phony trading floor on the sixth floor of the corporate headquarters. To convince visiting Wall Street analysts of how productive and energetic the firm was, they would pretend to be busy making deals. Employee Carol Elkin described the trading floor to the *Wall Street Journal* as "an elaborate Hollywood production."

More significantly, Enron used accounting magic to create the illusion of enormous profitability. It hid debt in "special purpose vehicles"—phony subsidiary companies designed for this purpose. It also claimed decades' worth of predicted future profit as present-day profit. This would be like claiming on a loan application that you make a salary of $300,000 because you expect to earn $30,000 a year for the next ten years. The company's supposed riches drove up the stock price, and company executives profited from the ballooning price by giving themselves generous stock options.

Enron executives kept up the pretense of profitability until the very end. In August 2001 Ken Lay sent his employees an e-mail that read, "I have never felt better about the prospects for the company." A little over three months later, after word of Enron's shady accounting practices began to leak out—causing its stock price to collapse—the company filed for bankruptcy, revealing it was over $16 billion in debt. It was the largest corporate bankruptcy in U.S. history.

Enronomics, n.: A form of economics not beholden to traditional standards of accounting (or to the laws of reality) that allows its practitioners to transform losses into profits and materialize revenues out of thin air.

Enronitis, n.: A communicable corporate disease that starts with rumors of questionable accounting practices and ends with a severely deflated stock price. After the 2001 collapse of Enron, many large corporations came down with a bad case of Enronitis, as investors became warier of the use of unorthodox accounting methods.

Arthur Andersen Syndrome, n.: A condition that causes its sufferers to believe wildly inaccurate financial information is true. Arthur Andersen was the accounting firm used by Enron. Somehow it never noticed, until the very end, that something was amiss at the energy company. The firm lost its accounting license as a result.

POLITICS 14

It's one of those chicken-and-egg mysteries: Are politicians full of b.s. by nature, or does the pressure of public life make them that way? Whatever the answer, the effect is the same: the complete "un-realification" of politics. Modern politicians, if they want long careers, must operate by certain core assumptions: that what they've done isn't as important as what people think they've done, that truth isn't as important as the appearance of truth, and that being honest isn't as important as putting on a convincing act of honesty. They disregard these principles at their peril, for they can be sure their opponents aren't disregarding them.

REALITY RULE 14.1

Politics is the art of looking good on TV.

Potemkin Photo Op, n.: A stage-managed event, created solely for media consumption, that offers a misleading picture of reality. Derives from the term Potemkin village, which described the fake villages Russian field marshal Grigori Aleksandrovich Potemkin allegedly built in 1787 along the route of Catherine the Great's tour of Crimea, to hide the poverty of the region from her.

Gesture Politics, n.: Political activity that focuses on showmanship rather than action.

Political Theater

Putting on a good show has always been an important part of politics, but modern political operatives have raised the use of stage-managed dramas performed for the benefit of the media to a fine (and totally shameless) art.

"Mission Accomplished"

On May 1, 2003, President Bush copiloted a navy jet that touched down on the USS *Abraham Lincoln,* where he was coming to meet victorious soldiers returning from war. Standing on the deck of the carrier, Bush announced the end of major combat operations in Iraq as a MISSION ACCOMPLISHED banner rippled in the breeze behind him. The moment was supposed to showcase a heroic, successful president who had once been a fighter pilot in the Texas Air National Guard. But critics derided the event as a carefully choreographed photo op. For instance, the president could have ridden to the carrier in a helicopter, but his handlers chose the jet because they thought it looked more dramatic—which meant the ship had to remain farther out at sea, delaying the soldiers' return home. Then there was the Mission Accomplished banner, whose message was at odds with the obvious reality of continued fighting in Iraq. The White House later claimed the banner had been the navy's idea, but the navy maintained the White House was to blame. It must have been one of those self-hanging banners, because no one would take responsibility for it.

The Trophy Turkey

For Thanksgiving 2003 President Bush made a surprise visit to the troops still in Iraq, where he helped serve a traditional holiday dinner. News photos

showed the president grinning as he carried a tray bearing a beautiful golden brown turkey. But the turkey wasn't real. It was a plastic prop known in the food service industry as a "trophy turkey." The food the soldiers actually got was served from cafeteria-style steam trays.

Let them eat turkey!

The Nigerian Market

Lest anyone think staged political events are an American phenomenon, there's the Queen of England's 2003 state visit to Nigeria, where she was photographed touring a village market and chatting with local people. Except security officials felt it would be too dangerous for the queen to go out in public, so a fake marketplace was constructed inside an armed compound. Actors were shipped in to man the stalls, and the queen was walked through what was essentially a movie set. However, it's unfair to say the photo op was entirely phony. Reportedly a few real Nigerian villagers did glimpse the queen through the compound's perimeter wall.

Ready-Made Crowd, n.: People bused in and paid to attend a political rally, so that TV cameras won't catch the politician speaking to an empty room.

Ovalitis, n.: A condition whereby residents of the Oval Office only hear news they want to hear. Also referred to as the "presidential bubble."*

---

*Richard Reeves, "The President Has Ovalitis," *Charleston Gazette,* October 1, 2004.

case file: Kerry's Fake Tan

In 1960 Senator John Kennedy and Vice President Richard Nixon participated in the first televised general election debate. Nixon was recovering from the flu and looked pale and unshaven. He didn't use makeup. Kennedy, however, looked tanned, relaxed, and energetic, and he did use makeup. According to popular legend, this helped him win the election. Learning from this, political handlers decided it wasn't enough to stage-manage events; the candidate also had to look good—or, at least, tanned.

John Kerry's campaign managers took this lesson to heart. The day before the first of the 2004 presidential debates, Kerry showed up in public looking positively pumpkin colored. Comedian Jay Leno wisecracked that an "orange alert" had been issued for the politician. It seemed his handlers had liberally slathered him with tanning lotion. Kerry's press office claimed that Kerry had simply caught some rays while playing touch football, but beauty experts identified the tan as definitely fake. But the important question is: fake or not, did it help Kerry? By general consensus he did win the first debate, but he ended up losing the election. So maybe, just maybe, a killer tan isn't the key to political success after all.

Milli Vanilli President, n.: A president given speaking points via a wireless receiver hidden in his ear. Refers to the speculation that during the September 2004 presidential debate President Bush was wearing such a device. This rumor began when attentive TV watchers spotted a mysterious rectangular bulge between the president's shoulder blades, with wires running over his shoulder, beneath his suit. The bulge could have been a receiving device. Bush, however, insisted it was simply the result of his poorly fitted shirt bunching up. At least one commentator decided Bush wasn't lying about wearing a receiving device—he was lying about wearing a defibrillator necessitated by an undisclosed health problem. Conspiracy theorists can take their pick.[*]

---

[*]Dave Lindorff, "Bush's Mystery Bulge," Salon.com, October 8, 2004.

case file: Boxgate

In late January 2003 President Bush delivered a speech in the warehouse of JS Logistics, a St. Louis trucking firm. The venue was chosen to highlight the supposed benefits of his proposed tax cuts for American small businesses. President Bush touted his plan in front of a screen that showed an enormous pile of boxes marked "Made in U.S.A.," with real boxes from the warehouse stacked on either side of him. The setting was very pro-American business, very "on message." But reporters were curious about the packing tape they noticed on the boxes on either side of the president. They peeled back the tape to discover the phrase "Made in China" stamped prominently on each box.

An embarrassed spokesperson immediately denied White House responsibility for the cover-up, blaming an anonymous volunteer who had prepped the area before the president's arrival. But even as it was denying responsibility, the administration was probably silently swearing never again to use real props. When you decide to go fake, it's usually best to go all the way—otherwise it's the details that get you every time.

Made in China?

REALITY RULE 14.2

In politics, as in poker, it all comes down to the art of the bluff.

Doublespeak, n.: Language intended to conceal rather than enlighten. Example: referring to the unemployed as "job seekers," or calling a drop in the stock market a "healthy correction." In use since the 1950s. Inspired by "newspeak," coined by George Orwell in his novel *1984*.

Greenscamming, v.: Deceptively using environmentally friendly rhetoric for non- or antienvironmental purposes. Example: The organization Concerned Alaskans for Resources and Environment may sound green, but in reality it lobbies for the expansion of clear-cut logging permits.

False Memory Syndrome

False memory syndrome causes its sufferers to recall events that never happened. Typically these events cast the person remembering them in a heroic light, or provide material for charming anecdotes.

Ronald Reagan was one of many presidents afflicted by this condition. In November 1983 Reagan told Israeli prime minister Yitzhak Shamir that during World War II he served as a photographer in the U.S. Army and was present at the liberation of Nazi death camps. Except that Reagan spent the war in California making training films as part of the First Motion Picture Unit of the Army Air Corps. He was never sent to Europe. However, it was a good story, so he repeated it a few months later during a meeting with Simon Wiesenthal.

California governor Arnold Schwarzenegger exhibited symptoms of this syndrome more recently. In an interview at the 2000 Republican convention, he described watching the 1968 Nixon-Humphrey presidential debate on TV shortly after his arrival in America, and being inspired to become a Republican. Schwarzenegger said, "When I came to this country, I was sitting in front of the television set, and I watched a debate between Hubert Humphrey and Richard Nixon, and I didn't even understand half of it because my English wasn't good enough then. I had a friend of [mine] translating." Nice sound bite, but Nixon never debated Humphrey on TV. This didn't stop the future governor from repeating the story in a May 2001 interview with talk show host Bill O'Reilly and tossing it into his speech at the 2004 Republican Convention in New York City. But by that time he no longer remembered a specific debate; instead he spoke only of having watched the "presidential race" on TV.

The opposite of false memory syndrome is sudden amnesia syndrome, the inability to recall things of a potentially embarrassing or incriminating nature. Politicians often develop this condition when forced to participate in committee hearings or criminal investigations.

Payola Punditry, n.: "Independent" commentary paid for with bribes. What you get when media talking heads accept money in exchange for secretly propagandizing for the government. Example: in early 2005 reporters for *USA Today* learned the Department of Education had paid conservative columnist Armstrong Williams $240,000 to "say nice things about" the No Child Left Behind Act. Williams later insisted he believed everything he said about the act, but he never bothered to tell his TV, radio, or print audiences about the financial arrangement.

"As If" Politics, n.: A political theory positing that if you act as if everything is going well, eventually it will. Act as if the economy is strong, and it will be strong. Act as if a military campaign is succeeding, and it will succeed. Reality will eventually conform to fantasy.[*]

---

[*]Tina Brown, *Times Online,* March 13, 2003.

---

case file: The African American Republican Leadership Council

In politics no problem's so bad clever marketing can't fix it. In fact, politicians usually try papering over a problem with a public relations campaign before doing anything more drastic, such as working on it. Because for many politicians, the difficulty isn't the problem, but the public's perception of it. Consider the African American Republican Leadership Council (hereafter the AARLC).

The Republican Party had an image of being indifferent to the concerns of black voters. This showed at the polls, with Republicans rarely achieving more than 10 to 15 percent of the black vote in any part of the country. What to do? Simple. Pretend the Republican Party *did* enjoy grassroots support from the black community. If the party pretended long enough, African Americans might be convinced to actually support it. And thus was born the AARLC.

The AARLC came into existence in 2002, billing itself "the only nationwide conservative Republican organization dedicated to elect Reaganite progrowth economic security African American Republicans to local, state, and the federal government." Its website declared the organization "dedicated to breaking the liberal Democrats' stranglehold over Black America," and underlined the group's commitment to black leadership by displaying pictures of great black Republican leaders such as Ronald Reagan and George W. Bush (*note: sarcasm*).

It looked and sounded great, but in early 2003 *Washington Post* reporter Gene Weingarten did a bit of digging and discovered exactly two of the organization's fifteen advisory panel members were black. The other thirteen were white. The honorary chair of the panel was black, but he had never heard of the group. All the candidates the AARLC supported in the November 2002 election were white. And an AARLC spokesman admitted the organization's primary financial contributors were "little old white ladies in Nebraska."

All of which begged the question: was the AARLC an African American organization if its leaders, supporters, and candidates were primarily white? Wouldn't a more accurate name have been the Caucasian Republican Leadership Council?

But to ask such questions is to miss the point. Because in the world of politics it matters not what anything is, but what it seems to be. So if the AARLC made it seem that the Republican Party was enjoying growing support from the black community, that was just as good as actually receiving or earning such support. Or, at least, in the eyes of the people making the decisions, it was a definite step in the right direction.

Renault Effect, n.: The phony shock and outrage expressed by officials when scandals they knew about (and may have been participating in) are uncovered. Named after the corrupt police chief in *Casablanca*, Louis Renault, who utters the classic line: "I'm shocked, shocked to find that gambling is going on here," just before collecting his winnings.*

REALITY RULE 14.3
Politics is a magnet for the egotistical, the criminal, and the insane.

Manchurian Candidate, n.: A media-friendly political candidate whose superficiality conceals the reality that he's a brainwashed drone, following the orders of a hidden master. Refers to the movie *The Manchurian Candidate,* originally starring Frank Sinatra, which tells the story of an American soldier who is captured, brainwashed, and programmed to become an assassin.

Danforth Syndrome, n.: The condition of living in a state of denial about the very real chance that a calamitous event will occur. Coined during the first Bush administration to describe people who could only deal with the idea that J. Danforth Quayle could become president by blocking the idea from their thoughts.[†]

Strange Political Candidates

In every election there are two kinds of candidates: those who seriously want to participate in the political process, and those who, ummm, aren't quite so serious. Or maybe they are. It can be hard to tell.

Joke Candidates

Some campaigns are obvious jokes. For instance, the supporters of Gay Penguin probably didn't really want to elect a homosexual penguin to the White House in 2004, though a few of their talking points were compelling: "Imagine a world where America has been ruled by a Gay Penguin since 2000: where would you be?"

---

*Lucas Hanft, "A Call to Avoid Casablanca-style Shock," *Yale Herald,* April 26, 2002.
[†]Clarence Page, "Buzzwords Say Much about Life in the '90s," *St. Louis Post Dispatch,* January 7, 1991.

Similarly, it's hard to take seriously the man who calls himself Vermin Supreme. He's repeatedly run for president on a platform that focuses almost entirely on dental hygiene, advocating "government-issued toothpaste containing addictive yet harmless substances; video surveillance through two-way bathroom mirrors; electronic tracking, moisture and motion sensor devices in all toothbrushes...or even preventative dental maintenance detention facilities." Strange stuff, though one argument he makes is difficult to counter: "All politicians are, in fact, vermin. I am the Vermin Supreme; therefore I am the most qualified candidate in this race."

The classic joke candidacy is Wavy Gravy's long-running "Nobody for President" campaign, which featured catchy slogans such as "Who cares? Nobody cares"; "Nobody will lower your taxes"; "Nobody has all the answers"; and "Nobody will defend your rights." (On second thought, maybe that campaign wasn't such a joke.)

Insane Candidates

Beyond the tongue-in-cheek campaigns are campaigns that may be jokes, or may not be. No one is quite sure, and that's what makes them so bizarre.

Eighteen twenty-four saw an effort to elect John Cleves Symmes Jr. president of the United States. Symmes came from a distinguished political family. His uncle of the same name (Judge John Cleves Symmes) founded the city of Cincinnati, and his uncle's daughter, Anna Symmes, married Lieutenant William Henry Harrison, who later became the ninth U.S. president. But the issue that Symmes Jr. devoted his life to promoting was a little off the beaten track: Symmes and his supporters wanted to fund a government expedition that would journey to the North Pole, enter the interior of the earth through the massive hole they expected to find there, and establish a profitable trade with the inhabitants within. Symmes didn't receive many votes, but it's interesting to speculate what course American history would have taken had he won.

Ferdinand Lop, an author who campaigned for the French presidency in the 1940s, rivaled Symmes for weirdness. The central plank of Lop's platform was his firm belief that the Avenue des Champs-Elysées should be extended all the way to the English Channel. Why? Just because. He also proposed eliminating poverty, but only after ten P.M.

More recent political campaigns include the efforts of Ferret Guy, who believes the top issue on the American government's agenda should be the legalization of domestic ferrets. He points out, "Ferret owners know only too well about how civil liberties can be taken away…People are asking, if government can't even handle the ferret issue, what can it handle?" Yes, I've often asked that. Or there's Albert "Al" Hamburg, the lead candidate for the Very Independent UNPOPULAR Party. (He, appropriately, is its only member.) In his campaign photos Hamburg sports a Nazi helmet, which is a nice touch.

Self-Appointed Emperors

While the campaigns described above may be a bit odd, they pay testament to the open, freewheeling spirit of democracy. Of course, democracy is not for everyone. Those who can't stomach the prospect of a long and grueling campaign that will end in almost certain disappointment have another option: appoint yourself emperor.

This was Joshua Norton's strategy, and it worked for him. On September 17, 1859, in a proclamation delivered to the *San Francisco Bulletin,* he declared himself Emperor of the United States. For the rest of his life he dutifully performed his role as Emperor Norton I, walking the streets of San Francisco in a uniform completed by a plumed hat, gold epaulets, and a sword. In 1880, ten thousand people attended his funeral, and there is serious talk today of renaming the Bay Bridge in his honor.

In 1950 a Washington lawyer named Russell Arundel declared himself King of the Grand Principality of Outer Baldonia, a small, rocky, uninhabited island off the coast of Nova Scotia, which had formerly been known as Outer Bald Tusket. The Outer Baldonian Declaration of Independence included "the inalienable right to lie and be believed; to drink, swear, and gamble; to sleep all day and stay up all night." The tiny principate entered into international diplomacy on March 9, 1953, when it declared war on the Soviet Union. Happily for both sides, the Soviet Union chose not to fight.

Finally, taking up Emperor Norton's mantle is current Los Angeles resident HRM Caesar St. Augustine de Buonaparte (that's what he likes to be called). In the 1990s Buonaparte sent President Clinton a letter declaring war on the United States. Buonaparte claims that Clinton's failure to respond means the

United States implicitly conceded defeat. Therefore, Buonaparte is now our emperor. All hail Emperor Buonaparte!

case file: The Milton Mule

In 1936 Boston Curtis ran for the post of Republican precinct committeeman in Milton, Washington. And he won—even though he was a mule. The voters had not been aware of his mulish nature. Mayor Ken Simmons had surreptitiously taken the mule down to the courthouse and placed its hoofprint on all the documents necessary to register it to run. Simmons wanted to prove that most people blindly vote along party lines, especially when it comes to the lower-ranking offices on the ballot—meaning they'll vote for anyone, or anything, with the right political affiliation. Evidently Simmons was correct. The joke was that Republicans voted in a cousin of the Democratic party's donkey symbol.

Although it's not unusual for animals to run for office (see Gay Penguin above), it is rare for them to win. The only animal (of a kind) to win an election in recent years was H'Angus the Monkey, a football club mascot voted in by the residents of Hartlepool, England. Since H'Angus ran on a platform of providing free bananas to the schoolchildren of Hartlepool, his victory is understandable.

REALITY RULE 14.4

"It's not who votes that counts; it's who counts the votes."*

Ghost Voting, v.: Voting on legislative measures while not physically present. Typically a lawmaker achieves this trick by jamming the "yea" or "nay" button at his desk to hold it down. The button racks up a great voting record

---

*Soviet dictator Joseph Stalin, 1879–1953. (Whether Stalin actually said this is disputed, but no other source for the statement is known.)

and the legislator gets paid a per diem for being there to vote, even if he was actually on vacation. In one notorious case in Pennsylvania, a button held down by a paper clip cast the deciding vote on a divisive 1991 tax bill.

Voting Irregularities

Hardly an election goes by without what are euphemistically termed "voting irregularities." Ranging from the trivial and slightly amusing to the far more serious and disturbing, these irregularities threaten the legitimacy of the entire electoral process, as well as our perhaps misguided belief that our votes are being counted and might actually make a difference.

In 2002 vote hackers realized it was relatively easy to log on to the New Zealand Electoral Centre's website and edit existing information or add names to the voter rolls. The break-in was discovered when a woman received a letter from the Centre asking her to confirm her name change from Fay to Fat Ass. Local papers also reported that "a basset hound with prolific toilet habits" had been added as a voter. Its occupation was listed as "cable layer." Along similar lines, a farmer in Newmarket, England, attempted to register her cows, Henry and Sophie Bull, as voters. She also tried to register her dog, Jake Woofles. But in a blow to the voting rights of animals, their applications were denied.

Given these pranks, election officials are on alert for obviously fake names such as Mary Poppins or Pippi Longstocking. In 1996 an official in Quebec cried foul when he learned a man registered to vote in his district was named Omar Sharif and supposedly lived with Martina Navratilova. Except in this case the son of the famous actor Omar Sharif really was living with a stockbroker named Martina Navratilova.

More disturbing are the rigged elections. The most legendary occurred in 1927 when Charles King was elected president of Liberia with over 240,000 votes cast for him—in a population with only 15,000 registered voters. The *Guinness Book of World Records* named this election the most fraudulent in world history—but that was before witnessing the Iraqi election of 2002, in which Saddam Hussein received 11 million votes without a single vote cast against him.

One would like to think such elaborate voter fraud couldn't happen in America, but our various political interests give it their best shot. Officials monitoring the 2004 presidential election caught a wide range of abuses, including voter registration cards completed in suspiciously similar handwriting, cards submitted with nonexistent addresses, and cards filled out by people who had been dead for twenty years. Someone tried to obtain absentee ballots on behalf of an entire neighborhood—everyone in it, by coincidence, was apparently going to be out of town on election day. These were just the cases that got noticed.

But these tricks pale in comparison to the possibilities for fraud associated with new electronic touch-screen voting technology. The backers of this technology assure everyone it's foolproof and hacker proof, which right away should raise red flags. Its detractors, such as the writer Bev Harris, warn that a few keystrokes could replace entire ballot counts with phony tallies, and no paper trail would record the fraud.

If even some of what the critics of electronic voting worry about comes true, voting machines could become mere mechanical placebos, lulling us into the belief we're voting, while the real vote count is entered by a hacker in a faraway office. If that ever occurs, it'll be the biggest election hoax in history. But something like that could never happen in America. Right?

Hanging-Chad Controversy, n.: A dispute that drags on and on, dwelling obsessively on details of increasing obscurity until the debate bears no relationship to the larger issue. Derives from the infamous examination of hanging chads after the 2000 election.

Money Party, n.: The monolithic political party rumored to govern the United States. Said to camouflage its monopoly on power by periodically hiring new actors to serve as presidents, senators, and congressmen.

Reality Check: **Bush Voters Have Lower IQs**
Is it true that states with higher average IQs went to Al Gore in the 2000 presidential election, whereas states with lower average IQs went to George Bush?

Smart people vote Democratic. Stupid people vote Republican. That, at least, was the implication of a chart that circulated on the Internet during the early part of 2004, and showed that American states whose populations possessed on average higher incomes and IQs voted for Gore in the 2000 presidential elections, whereas their poorer, dumber counterparts voted for Bush. The source of this chart was supposedly an academic book titled *IQ and the Wealth of Nations* by Richard Lynn and Tatu Vanhanen. Except that the real source was a guy using the screen name Robert Calvert, who posted the data to a Mensa Internet newsgroup in 2002. Apparently he just made it up. His phony chart lingered in newsgroup obscurity for two years until it was rediscovered around April 2004—at which point it appeared everywhere. It was soon debunked, but that didn't stop major newspapers and magazines, such as the *St. Petersburg Times* and the *Economist,* from printing it as fact. After the election the chart started circulating again. Look for versions of it to appear as the 2008 election approaches.

Realitician, n.: Someone who freely distorts reality by telling people only what they want to hear, much like a politician.

Phony Election Coverage

On March 20, 2004, television audiences in Taiwan sat glued to their sets watching real-time presidential election results flash across the screens. TV commentators reported the election like a sporting event: "More vote numbers are now coming in... The figures are jumping faster and faster... The election outcome is getting unpredictable at every minute."

On some channels opposition candidate Lien Chan took an early and commanding lead; other stations had incumbent Chen Shui-bian ahead. But it didn't really matter which channel you were watching because the election committee hadn't released any figures. The stations were inventing numbers out of thin air. When the committee finally did release early results, only two hundred thousand votes, out of a total of thirteen million, had been counted—a contrast to the three million many stations had reported. The stations quietly revised their figures downward, and Chen Shui-bian won the election by a thin margin of thirty thousand votes.

The Taiwanese stations were guilty of posting phony election results to boost ratings, but at least they waited until the polls had closed. American networks could never wait that long. Of course, the networks would vigorously deny doing anything as questionable as inventing results while people are still casting votes. They say they predict election outcomes based on a complex system of exit polls and statistical analysis. But recent history suggests exit polls are about as reliable a method for calling elections as plucking numbers out of thin air. In 2000 networks first called the election for Gore, then said it was too close to call, then said Bush was the winner before finally saying, again, that it was too close to call. In 2004 the networks were more cautious, but still got bitten when exit polls seemed to show a Kerry win, though Bush walked away with the victory. However, one theory holds that the 2004 exit polls were right and it was the official election results that were made up (see Voting Irregularities, above). What's the truth? Honestly, who can tell anymore?

Bushlips, n.: Insincere election promises. Derives from the first President Bush's campaign promise not to raise taxes ("Read my lips. No new taxes."), and his subsequent breaking of that promise once in office. The term was voted New Word of the Year by the American Dialect Society in 1990, but despite this endorsement, never really caught on.

REALITY RULE 14.5
In politics it doesn't matter if an accusation is true or false, only that it sticks.

Swift Boat, v.: To smear a person's reputation. Refers to the organization Swift Boat Veterans for Truth—founded to oppose John Kerry's 2004 presidential bid—that alleged Kerry faked injuries while serving as a commander of a swift boat in Vietnam in order to receive Purple Hearts. Veterans who served with Kerry denied these claims.*

Dirty Trick Campaigns
Political campaigners don't like to leave anything to chance, especially in a close race. To make sure their candidate has an edge, they'll lie, cheat, and steal.

---

*Frank Rich, "The Swift Boating of Cindy Sheehan," *New York Times,* August 21, 2005.

Such tactics are known as dirty tricks, and like voting irregularities, they range from the lighthearted and amusing to the low-down and despicable.

The twentieth-century master of the lighthearted dirty trick was Dick Tuck, whose target of choice was Richard Nixon. In 1956 Tuck hired dump trucks to drive past the site of the GOP convention in San Francisco (where Nixon was running as Eisenhower's vice president) with the words DUMP NIXON painted on their sides. In 1968 he hired pregnant women to attend Nixon rallies carrying signs that read NIXON'S THE ONE! But Tuck's most famous stunt (which may be an urban legend) was dressing up as a conductor and signaling a train to leave the station . . . as Nixon tried to deliver a speech from the caboose. Tuck's antics drove Nixon so crazy Nixon eventually told an aide that the Republicans needed to develop a "Dick Tuck capability" of their own.

Such efforts continue today. In 2004 Democratic pranksters engineered it so that if you typed "miserable failure" into Google, President Bush's biography was the first thing to come up. Republican pranksters responded by making sure John Kerry's website was the first hit when anyone searched for "waffles."

Unfortunately, many political pranks are not so harmless. In 2004 some Pennsylvania voters received flyers explaining that, because of expected heavy voter turnout, the election would be extended for a day. Republicans were scheduled to vote on Tuesday, November 2, but Democrats were asked to wait till Wednesday to go to the polls. It doesn't appear anyone fell for this obvious trick.

But the really low-down tricks revolve around character assassination, that art of insinuation whereby politicians accuse one another (usually through proxies) of all manner of vice and sin, regardless of proof.

Character assassination is a time-honored tradition. Aaron Burr was defeated in New York's 1804 gubernatorial campaign, in large part owing to an accusation that he frequented brothels. The *American Citizen* claimed to have a list of twenty prostitutes, all willing to declare he was their favorite customer. In 1844 the opponents of James Polk, furious that they couldn't find dirt on the squeaky-clean Democratic presidential candidate, invented a story about one Baron von Roorback encountering a group of Polk's beaten and abused slaves while traveling through America. In reality neither the slaves nor Baron von Roorback existed, and "roorback" became slang for a political dirty trick throughout the rest of the nineteenth century.

You don't have to look hard to find mudslinging in recent campaigns. In

2004 Republicans cooked up a Kerry affair with an intern and suggested he had faked injuries while serving in Vietnam. Democrats fought back with rumors about Bush snorting cocaine at Camp David and arranging for a girlfriend to have an abortion. Whether the accusations had much substance behind them didn't matter. In the world of political campaigning all that matters is that an accusation be believable enough to sow seeds of doubt.

Frequent Liar Miles, n.: What people earn by lying frequently. Politicians tend to accrue a lot of them. (Possible first usage: August 4, 2000, in the *San Francisco Chronicle*, to describe the many air miles logged by candidates during the presidential campaign.)

> Reality Check: **Lynne Cheney's racy novel**
> Did Lynne Cheney, wife of Vice President Dick Cheney, once write a racy novel that included descriptions of a lesbian love affair? Or were allegations of such a novel part of a smear campaign against her?

Lynne Cheney is well known for her conservative views on morality and for her support of a constitutional amendment banning same-sex marriage. So it may seem unlikely that in her younger, wilder days she penned a novel featuring brothels, attempted rapes, and lesbian love affairs, but it is true. The book, set on the American frontier and titled *Sisters,* was published by New American Library in 1981. It includes such classic lines as "In the evenings I shall read to you while you work your cross-stitch in the firelight. And then we shall go to bed, our bed, my dearest girl." The book has long been out of print, but shortly before the 2004 presidential election those hoping to embarrass the Cheneys tried to get it republished. However, its publisher eventually decided not to reprint, at the request of its author, who said she did not consider it "her best work."

Black, White, and Gray Propaganda

Propaganda is defined as information disseminated to influence public opinion. That's common knowledge. Less well known is that propaganda comes in three varieties—white, black, and gray—all used widely during political campaigns.

White propaganda—information openly distributed by an organization promoting itself—is the most common. Political ads are good examples. But sometimes it's more effective to put embarrassing or misleading words into your opponent's mouth. When this is done it's known as black propaganda (or a "double dirty trick").

For example, in November 2003 flyers advertising the Young Democrats' rally for Democratic candidate Howard Dean appeared on the Dartmouth

Confederates for Howard Dean

College campus. The flyers were decorated with an image of the Confederate flag—a reference to Dean's remark that he wanted to be "the candidate for guys with Confederate flags in their pickup trucks." Was this poster part of the Young Democrats' effort to take Dean's statement seriously and reach out to Confederate sympathizers in New England? Of course not. The flyers were black propaganda created to embarrass the Dean campaign.

Gray propaganda is similar to black propaganda, except it never pretends to be from a particular source. It just floats unclaimed in the public arena, sowing doubt and discord.

In Lauderdale County, Tennessee, shortly before the 2004 election, leaflets were found showing President Bush's head pasted onto the body of

Democratic joke, or Republican dirty trick?

a handicapped runner, accompanied by the caption: "Voting for Bush is like running in the Special Olympics. Even if you win, you're still retarded." Republican officials denounced the offensive leaflets and accused Democrat Craig Fitzhugh of having sponsored their creation, since they had appeared outside his office. But Fitzhugh fired back, claiming Republicans were responsible. The Tennessee Democratic Party even issued this statement: "This disgusting flyer is a dirty trick by Republicans to try and smear Craig Fitzhugh and the Democratic

Party in Tennessee. We are shocked and appalled that they would stoop to this level to try and score political points."

So who created the flyer? No one knows, and it hardly matters. The mystery of its origin created doubt and controversy, which, one must assume, is exactly what the flyer's creator intended.

Vast Right-Wing Conspiracy, n.: A supposed cabal of conservatives, working out of think tanks and foundations, that now controls much of the media and government. First used by First Lady Hillary Clinton in an interview on NBC's *Today* show in January 1998: "For anybody willing to find it, and write about it, and explain it, is this vast right-wing conspiracy that has been conspiring against my husband since the day he announced for president. A few journalists have kind of caught on to it and explained it, but it has not yet been fully revealed to the American public." Ironically, the term has now been embraced by conservatives.

Political Photo Fakes

A photo that circulated on the Internet in 2002 showed President Bush sitting next to a child. Both were holding books, and the girl appeared to be reading aloud from hers while the president looked on admiringly, seemingly unaware his own book was upside down. Another image showed Senator Tom Daschle preparing to recite the Pledge of Allegiance with his hand held over the wrong side of his chest, as if unfamiliar with this American tradition. And then there was the photo of President Bush peering intently through a pair of binoculars, oblivious to the fact that the lens cap was still on.

One of the most popular photo genres on the Internet is the political photo spoof. Apparently there's no end to the fun to be had by gawking at politicians caught in awkward, embarrassing, or compromising poses (and let's be honest—there is no end to such fun. It's always entertaining to see politicians looking stupid).

Most of these images have been photoshopped (see chapter 5). For instance, Bush's book was digitally flipped around, as was Senator Daschle's hand. But sometimes the photos are real. The image of Bush with the binoculars appears to be untouched.

While the Internet and modern photo technology have provided fertile ground for altered photos, the phenomenon is not new. During the 1930s what was supposedly an Adolf Hitler baby picture spread throughout England and America. It was definitely a scary-looking baby, but it wasn't Hitler. It was actually a Connecticut-born baby who looked much cuter in the original, undoctored photo (on the right). As with many hoax photos, the doctorer's identity was never discovered.

Far more serious is when fake political photos are used for propaganda purposes. The government of the Soviet Union was notorious for constantly rewriting its history by airbrushing out of photos those people who had fallen out of political favor. One day you were standing next to Lenin; the next day you were gone. But what people really worry about is a fake photo being used

Baby Adolf

as part of a dirty-tricks campaign to influence an election. Though, of course, this has already happened. In 1950 Senator Millard Tydings (correctly) called Senator Joseph McCarthy's allegation that hundreds of "card-carrying Communists" were working in the State Department "a fraud, a hoax, and a deceit." As payback, McCarthy's staff faked a picture of Tydings chatting with Earl Browder, head of the American Communist Party. The publication of this photo contributed to Tydings's subsequent defeat at the polls. In reality, Tydings and Browder had never met.

Ironically, the huge number of fake photos circulating on the Internet makes it harder for a doctored photo to have an impact on a political campaign, because the easier photos are to fake, the harder it is to get anyone to believe they're real. The first thing jaded Internet users now say when they see an eyebrow-raising photo is a skeptical, "Is that real or fake?"

Brainwashington, n.: More a state of mind than an actual place. The propaganda-fed version of reality that emanates from the Washington establishment.*

---

*Mathias Broeckers, "Welcome to Brainwashington, D.C.," lecture at the Chaos Communication Camp, August 9, 2003.

WAR 15

Wars are won by figuring out what your opponent is doing, and deceiving him about your own plans—controlling how the enemy perceives reality. This was just as true when ancient Greeks won the Battle of Troy by hiding inside a giant wooden horse as it is today, and there's nothing particularly bizarre about it. It's simply part of the military's job. Things only start to get surreal when the boundaries of the battlefield dissolve, allowing war-related deception to seep into the general culture.

REALITY RULE 15.1

Truth is the first casualty of war.

Weapons of Mass Deception, n.: War propaganda. Specifically, the public relations techniques used to convince the American public of the necessity of invading Iraq in 2003. The widely used term (it appears in the titles of at least three books published since the invasion) alludes to the weapons of mass destruction that Saddam Hussein's regime was said to possess, and which were the central point in the argument for going to war, but which have, to date, never been found.

Wag the Dog, v.: To create a phony foreign military crisis in order to distract the public from a domestic political scandal. Derives from an old axiom characterizing backwardness as "the tail wagging the dog." Popularized by a 1997 movie of the same name, in which a Hollywood producer and a political campaign manager invent a war in order to cover up a White House sex scandal. When the Clinton administration launched a military strike against a terrorist training camp in Afghanistan on the same day in 1998 that Monica Lewinsky concluded her testimony before the grand jury investigating the president's relationship with her, many critics denounced the strike as a wag-the-dog maneuver.

case file: The Department of Disinformation

In late February 2002 the *New York Times* learned of the Office of Strategic Influence (OSI), a program newly created by the Department of Defense. The OSI's mission was to manage a global PR campaign that would promote U.S. interests in the war on terror, not only through traditional propaganda techniques such as handing out leaflets in foreign countries, but also by planting fake stories in newspapers and otherwise spreading misinformation. In the words of the *New York Times*'s source, the office's duties would go "from the blackest of black to the whitest of white." It would be, in other words, a department of disinformation, charged with the task of telling lies.

The OSI was not yet an official program, not having received presidential approval. But it had been allocated a staff, a multimillion-dollar budget, and a director. It had also hired a Washington consulting firm to aid its efforts.

The media was quick to point out the paradox created by an official department of disinformation (as opposed to the unofficial misinformation campaigns the CIA and other arms of the government had long been known to operate). Once the Pentagon admitted that at times it might be lying, how could anything it said be trusted? How could reporters even be sure the OSI was real and not a lie designed to throw America's enemies off guard? It recalled the paradox formulated by the Cretan philosopher Epimenides when he stated, "All Cretans are liars."

At first the Pentagon insisted the OSI would only spread misinformation of a tactical, military nature—for instance, about the timing and scope of future attacks on enemy combatants. But eventually, faced with escalating media criticism, Secretary of Defense Donald Rumsfeld announced the OSI would be shut down. "The office is done," he said. "What do you want? Blood?"

Cynics noted the OSI's closure may have been the first news item issued at the direction of the OSI.

Mighty Wurlitzer, n.: A media echo chamber of lies. The effect of feeding false information to one news organization and then arranging to have it echoed by other media sources. After hearing the information repeated often enough, the public believes it must be true. Coined by the CIA.

Reality Check: CIA Stories

The CIA is always the focus of the weirdest conspiracy theories. Over the years it's been accused of plotting to introduce mind-altering drugs into the water supply, training psychics to use their powers to kill, and creating the AIDS virus. These theories may be pretty dubious, but what about the following rumors?

The CIA Muezzin School

Does the CIA run a school in Virginia that trains agents to pose as muezzins (the men who call Muslims to prayer five times a day from the minaret towers of mosques) because the agency believes muezzins are in a special position to view everything going on in Muslim communities?

A news story reprinted on numerous Islamic websites asserts the CIA is indeed training agents to pose as muezzins as part of its effort to infiltrate Muslim society. This muezzin school has six minarets from which agents practice the *adhan,* the Muslim call to prayer. Over one hundred agents graduate from the school each year, then relocate to Muslim countries and take up their lonely vigils in minarets, diligently spying on the populations below. The Islamic sites carrying this story appear to take it seriously, making this another example of satire mistaken as news (see chapter 10). The faux news report actually comes from the *Rockall Times,* a British humor website.

Acoustic Kitty

Did CIA researchers once transform a cat into a mobile bugging device—by implanting a microphone in the cat's ear and running an antenna up its tail—as an inconspicuous way to spy on Soviet agents?

Operation Acoustic Kitty was described to London's *Daily Telegraph* by former spy Victor Marchetti in 2001 and in documents declassified from the CIA's science and technology directorate. Throughout much of the 1960s, CIA researchers toiled to insert wires and batteries into a cat without killing it in the process. Unfortunately, once wired up, the willful feline proved difficult to control—wandering off in search of food, or chasing after cats of the opposite sex. Finally Acoustic Kitty was deemed ready and was released in a real-world trial. It promptly got run over, bringing the million-dollar operation to an end.

Classified Santa Claus

Did the CIA keep reports of terrorist threats against Santa Claus classified for twenty-nine years?

In a top-secret report created to identify terrorist activity around the world and delivered to President Gerald Ford on December 17, 1974, the CIA noted that an organization known as the Group of the Martyr Ebenezer Scrooge had plotted to sabotage Santa Claus's flight from the North Pole. The report also described incidents such as a bomb found at the British consulate in Buenos Aires, and threats to hijack British Airways flights. The entire report was classified until 1999, at which point most of it was declassified—while the sections relating to Santa Claus remained blacked out. It was only in 2003 that they were revealed to the public, as part of the National Security Archive's effort to end the overclassification of government documents. The Santa Claus reference was evidently a bit of Christmas humor. That it was kept classified for twenty-nine years was evidently the result of a government censor's lack of humor.

Plausible Deniability, n.: The ability of political leaders to deny knowledge of their subordinates' actions, thereby shielding themselves from fallout or legal consequences should those actions go wrong. According to this doctrine of political oversight, first formulated by the CIA in the 1950s, leaders should maintain a state of guilt-free ignorance by refusing to find out the details of what those under their command are doing.

case file: The Islamic Hostage Action–Figure Hoax

When word of yet another hostage taken in Iraq spread on February 1, 2005, the public braced for the worst. News broadcasts showed a photo of a U.S. soldier sitting on the ground with a rifle pointed at his head. The photo had been posted on an Internet bulletin board frequently used by Iraqi rebels, accompanied by the statement: "Our mujahideen heroes of Iraq's Jihadi Battalion were able to capture American military man John Adam after killing a number of his comrades and capturing the rest. God willing, we will behead him if

U.S. soldier John Adam, aka action-figure Cody

our female and male prisoners are not released from U.S. prisons within the maximum period of 72 hours from the time this statement has been released."

The Mujahideen Squadron had kidnapped a Brazilian engineer the previous month, so though the U.S. military denied any soldier was missing, the threat seemed credible—at least to the major news networks.

Bloggers were a bit more skeptical. A few pointed out that the soldier was strangely ex-

Elmo captured by insurgents

Barbie taken hostage

pressionless for someone with a rifle pointed at his head and his arms twisted behind his back. And the gun didn't look too real, either.

Within hours American toy manufacturer Dragon Models USA Inc. issued a statement noting that John Adam closely resembled its Cody action-figure doll, right down to their identical uniforms. A side-by-side comparison revealed the two to be one and the same. Apparently the rebels had gotten so desperate they were holding toy dolls hostage. Photos of Hostage Elmo—and the inevitable Hostage Barbie tableau—immediately appeared online.

A week later on a Jihadist message board, an anonymous "20-year-old Iraqi young man . . . unarmed [and] independent" took responsibility for the hoax, insisting it was just "a scheme that I made up with a toy that I bought with $5." Accompanying his confession, a photo showed the hostage scene from a different angle, the tiny rifle held between someone's fingers. A few bloggers noted that the new photo could be interpreted another way. It could mean soldier John Adam had been taken hostage by giants.

Incestuous Amplification, n.: What happens when leaders shield themselves from reality (or potentially disturbing news) by refusing to entertain advice from people who disagree with them. Also known as the policy of No Bad Information Invited.

Reclassify, v.: To take information that's public knowledge and declare it secret. Example: after 9/11 almost every major newspaper reported that an

FBI investigator had warned his superiors before the attack that al-Qaeda agents who were enrolling in flight schools posed a potential threat. Government officials later decided that this warning's existence was highly sensitive information and should be classified. A Bush spokesman noted, "Just because something had been inadvertently released, doesn't make it unclassified." Millions of people were apparently supposed to forget they knew about the warning.

case file: Operation Take One for the Country

No one could accuse Operation Take One for the Country (OTOFTC) of having modest goals. Its website, which appeared in early 2004, declared it a movement of women "who have covertly organized into groups to frequent eating and drinking establishments near armed service bases where troops are preparing to ship out overseas, and take one for the country, so to speak." To put it more bluntly, these women were on a mission to offer no-strings-attached sex to soldiers departing for Iraq.

OTOFTC immediately attracted suspicion. It wasn't that people doubted some women were willing to sleep with a soldier simply because he was about to deploy. During World War II women who offered themselves to departing soldiers were called "charity girls" or "patriotic prostitutes." What aroused suspicion was the claim that OTOFTC represented a coordinated network. Its website even declared several sororities would descend en masse on San Diego to participate in the operation during spring break. In fact, there was no evidence of any organized effort, nor was there indication that OTOFTC represented anything but a cheeky attempt to sell T-shirts, available on its website.

Given the nature of the operation, there was a good possibility Reality Rule 3.4 (see page 52) would come into play, but by the end of the year the OTOFTC website had been replaced by a blank page.

Baghdad Bob, n.: The nickname given to Muhammed Saeed al-Sahaf, Saddam Hussein's beret-wearing information minister, who distinguished himself during the invasion of Iraq by insisting U.S. troops were losing, even as they practically rode over him in a tank. The nickname has more recently come to signify anyone who insists on proclaiming victory despite overwhelming evidence to the contrary. When Vice President Cheney declared in May 2005 that the Iraqi resistance was in its "last throes," Greg Mitchell of *Editor & Publisher* questioned whether Cheney was "the new Baghdad Bob."

Phony Veterans

Con artists have successfully impersonated students, doctors, and even royalty, so it shouldn't surprise that some people—probably thousands—pose as military veterans. There's a big incentive, given the admiration military heroes receive. The only surprising thing is how far some fakers advance in their careers—becoming judges, Pulitzer Prize-winning authors, or congressmen—before their phony heroism is challenged.

Douglas R. Stringfellow

Republican Douglas Stringfellow's boasts about his World War II exploits as an agent of the Office of Strategic Services (OSS) were a central part of his 1952 congressional campaign. He claimed to have helped rescue German physicist Otto Hahn from behind enemy lines; to have been captured himself and held in Belsen Prison, where the torture he endured made him a paraplegic; and to have escaped from Belsen with the aid of the anti-Nazi underground. He also said he had been awarded a Silver Star. None of this was true, not even the part about being a paraplegic, as his Democratic opponents revealed shortly before his 1954 reelection campaign. Stringfellow had been a private in the Army Air Forces and was wounded by a mine explosion during a routine mission in France, but he could walk with a cane. Stringfellow confessed to his deception and bowed out of the campaign. He ended up working at various Utah radio stations under a pseudonym.

Judge Patrick Couwenberg

Judge Couwenberg told many exciting stories about his adventures working for the CIA in Laos, his service in Vietnam, and how he got shrapnel embedded in his groin (a wound that caused him to miss an occasional day of work). It was partly because of this past heroism that California governor Pete Wilson, himself an ex-Marine, appointed Couwenberg to the Los Angeles

Superior Court in 1997. The trouble was that none of Couwenberg's stories were true. His actual service was limited to a stint in the navy reserves. When confronted with his lies, Couwenberg conceded he had made a lot of stuff up, but argued it wasn't his fault because he suffered from a mental condition called pseudologia fantastica. This explanation didn't sway the state's Commission on Judicial Performance, which removed him from the bench.

Joseph Ellis

Pulitzer Prize–winning historian Joseph Ellis was fond of regaling students in his Vietnam War class at Mount Holyoke College with tales of the 1960s. He told them that he had commanded a platoon of paratroopers in Vietnam, and that his experiences there led him to join the peace movement upon his return home—eventually taking him to Mississippi, where he was active in the civil rights movement. He repeated these claims in an interview with the *Boston Globe*. Unfortunately for him, *Globe* reporters did some fact-checking. The truth, they found, was that Ellis had served in ROTC as an undergraduate and had later taught history at West Point, but he had never been sent to Vietnam. Nor had he participated in either the civil rights or the peace movements. The mystery was why he had made all this up, since the stories hadn't directly helped his career. Perhaps it was vanity. Ellis attributed his lies to a nagging insecurity stemming from growing up in a dysfunctional family with an alcoholic father. Mount Holyoke suspended Ellis without pay for a year, but he's since returned and seems as popular with his students and as well respected by fellow historians as ever.

DEATH 16

Dead men tell no lies. But how do you know they're really dead? Because even with death—that great equalizer, that one unavoidable fact of life—not everything is always as it seems.

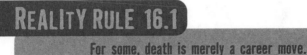

REALITY RULE 16.1

For some, death is merely a career move.

Elvis Spotting, n.: A sighting of someone who is supposed to be dead walking around in public.

How to Fake Your Death

Feeling depressed? Weighed down by debt and obligations? Looking to start over with a clean slate? Have no fear. There's a solution to all your problems. Just fake your death. It's the "get out of jail free" card of life. People do it all the time.

The most popular, least messy way of checking out (without really checking out) is forging a death certificate. What people who choose this method often forget, however, is that once they're officially dead, they need to stay dead, which means under the radar. Inevitably, after living for a few years with a new identity, they get arrested for a minor offense, the police check their fingerprints, and the game is up. In 1997 William Peterson filed a death certificate for himself rather than face up to a drunk-driving charge, and spent the next eight years living carefree as William Arksey—until he was arrested for forgery. At his trial Arksey/Peterson pleaded for mercy, telling the judge his criminal life was in the past and noting, "I was a different person then." Despite the obvious truth of this statement, the judge was not sympathetic.

Another strategy is to go missing. This is particularly popular among those with an accomplice, such as a spouse, who can claim any life insurance due. The major problem with this method, as Nikole Nagle discovered in 2003 when she reported her common-law husband missing, is that insurance companies don't pay up right away if there's no body. They wait a long time, especially if the policy was issued four days before the person vanished. It also doesn't help if the supposedly dead husband phones the police to report seeing his own body drift out to sea.

The most traditional, and seemingly convincing, way to stage your demise is to leave behind a body the police will think is yours. But sophisticated forensic techniques, such as DNA analysis, have made this much, much harder to pull off. At the very least a would-be death faker needs a body that's an approximate match to his own—of the same gender, height, and weight. It was the weight that gave Joseph Kalady away after he killed a handyman in 2001, disguised the victim's body as his own, and did a runner. Since Kalady weighed over 450 pounds, and the dead body didn't, the police knew something was up. Police arrested Kalady two years later, but while being held awaiting trial he sneakily eluded justice a second time by dying. This time it was for real (or so the police believe).

As people spend more time on the Internet, they're now faking their deaths online. Killing off your online persona is a great way to get out of conversations with which you've grown bored, or to rubberneck at your own virtual funeral, watching as your Internet buddies weep and moan about your passing.

September 11 brought a glut of fake online deaths as people tried to look like instant heroes (or tragic victims) in the eyes of their computer friends. One person's elaborate ruse convinced everyone in the LiveJournal community that he had died rushing into the burning World Trade Center to save people. The outpouring of grief and commiseration that followed turned to disgust when the hoax was exposed.

The phony online suicide, announced in advance, is also a guaranteed attention-getter. One wag's "countdown to oblivion" weblog declared he would take his own life in a few days: "My name is Jerry Romero, and I am 23 years old," he wrote. "On January 13th, I am going to kill myself." Much virtual handwringing and pleading to reconsider ensued, but when January 13 arrived, visitors to his site were met with a single word: PWNED (see chapter 6).

Death by Cop, n.: Suicide committed by intentionally provoking the police to use deadly force.

Death by Sims, n.: The result of the decision to kill off the character that symbolically represents you in a *Sims* game.

Elvis Lives: Fake Celebrity Deaths

Some celebrities never die; they just go into hiding.

It's not clear why some celebrity deaths inspire death-hoax rumors while others don't; but once a rumor takes hold, it can have amazing staying power.

And no celebrity clings more stubbornly to life after death than Elvis Presley. The official story is that he died on August 16, 1977. The unofficial story is that the corpse in his coffin was a wax dummy, and no body was buried in the meditation garden at Graceland. As his loyal fans argue, if Elvis was buried at Graceland why does his tombstone misspell his name—Elvis Aron Presley—as Elvis Aaron Presley? Why the extra a? Does it stand for "alive"? Inquiring minds want to know.

Some say Elvis went into the Federal Witness Protection Program after getting mixed up with the Mob. Others say he decided to do a runner after getting tired of the pressures of stardom. Still others insist he was abducted by aliens. In any case, people keep seeing him all over the place: pumping gas in the Australian outback; eating cheeseburgers in St. Paul, Minnesota; or ordering double lattes in Pensacola, Florida.

In 2002 psychiatrist Donald Hinton published a book in which he claimed he had been treating Elvis for back pain since 1997. According to Hinton, Elvis called it quits in 1977 because of his failing health and took up a more stress-free life under the name Jesse, in honor of his stillborn twin brother. He lived in Apopka, Florida, for a while before settling in Missouri. Hinton promised Elvis would return to public life on the twenty-fifth anniversary of his death, but Elvis pulled a no-show. The aging star must have gotten last-minute jitters.

Then there's Jim Morrison, lead singer of the Doors, who supposedly died of a heart attack (or a heroin overdose) in Paris on July 3, 1971. Businessman Gerald Pitts claims he found Jim "living on a ranch in the Pacific Northwest in the summer of 1998." Apparently the singer had tired of the celebrity rat race and decided to become a gun-toting cowboy. Pitts will tell you all about it in a video he sells for $24.95.

And what about rap star Tupac Shakur? Was he really killed in a drive-by shooting on September 7, 1996? Seven-day theorists—inspired by clues Tupac supposedly left in his final album, *The Don Killuminati: The Seven Day Theory*—argue the rapper faked his death with a plan to resurrect himself after seven years. His death's seventh anniversary passed without incident, which put a dent in that theory. But in April 2005 a fake CNN news story raced around the Internet claiming Tupac had showed up to do a little shopping at some high-end stores in Beverly Hills. He mustn't have found anything he liked, because he hasn't been seen since.

To date, no celebrity has justified death-hoax rumors by returning from the grave, unless you count the brief comeback of comedian Andy Kaufman.

During his life Kaufman often talked of faking his death, though he said if he ever did "pull an Elvis" he would return twenty years later to tell everyone about it. Then he died of lung cancer on May 16, 1984. Or did he? On May 16, 2004, a press release announced his return and his blog appeared online. Where had he been hiding out? On New York City's Upper West Side, said the resurrected Kaufman. A buzz of Internet speculation ensued. Had Kaufman really pulled off the greatest hoax in history? Sadly, no. After a week or so the joke got old for whoever was behind it, and new posts stopped appearing on Andy's blog.

So make that zero times a celebrity has come back from the grave. Which is a pity. Just once, someone ought to do it for real.

Dead as Elvis, adj.: Really, really dead, with no chance for recovery. Example: "My love life is as dead as Elvis."

How to Fake Someone Else's Death

If you can't stomach the thought of faking your own death, you can always fake someone else's. Why would you do this? Two reasons: to get sympathy (and thereby financial help), or just for fun.

After 9/11 Maureen Curry of Vancouver, Canada, reported her daughter killed in the terrorist attack, and complained her employer had refused her request for bereavement leave. Friends and politicians quickly raised over $2,000 for her, only to learn her daughter was alive and well and living in Winnipeg, though the two had been estranged for years. Likewise, Cyril Kendall's report that his son Wilfred had died in the World Trade Center netted him $160,000 in compensation from the Red Cross. There was just one problem: He didn't have a son named Wilfred. But he did have a shiny new car thanks to the Red Cross money. He subsequently lost the car when he was thrown into jail for thirty-three years.

The false-death claim as prank was pioneered by eighteenth-century satirists such as Jonathan Swift and Benjamin Franklin. Both publicly predicted the deaths of famous astrologers and then declared their predictions had come true—much to the annoyance of the astrologers, who were alive.

In modern times the fake-death prank is most often perpetrated by random jokers who doctor webpages to resemble official news reports. The faux deceased are usually entertainers, not astrologers. In fact, one measure of a celebrity's star power is whether her death has been falsely reported. To have enough obsessive fans that someone would find it funny to scare them with news of your death is the ultimate sign of success.

Just to clear things up, these celebrities have not died (as of this writing), despite Internet reports to the contrary:

Eminem didn't die in a car crash in December 2000.

Nor did Britney Spears suffer a similar fate, either in June or October of 2001.

Johnny Knoxville, star of MTV's *Jackass,* didn't die "while being filmed parachuting from a biplane whilst eating a catering sized tub of Heinz baked beans, when his parachute failed to open."

Michael Jackson never committed suicide in April 2004.

Jon Heder, star of *Napoleon Dynamite,* didn't crash and die while driving to Oregon.

Portly actor John Goodman didn't collapse from a heart attack in January 2005.

And William Hung, the antistar of *American Idol,* never OD'd from heroin, nor did he ever leave a suicide note that read: "I have no reason of living . . . my art which is my importance to the best everybody laugh to . . . I make end here . . . goodbye world of cruel."

Dead But Still Productive

After death many artists prove far more prolific than they ever were while alive. Tupac Shakur has released seven albums since dying, which explains why so many people think he's still hanging out somewhere. Meanwhile, Jimi Hendrix has produced hundreds of albums postmortem, compared to just three premortem. Ernest Hemingway is known to publish a new work every few years,

on the public. Far more remarkable are th____
dead. One of the more notorious examples is ge___ novelist V. C. Andrews, who has churned out bestsellers ever since dying in 1986. Her ghostwriter, Andrew Niederman, channels her creative spirit—occasionally even making publicity appearances as her (not in drag, as far as I know). This bait and switch was not made clear to Andrews's fans until years after her death. Niederman's name didn't appear on the books, and the publisher implied (falsely) that Andrews had largely completed these novels before her death. Even today many people continue to buy Andrews's books, believing they were actually written by her.

REALITY RULE 16.2
Dead men tell no tall tales. (They leave that to the living.)

Young Male Immortality Syndrome, n.: The failure of many young men to understand that they too will die. And it'll happen sooner rather than later if they think they can do all the stunts they see on TV, such as jumping off buildings or dodging bullets.

Reality Check: Weird Deaths
We're all fascinated, for purely self-interested reasons, in the strange ways other people have met their ends. As a result, tales of unlikely deaths—some true, some false—circulate throughout our culture. Which of the following are true, and which are urban legends?

Death by Lava Lamp
Did a man heat a lava lamp on his stove in an attempt to make it bubble faster, only to have the lamp explode and spray out shards of glass, one of which punctured his heart and killed him?

np|

Call this a case of curiosity killed the lava lamp owner."

Deadly Urine

Was a British woman strolling across a park struck, literally out of the blue, by a shaft of frozen urine falling from a plane's leaky toilet?

The Day Today, a spoof news program that aired in Britain during the 1990s, ran a brief segment about a woman who died in this fashion. The story was a joke, but an accompanying picture of a woman lying on Wandsworth Common, a large urine icicle lodged in her side, made its way onto the Internet and has circulated there ever since. I couldn't obtain permission to reproduce the image, but if you do a Google search for "frozen urine," you'll find it easily enough. It's quite lovely.

Rocket Man

Did a man, in an attempt to break the land-speed record, attach a solid-fuel rocket to his 1967 Chevy Impala and fire up the engines on a lonely stretch of highway in the Arizona desert, where the vehicle quickly achieved speeds in excess of 300 mph and, when it hit a bump in the road, launched into the air and flew into a cliff one-and-a-half miles away?

For many years this story circulated on the Internet and was believed to be true. Supposedly the highway patrol deduced what happened after finding burn marks on the road and a large crater in the side of a cliff. The tale's popularity helped launch the tradition of giving Darwin Awards to people whose extreme poor judgment resulted in their deaths (their stupidity thereby deselecting them from the gene pool—making them examples of Charles Darwin's theory of natural selection). However, the Arizona Department of Public Safety has no record of anyone dying in such a fashion. In other words, the story is an urban legend.

Xenacate, v.: To kill a TV or movie character off so completely that no chance remains of bringing her back from the dead, whether in a future episode or a sequel. Inspired by the TV show *Xena: Warrior Princess* (which is ironic, since Xena herself often died and magically came back to life). Example: almost all of the red-shirted characters (except for Mr. Scott) in the original *Star Trek* series.

Reality Check: Strange Funerals

Funeral customs vary around the world. For instance, some Tibetans perform sky burials, in which vultures feed on the corpse and carry parts of it into the air. Traditionally, in the West, you were either buried or cremated. But more and more people are experimenting with alternative ways of saying good-bye to their loved ones. How far out are they willing to go? See if you can guess which of these funeral practices are real, and which are fake.

Final Curtain

Does a New Jersey real estate development company operate a chain of cemetery theme parks, where visitors can dine at fine restaurants, shop, and go on rides, in addition to visiting their loved ones' graves?

In March 1999 ads announcing the imminent launch of a Final Curtain cemetery theme park chain—motto: "Death got you down? At last an alternative!"—appeared in a variety of magazines. Numerous newspapers and TV stations (including the *New York Daily News,* the *Boston Herald,* and Fox TV) also reported this unusual cemetery concept. However, the media had been taken in by inveterate prankster Joey Skaggs, with the help of a website, a dedicated phone number, and a lot of friends. He later explained he perpetrated the hoax to draw attention to the death-care industry, which he described as "a giant corporate scam, exquisitely successful at commercializing death."

Piranha Food

Did a man arrange to have his body fed to piranhas after he died?

When German artist Karl Friedrich Lentze read in 2004 about a Dutch man who requested his body be fed to snails after his death, he was inspired to write to various zoos to inquire whether they would feed his corpse to piranhas. He suggested the event would serve an educational purpose. The director of the Cologne Zoo responded that piranhas prefer live flesh, so Lentze would really have to be fed to them while he was alive. Lentze demurred, but did propose the zoo staff poke his dead body with a stick to make it look like he was moving. The director didn't think this would work, which put an end to the piranha funeral.

Oscar Mayer Wiener Funeral

When the driver of the Oscar Mayer Wienermobile died, did the hot-dog-shaped car lead his funeral procession as ceremony attendees sang "I'd love to be an Oscar Mayer wiener" to the accompaniment of hot-dog-shaped whistles?

When George Molchan died in April 2005, he was honored in this fashion. He had portrayed Little Oscar, the mascot of the Oscar Mayer company, so his friends and family thought he would appreciate a wiener-themed funeral.

Dead Wife as Coffee Table

Did a man preserve his wife's body in an airtight glass container that he now uses as a coffee table?

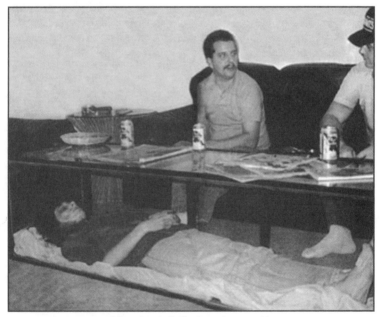

Jeff wonders why his friends are reluctant to visit.

A picture, which has circulated on the Internet since at least 2000, shows a man enjoying a beer with a friend, oblivious to a woman lying in the glass case on which his beer is resting. The attached story tells of Jeff, who—unable to bear the thought that his young wife Lucy had died—had her preserved in an airtight glass case that he now uses as a coffee table. In reality a body couldn't be preserved this easily. Lenin's body has been displayed in a glass case for years, but it requires constant maintenance by a team of embalmers. The dead-wife-as-coffee-table story is actually a decades-old urban legend. The picture of Jeff seems to be an attempt to re-create it. The photographer is unknown.

Diamonds Are Forever

Will a company turn the cremated remains of your loved one into a diamond?

The company is called LifeGem, and it is real. Its website promises "a certified, high-quality diamond created from the carbon of your loved one as a memorial to their unique life." Prices range from $2,000 to $18,000. The bodies must be cremated first (so don't deliver Uncle Joe's corpse straight to the company's door), but LifeGem happily accepts animal cremains as well. So Fluffy can be with you forever, on a ring around your finger.

Human Taxidermy

Will a company freeze-dry and mount the body of your loved one, allowing you to keep Grandma permanently on display in your home?

The company is called Preserve A Life, but it isn't real. According to an October 2004 spoof article in the Phoenix New Times, Preserve A Life had pioneered the art of humidermy (human taxidermy), which allowed the permanent preservation of bodies in posed positions. "Children have been posed on bicycles and skateboards, grandmothers in rocking chairs, and grandfathers playing boccie ball," the article stated. What made this claim semibelievable was that the article discussed Preserve A Life in the context of real companies offering "post-life alternatives"—such as the Utah-based Summum, which specializes in Egyptian-style mummification. If you could mummify Grandma Martha, why couldn't you freeze-dry her? It sounded logical, but that's not the case. Not yet.

case file: Push-button Bugles

Military funerals are full of time-honored traditions: soldiers standing at attention, a flag-draped coffin, a bugler playing taps. But a number of years ago the military began to run out of trained bugle players. Its solution was to invent a push-button bugle that allows someone to flip a switch, put the instrument to his lips, and maintain that pose as an electronic chip plays a recorded version of the memorial music. It's Milli Vanilli taps.

The introduction of these phony bugles inspired a few veterans to create Bugles Across America, a network of volunteer buglers who fill in at funerals when military buglers aren't available. But even this effort can't make up for the bugler shortfall. So push-button bugles remain in frequent use at services. And most people admit they look better than a boom box.

As it happens, the push-button bugles play a version of taps performed by U.S. Army Sergeant Major Woodrow "Woody" English, who is still alive. This means that someday, in a twist worthy of the times in which we live, Sergeant Major English could be playing taps at his own funeral.

Postmortem Divorce, n.: A clause in a will stating that a husband and wife should not be buried next to each other. They may have pretended to tolerate each other in life, but they'll be damned if they'll spend eternity together.

Contacting the Dead

Every culture has different beliefs about communicating with those in the afterlife. In ancient Roman myth, plucking a golden bough from a magical tree would allow you to travel to the land of the dead and back. During the nineteenth century elaborate séances became the rage. Today afterlife communication has gone high tech. Still, no technique is guaranteed to work any better than the golden-bough trick.

The Phone Angel

In 2005 German inventor Jürgen Bröther debuted the Phone Angel—basically a weatherproof cell phone designed to be buried in a grave, with an attached speaker pointing down at the coffin. Mourners can call from anywhere in the world, and the Phone Angel broadcasts their voices, via the microphone, toward their loved one. Hopefully no one ever talks back, but imagine the terror a crossed line could cause.

Endless Echoes

Operating on the theory that the souls of dead people float in outer space, the Endless Echoes company uses a satellite dish antenna to blast messages into the heavens (for a price of $24.95 per minute). You phone the company, leave your message on its answering machine, and it takes care of the rest. Endless Echoes advertises its service as a way to get one final message to a loved one "when you never had a chance to say 'good-bye.'" I imagine messages like, "You left the oven on, Idiot!"

Afterlife Telegram Service

The Afterlife Telegram service maintains a team of terminally ill patients who promise, for a fee of five dollars per word, to memorize any message you want to send to someone in the great beyond, and to deliver it personally when they reach the other side. The service acknowledges that many things could go wrong and guarantees nothing—noting, "Reincarnation could cause a problem," and also, "If the afterlife is segregated into heaven, hell and purgatory, it is possible that the messenger will not be sent to the same place as the addressee." Perhaps the company should specify whether each messenger is a sinner or a saint.

Text Message from Jesus

A Finnish phone company rolled out a service allowing customers to send a prayer to Jesus via text message. What made this interesting was that the company promised Jesus would respond. A Finnish newspaper sent a prayer for help, as a test. Jesus replied, "Unless you follow God's will much better than priests and pharaohs, you will not be allowed into the heavenly kingdom." Apparently Jesus was in a mood to be as cryptic as a fortune cookie. The phone company subsequently shut down the service after receiving numerous complaints.

Afterlife Bill Payment

Sometimes the reason for contacting the dead is financial, not personal. If someone dies without settling his debts, a company might still want to collect.

What should it do? Sprint came up with an ingenious solution. The phone company sent an unpaid bill directly to the grave of its former customer—correctly listing not only the address of the cemetery, but also the section of the plot in which the debtor lay. (Sprint denied any knowledge of how the cemetery plot address got into its records.) The total amount he owed? $3.95. The cemetery eventually passed the bill along to the town clerk, who warned that if the deceased customer didn't pay up, his lapse would affect his credit rating.

Acknowledgments

Without the help of my agent, Alička Pistek, this book would not exist. She was the first person, back in 2003, to listen to me explain my idea for a book about "fake reality," and her efforts on my behalf allowed it to happen. I'm also grateful to my editor at Harcourt, Stacia Decker, for her enthusiasm and for the many improvements she made to the manuscript.

Then there are all the usual suspects to thank: Beverley, for putting up with me with her usual good humor; my parents, for their constant love and support; Charlie, for staying out of trouble; Boo, for being her catlike self (including her annoying but lovable habit of lying on the keyboard as I'm trying to write); Ted, for traveling from Boston to supply movie, coffee, and Guinness breaks; Uncle Rudy, for providing such an inspiring example of enlightened skepticism; and Kirsten, Ben, Astrid, and Pippa, for beaming positive energy to me all the way from Malawi.

Warm thanks also to the many visitors to my site whose comments provided humor and insight. I owe a special debt to those few who selflessly served as moderators, preventing the site from sliding into anarchy while I was preoccupied with writing the book: Charybdis, Boo (no relation to my cat), Hairy Houdini (and Raoul), Maegan, Myst, Smerk, and Stephen Walden (full name by request). If I could list all the other regulars who help make the site such a fun place, you know I would. But there's not enough space (and I'd be afraid of overlooking someone). However, you can be sure you're all appreciated.